Advances in Spatial Science

The Regional Science Series

This series contains scientific studies focusing on spatial phenomena, utilising theoretical frameworks, analytical methods, and empirical procedures specifically designed for spatial analysis. Advances in Spatial Science brings together innovative spatial research utilising concepts, perspectives, and methods relevant to both basic science and policy making. The aim is to present advances in spatial science to an informed readership in universities, research organisations, and policy-making institutions throughout the world. The type of material considered for publication in the series includes: Monographs of theoretical and applied research in spatial science; state-of-the-art volumes in areas of basic research; reports of innovative theories and methods in spatial science; tightly edited reports from specially organised research seminars.

The series and the volumes published in it are indexed by Scopus.

For further information on the series and to submit a proposal for consideration, please contact Johannes Glaeser (Senior Editor Economics) Johannes.glaeser@springer.com.

Yee Leung

Digital Twins of Cities

Modeling Urban Dynamics and Complexity

Springer

Yee Leung
Department of Geography and Resource
Management
The Chinese University of Hong Kong
Shatin, Hong Kong

ISSN 1430-9602 ISSN 2197-9375 (electronic)
Advances in Spatial Science
ISBN 978-3-032-07965-7 ISBN 978-3-032-07966-4 (eBook)
https://doi.org/10.1007/978-3-032-07966-4

This Springer imprint is published by the registered company Springer Nature Switzerland AG
The registered company address is: Gewerbestrasse 11, 6330 Cham, Switzerland

In memory of my mother
Siu Fong Chan (陳少芳)

To
My wife Sau Ching (秀清) Sherry
My son Hei (熹)
My sisters
Sin Mui (倩梅), Wai Chun (惠珍) Christine
My brothers
Sun (晨), Sing (醒), Kok (覺) Arthur
for their love and care from near and far

Preface

Though the development of digital twins of cities is still in the infancy stage, it promises to be a ground-breaking paradigm shift in the modeling of cities—particularly the dynamics and complexity of their evolutions. It is argued in this book the importance of incorporating dynamics and complexity into digital twins of cities for effective and efficient modeling, simulation, prediction, and management of cities which are ever-evolving dynamical complex systems. Until now, too much emphasis has been placed on the data and information aspects in the building of digital twins of cities. Exactly how to instill urban theories—the most fundamental pillar of urban science and practical city management—into digital twins of cities has not received the kind of attention it deserves in the current literature. Since cities are dynamical complex systems, urban dynamics and complexity should serve as the backbone of the digital twins. Data and information alone will not make us more intelligent in the analysis and management of our city developments. It is the theories on city evolution that will inspire the search for solutions to our urban problems. Intelligent integration of theories and data into digital twins of cities will play a definitive and pivotal role in the modeling and management of our complicated city development process. Dynamics and complexity of city evolution are undoubtedly the most crucial theoretical foundation on which digital twins of cities should be built. Due to the many-faceted nature of dynamics and complexity of cities and the variety of approaches for their discovery and analysis, having a unifying framework will be foundational to the construction of digital twins essential for the real-time, near real-time, and life-time management and solution of our ever-evolving city problems.

The purpose of this book is to develop a general framework within which urban dynamics and complexity can be unraveled and incorporated into digital twins of cities under various circumstances. Such a framework is non-existent in current literature but is of paramount importance for our investigations. However, the underlying dynamics and complexity can be very complicated about which we may have good knowledge, limited knowledge, or even no knowledge. How to unravel the underlying dynamics is thus crucial to the deployment of digital twins to solve complex city problems. The proposed framework targets the enablement of digital twins to acquire theories and to capitalize on the power of information technologies as well as the richness of data to solve our city problems in real time, near real-time, and on a long-term basis. When the governing equations of urban dynamics are known but their solutions rely on exorbitantly high-dimensional models, we build digital twins by learning the corresponding reduced-order models of much lower dimensions via low-dimensional manifold learning from snapshots generated by the high-dimensional models over a range of parameter values at different points in space and time. When we have very limited knowledge or no idea about the governing equations, we use data-driven methods to build digital twins by learning the reduced-order models from spatiotemporal time series obtained through observations or experiments. To make the data-driven approach interpretable and conformed to certain urban theories, we inject urban theories into data-driven learning to make digital twins urban theory-informed. The framework also allows for modeling cities as complex dynamical networks from which reduced-order models can be derived. To address emergence arising from interactions of individual city agents at the microscopic level, we can incorporate dynamics and complexity into digital twins of cities by learning the reduced-order models of adaptive dynamical networks with agents interacting within complex network communication topologies. The issues of scale, urban sensing, uncertainty, and data quality—essential to the modeling of urban dynamics and complexity via digital twins of cities—are also examined in this book. To make building digital twins a dynamic process, feedback loops between models and data are enforced so that models and data are made mutually informed in the modeling of our ever-changing complex urban systems. The interoperability between models and data ensures that models closely capture the underlying mechanisms that govern the development of cities throughout their life cycles and can be dynamically updated according to the changing reality and updated information, and data can be made model-informed and dynamically collected to better empower our simulations of the urban process and decision-making in city management.

The proposed framework advances our understanding of the dynamics and complexity of city evolution and their modeling through digital twins of cities. It is an exciting undertaking in novel urban modeling in the era of rapid advancement of artificial intelligence and explosive growth of multisource, multitype, and multiscale spatiotemporal data. With this, we can successfully ride the tide of conceptual and theoretical developments in urban science, information technology, artificial intelligence, and data science. It will take us to a new frontier of modeling geographical systems in general and urban systems—together with their digital twins—in particular. The framework can also be extended to build digital twins for other dynamic and complex human and physical systems. Facing us is a host of theoretical and practical problems that need to be solved. It is hoped that the proposed framework in this book will lay a foundation for and stimulate interest in such investigations to achieve city resilience and sustainability.

This book is a research monograph targeting researchers in geography, urban planning, regional science, urban economics, artificial intelligence, machine learning, physics, applied mathematics, and probability/stochastic process/statistics. I hope it can stimulate interest in this exciting field of interdisciplinary research whose advancement calls for the concerted effort of experts from relevant disciplines to tackle novel theoretical and applied research problems whose wholistic solutions go beyond a single discipline. Involvement of researchers in these fields will make our investigations theoretically solid, empirically verifiable, and real-life relevant. The monograph can also be used as advanced textbook or a reference for graduate students and advanced undergraduate students. Since the purpose is to bring theories and technologies to practice, the book is also intended for governments and practicing professionals committed to build resilient and sustainable cities over time and space. Though our concern is digital twins of cities, issues and problems that we address apply to other dynamical complex human and physical systems also.

Shatin, Hong Kong Yee Leung
July 2025

Acknowledgments I would like to thank Alan G. Wilson for the valuable comments and suggestions on the earlier versions of the book. Deep appreciation also goes to Manfred M. Fischer, Johannes Glaeser, and Alan G. Wilson for the suggestion of having the book published in the Advances in Spatial Science series.

I would like to thank the owners of the copyrights for permission to adopt some figures in this book from their originals: Elsevier for Figure 4.10 and 9.6; IOP Publishing Ltd. for Figures 9.3 and 9.4; Taylor & Francis for Figure 9.5; American Physical Society for Figure 9.7; Springer Nature for Figure 10.3 and Figure 10.4. To make the book self-contained as much as possible, reference is drawn to some of my previous co-authored publications. Part of Section 3.2 is abridged from Tsang and Leung (2011); Parts of Section 4.6 on RCMD method and Section 4.8 on dual neural network for EM model are shortened from Leung et al. (2001) and Leung et al. (2004e), respectively; the description of MEMD-SCA-LSTM in Section 9.4 is condensed from Shi et al. (2024); the discussion of PHD-filter-based sensor network in Section 10.2 is abridged from Leung et al. (2013) and Wu et al. (2020); part of the discussion on error propagation in MBGIS in Section 10.3 is simplified from Leung et al. (2004a).

To my wife Sau Ching Sherry and my son Hei, their support, understanding, and love made the writing of this book a pleasant journey, my unfeigned appreciation. I am also grateful to Hei for his format editing of and graphical illustrations for the book.

Competing Interests The author has no competing interests to declare that are relevant to the content of this manuscript.

Contents

About the Author

Yee Leung is Emeritus Professor of the Department of Geography and Resource Management, and Honorary Senior Research Fellow of the Institute of Space and Earth Information Science at The Chinese University of Hong Kong, Hong Kong SAR, P. R. China. He is a pioneer of the theory and applications of fuzzy sets approach to geographical research and has done novel research on uncertainty analysis in geographical modeling and spatial information using probability, statistics, fuzzy set, rough-set, and granular computing. His research also covers artificial intelligence in general and machine learning, deep learning, neural network, evolutionary computation, and optimization in particular. He has published six monographs and over 200 articles in reputed international journals mainly in geography, geographical information science, artificial intelligence, computer science, and information science. His research is holistically reflected in the landmark research monographs: Leung Y (1988) Spatial Analysis and Planning under Imprecision, Amsterdam: Elsevier Science; Leung Y (1997) Intelligent Spatial Decision Support Systems, Berlin: Springer-Verlag; and Leung Y (2010) Knowledge Discovery in Spatial Data. Berlin: Springer-Verlag. This monograph stitches into the mosaic of his investigations.

Acronyms and Abbreviations

AI	Artificial Intelligence
CA	Cellular Automata
CNN	Convolutional Neural Network
DFA	Detrended Fluctuation Analysis
DMD	Dynamic Mode Decomposition
EM	Entropy Maximization
EMD	Empirical Mode Decomposition
GA	Genetic Algorithm
GAM	Generalized Additive Model
GMM	Gaussian Mixture Model
IMF	Intrinsic Mode Function
KF	Kalman Filter
LLM	Large Language Model
LSTM	Long Short-Term Memory
MAS	Multiagent System
MEMD	Multivariate Empirical Mode Decomposition
MFDFA	Multifractal Detrended Fluctuation Analysis
MSE	Mean Squared Error
ODE	Ordinary Differential Equation
PCA	Principal Component Analysis
PDE	Partial Differential Equation
PHD	Probability Hypothesis Density
PINN	Physics-Informed Neural Network
POD	Proper Orthogonal Decomposition
RCMD	Regression-Class Mixture Decomposition
ROM	Reduced-Order Model
RPS	Reconstructed Phase Space

SCA	Spatial Cosine Attention
SINDy	Sparse Identification of Nonlinear Dynamical Systems
SLM	Small Language Model
SVD	Singular Value Decomposition

List of Figures

Chapter 1
Introduction

1.1 On Digital Twins of Cities

Since its inception, the concept of digital twin (Grieves 2005)—which was first applied to construct physical simulators to simulate outer space conditions for decision-making in aeronautics and space missions (Shafto et al. 2010)—has found its applications in a variety of disciplines including manufacturing (Grieves 2014, 2016), mechanical engineering (Schweigert-Recksiek et al. 2020), medical services (Martinez-Velazquez et al. 2019), atmospheric and climate sciences (NASEM 2023b), robotics (Zhang et al. 2021), etc. A digital twin, in short, is a realistic digital representation of and is closely connected to something physical with feedback loops (Centre for Digital Built Britain 2020). More substantially, it is defined as "A set of virtual information constructs that mimics the structure, context and behavior of an individual/unique physical asset, or a group of physical assets, is dynamically updated with data from its physical twin throughout its life cycle and informs decisions that realize value" (AIAA and AIA 2020). Extended on this, "The bidirectional interaction between the virtual and the physical is central to the digital twin" is added to the definition in NASEM (2023a). In short, the conceptualization is characterized by a coupled system with a tight connection between the physical asset and its digital replica—the digital twin. Through digital twins, we can simulate changes, predict needs, optimize structures and processes, manage/control developments, and monitor performances of the physical systems throughout their life cycles.

Recently, the concept has taken on a broader and looser meaning to include simulation models that run by the side of real-life structures and processes in physical and human systems (Batty 2018). As a result, there emerges the concept of digital twins of cities in urban analysis and city planning (Wan et al. 2019; Shahat et al. 2021; Batty and Milton 2023; Goodchild et al. 2024). Heretofore, the main emphasis on developing digital twins of cities has been centered around the development of information infrastructure—including multimodal micro sensors, internet of tings (IoT), and other conventional data sources—that enables the digital characterization

Y. Leung, *Digital Twins of Cities*, Advances in Spatial Science,
https://doi.org/10.1007/978-3-032-07966-4_1

of cities in a more informative and realistic way (Ivanov et al. 2020; Lei et al. 2023; Wang et al. 2023; Wu et al. 2023; Goodchild et al. 2024). Though such an undertaking is essential, it is, however, far from sufficient in making digital twins an effective means for the analysis and simulation of complex urban processes that are essential for our understanding, prediction, and management of the ever-evolving cities. Since cities are complex adaptive systems, it is of paramount importance to incorporate complexity into digital twins of cities (Caldarelli et al. 2023). Because a complex world is dynamic, complexity is not static and must be studied in the dynamic context and evaluated on a time-varying basis over long-time scales. Therefore, to incorporate complexity, we also need to incorporate dynamics—which studies how objects or systems change and interact with feedback loops in time—into digital twins of cities.

Apparently, concentrating on big data alone is a far cry from the ideal digital twins of cities useful for urban research and practical applications. Big data needs big theory (Coveney et al. 2016). Digital twins are just as good as the theories embedded into them. Therefore, digital twins of cities must be based on or informed by relevant urban theories that capture closely the lifecycle evolution of cities. They themselves are also ever-evolving models of the physical systems/twins with continuous knowledge and data updates. Dynamical system theory (Holmes 1990; Katok and Hasselblatt 1995) and complexity theory (Weaver 1948; Turner and Baker 2019) are thus complementary theoretical constructs pivotal to the study of real-life city evolution—which is dynamic, self-organized, emergent, and nonlinear—exhibiting high degree of complexity beyond the concealment of time and space. Complexity theory (Weaver 1948; Prigogine 1987) and complexity science (Krakauer 2024) render a means to understand how systems grow, adapt, self-organize, and evolve across multiple scales (Sammut-Bonnici 2014), and dynamical analysis offers a way to analyze time dependence of qualitative system behavior, resulting in complex structures and processes. Dynamics and complexity are, for instance, linked by the concept of emergent behavior through complicated interactions of system components. Nonlinear dynamics is a source of complex behavior. Chaos and fractals are, for example, part of dynamics (Waldrop 1993; Strogatz 1994), and they are closely related. So are bifurcations and self-organization. Knowing the dynamics of a system is fundamental to the detection, simulation, and prediction of complex system behavior in the spatiotemporal domain that is essential to educated decision-making. Therefore, they should serve as a backbone of the development of digital twins of cities for the modeling of urban dynamics and complexity.

1.2 Organization of the Book

The purpose of this book is to develop a general framework for the incorporation of dynamics and complexity into digital twins of cities to ensure that models closely capture the underlying mechanisms that govern the development of cities throughout their life cycles, and can be dynamically updated according to the changing reality, and data can be made model-informed and dynamically updated to better empower our analysis and decision-making in city management. This book is a substantial extension of my unpublished short book on the incorporation of dynamics and complexity into digital twins of cities (Leung 2024). For simplicity and without confusion, the term digital twin means an individual twin or a system of interconnected twins—depending on the context of our discussion in this monograph.

The remainder of this book is structured as follows. I first give a brief argument in support of incorporating dynamics and complexity into digital twins of cities and identifying the mission of digital twins of cities in Chapter 2. In Chapter 3, a discussion is made on the learning and modeling of dynamics and complexity of cities where the governing equations are known, and the derivation of the low-dimensional surrogate models through dimension reduction manifold learning for efficient simulation and prediction. In Chapter 4, I explore plausible methods in the data-driven approach to learn and incorporate dynamics and complexity into digital twins of cities when the underlying dynamics of the systems are not known, and we must rely solely on data available. To make the data-driven approach interpretable and respect theories, I examine how we can make the data-driven approach urban theory informed in Chapter 5. Making a slight but related diversion from the macroscopic approaches in Chapters 3 to 5, I show how to incorporate dynamics and complexity into digital twins of cities when cities are conceptualized as dynamical complex networks in Chapter 6. In Chapter 7, I discuss the incorporation of dynamics and complexity into digital twins of cities at the microscopic level via the multiagent approach. In Chapter 8, I reflect on the macro–micro dichotomy, and the necessity to analyze dynamics and complexity of cities on multiple scales. To drive home the importance of synchronizing models and data in the construction of digital twins of cities, I highlight in Chapter 9 the interoperability between models and data through which models and data can be made mutually informed, and the dynamic updating of digital twins can be made throughout the life cycles of cities. Finally, sensor networks and the issue of data quality and error propagation in digital twins are briefly discussed in Chapter 10. I then conclude the book with a summary and outlook for further research in Chapter 11. To make the book self-contained to a certain extent, abridged descriptions of relevant methods in the literature are given at appropriate places to facilitate our discussion. Matrices and vectors are put in bold throughout.

For simplicity and without confusion, digital twins of cities can mean standalone digital twins of urban entities/processes or a system of interconnected digital twins in our discussion throughout. For example, we can have a digital twin of a room, a building, a built environment, a transportation network, a power grid, an urban land development process, a public service, a city, a system of cities, etc. To simplify, acronyms will be employed for some terms repeatedly used in the text, for instance, ROM is the acronym for reduced-order model, and PDE is the acronym for partial differential equation, etc. For convenience, a glossary of acronyms and abbreviations is given on pages xxiii-xxiv for easy reference. Concrete examples on the modeling of urban dynamics and complexity by means of digital twins of cities are used to substantiate the conceptual arguments wherever appropriate. Directions for further research are suggested in the remarks or relevant places throughout the book.

References

AIAA (American Institute of Aeronautics and Astronautics) and AIA (Aerospace Industries Association (2020) *Digital twin: definition & value*. AIAA and AIA position paper.

Batty M, Milton R (2023). Building a digital twin for British cities. *Physics and Society*. arXiv:2312.03674. https://doi.org/10.48550/arXiv.2312.03674.

Batty M (2018) Digital twins. *Environment and planning B: Urban analytics and City Science*. *5*(45): 817–820. https://doi.org/10.1177/2399808318796416.

Caldarelli G, Arcaute E, Barthelemy M, Batty M, Gershenson C, Helbing D, Mancuso S, Moreno Y, Ramasco JJ, Rozenblat C, Sánchez A, Fernández-Villacañas JL (2023) The role of complexity for digital twins of cities. *Nature Computational Sciences* 3: 374–381.

Centre for Digital Built Britain (2020) *The Gemini Principles*. https://www.cdbb.cam.ac.uk/Resources/ResoucePublications/TheGeminiPrinciples.pdf.

Coveney PV, Dougherty ER, and Highfield RR (2016) Big data need big theory too. *Philosophical. Transactions of Royal Society A* 374: 20160153.

Goodchild MF, Connor D, Fotheringham AS, Frazier A, Kedron P, Li W, Tong D (2024) Digital twins in urban informatics. *Urban Informatics 3:16*. https://doi.org/10.1007/s44212-024-00048-6.

Grieves M. (2005) Product lifecycle management: the new paradigm for enterprises. *International Journal of Product Development* 2(1/2): 71–84.

Grieves M (2014) *Digital Twin: manufacturing excellence through virtual factory replication: A whitepaper*. original edition. http://innovate.fit.edu/plm/documents/doc_mgr/912/1411.0_Digital_Twin_White_Paper_Dr_Grieves.

Grieves, M (2016) Origins of the Digital Twin Concept. https://doi.org/10.13140/RG.2.2.26367.61609. www.researchgate.net/publication/307509727.

Holmes P (1990) Poincaré, celestial mechanics, dynamical-systems theory and chaos. *Physics Reports* 193(3): 137–163.

Ivanov S, Nikolskaya K, Radchenko G, Sokolinsky L, Zymbler M (2020) Digital twin of city: concept overview. *2020 Global Smart Industry Conference* (GloSIC). https://doi.org/10.1109/GloSIC50886.2020.9267879.

Katok A, Hasselblatt B (1995) *Introduction to the Modern Theory of Dynamical Systems*. Cambridge: Cambridge University Press.

Krakauer DC (ed.) (2024) *Foundational Papers in Complexity Science Volume 1–4*. New Mexico: Santa Fe Institute.

Lei B, Janssen P, Stoter J, Biljecki F (2023) Challenges of urban digital twins: a systematic review and a Delphi expert. *Automation in construction* 147: 104716. https://doi.org/10.1016/j.autcon.2022.104716.

Leung Y (2024) Incorporating Dynamics and Complexity into Digital Twins of Cities—A General Framework. (unpublished).

Martinez-Velazquez R, Gamez R, Saddik E, Cardio A (2019) Twin: A digital twin of the human heart running on the edge. *Proceedings of the 2019 IEEE International Symposium on Medical Measurements and Applications (MeMeA)*, 1–6.

NASEM (National Academies of Sciences, Engineering, and Medicine) (2023a) *Foundational research gaps and future directions for digital twins*. Washington DC: National Academies Press.

NASEM (National Academies of Sciences, Engineering, and Medicine), National Academy of Engineering, Division on Earth and Life Studies, Division on Engineering and Physical Sciences, Board on Life Sciences, Board on Atmospheric Sciences and Climate, Computer Science and Telecommunications Board, Board on Mathematical Sciences and Analytics, Casola L, editor (2023b) Opportunities and Challenges for Digital Twins in Atmospheric and Climate Sciences. *Proceedings of a Workshop—in Brief*. Washington DC: National Academies Press (US). ISBN-10: 0-309-70128-7.

Prigogine I (1987) Exploring complexity. *European Journal of Operational Research 30(2)*: 97–103.

Sammut-Bonnici T (2014) Complexity Theory. In Cooper CL (ed.) *Wiley Encyclopaedia of Management*. Hoboken: John Wiley & Sons.

Schweigert-Recksiek S, Trauer J, Engel C, Spreitzer K, Zimmermann M (2020) Conception of a digital twin in mechanical engineering-a case study in technical product development. *Proceedings of the Design Society: DESIGN Conference* Vol 1: 383–392. https://doi.org/10.1017/dsd.2020.23.

Shafto M, Conroy M, Doyle R, Glaessgen E, Kemp C, LeMoigne J, Wang L (2010) *Draft modeling, simulation, information technology & processing roadmap. Technology Area 11.* National Aeronautics and Space Administration.

Shahat E, Hyun C.T, Yeom C (2021) City digital twin potential: a review and research agenda. *Sustainability* 13:3386. https://doi.org/10.3390/su13063386.

Strogatz SH (1994) *Nonlinear Dynamics and Chaos*. Reading: Addison-Wesley.

Turner JR, Baker RM (2019) Complexity theory: an overview with potential applications for the social sciences. *Systems* 7(1): 4. https://doi.org/10.3390/systems7010004.

Waldrop MM (1993) *Complexity: The Emerging Science at the Edge of Order and Chaos*. NY: Simon and Schuster.

Wan L, Nochta T, Schooling D (2019) Developing a city-level digital twin-propositions and case study. *International Conference on Smart Infrastructure and construction 2019 (ICSIC)*. https://doi.org/10.1680/csic.64669.187.

Wang H, Chen X, Jia F, Cheng X (2023) Digital twin-supported smart city: status, challenges and future research directions. *Expert Systems with Applications* 217 (2023) 119531. https://doi.org/10.1016/j.eswa.2023.119531.

Weaver W (1948) Science and complexity. *American Scientist* 36: 536–544.

Wu H, Ji P, Ma H, Xing L (2023) A comprehensive review of digital twin from the perspective of total process: data, models, network and applications. *Sensors* 23: 8306.

Zhang Y, Meina A, Lin X, Zhang K, Xu Z (2021) Digital twin in computational design and robotic construction of wooden architecture. *Advances in Civil Engineering* 1:1–14. https://doi.org/10.1155/2021/8898997.

Chapter 2
Dynamics and Complexity of Cities

2.1 Cities as Dynamical Complex Systems

Cities are dynamical complex systems with ever-changing structures over time—exhibiting nonlinear dynamics, complex emergence, and self-organizing behavior (Allen 1984). These systems generally contain a very large number of elements/parts/agents at different levels of the hierarchy. The connectivity within a city is high and the heterogeneous interactions among elements and constituent parts of the system in time and space are usually strong and nonlinear—leading to complicated phase transitions in the phase space within which a system may settle down to an equilibrium, cyclic, or complicated set like fractals (Fractal is an irregular geometric structure or process containing detailed structure at arbitrarily small scale, exhibiting self-similarity on all scales). A point in the phase space specifies the state of a dynamical system. By studying the trajectories of a system in the phase space, we can draw insights into the stability and behavior of the system. It is the multiplicity of equilibrium states and the transitions among them that are most interesting in the dynamical study of urban systems (Wilson 2000). Patterns that characterize urban growth and form emerge as consequences of such interactions among city agents, flows of energy and information (Batty 2013). Patterns are structured states which may be formed by exogeneous imposition—internally generated through self-organization without external control, or both. Thus, the synergistic interdependence with positive and negative feedback loops changes the state of a complex system over time. With positive feedback, we increase the rate of change in a variable in a certain direction, and with negative feedback, we reverse its direction of change. Growth or decline of a city, for example, implies a positive or negative feedback or cumulative causation that moves the system into a continual state of equilibrium or disequilibrium (Batty 2013). In other words, self-emergence shapes the properties, order, and structures of a system by the spontaneous micro behaviors of its elements, the relationships between its various parts, and the interactions with its environment. Cities can thus be modeled from the microscopic perspective as living organisms which evolve through

Y. Leung, *Digital Twins of Cities*, Advances in Spatial Science,
https://doi.org/10.1007/978-3-032-07966-4_2

adaptation to its interaction with other agents and the environment—resulting in complexity of urban forms (Jacobs 1961; Allen 1984). It is a bottom-up approach to study dynamics and complexity of cities.

On the other hand, dynamic behavior and complexity can be studied from the macroscopic perspective via deterministic or stochastic governing equations from top down. Through them, we can study discrete-time and continuous-time dynamics of urban systems (Forrester 1969; Wilson 1981; Allen 1997). Parameters in the governing equations describing the dynamics of such systems may have critical values at which there can be discrete jump from one kind of equilibrium state to another due to nonlinearity—resulting in complex structures across multiple scales at many levels in the city systems (Wilson 2000)—making the non-equilibrium phenomena more important and revealing in emergence and self-organization of cities (Allen et al. 2008). In general, complex systems have top-down and bottom-up dynamics. The macro structure and process may affect or restrain the microscopic behaviors of its constituents. Processes at the macro level possess their own dynamics that need to be studied in their own right. Therefore, both the macroscopic (macro dynamics) and microscopic (micro dynamics) perspectives should be incorporated into digital twins of cities so that the top-down and bottom-up approaches to complex urban systems and their synergy can be studied with deeper revelation. To be complete, multilevel dynamics should be incorporated into digital twins of cities (The issue of scale is further discussed in Chapter 8).

2.2 Reduced-Order Models for Dynamic and Complex Urban Processes

Therefore, to make digital twins a facilitator for our understanding of and decision-making on cities, dynamics and complexity must be incorporated into the construction of digital twins of cities. Through such formulation, we can harness the power of both the model and data to make reliable predictions of and effective strategies for the development of complex adaptive urban systems. Since dynamical models are generally complex and high-dimensional, the search for their simplified representations on the low-dimensional manifold is instrumental in the construction of the corresponding digital twins, and the mitigation of computational complexity. Complicated systems can often be approximated by simpler systems exhibiting similar behavior. Reduced-order model (ROM) (Lucia et al. 2004; Lu et al. 2021)—the low-fidelity model—for high-dimensional construct—the high-fidelity model—thus plays a crucial role in the efficient and successful simulation of urban processes—particularly those which are difficult to comprehend and manage—via digital twins of cities. It is particularly important to handle fast dynamics problems—such as pedestrian flows, traffic congestions, and microclimates of built environment, and to mete out instant responses and regulatory measures for their management. It is also instrumental in efficiently simulating slow or long-run dynamics to explore future horizons of dynamical urban systems, and learn new dynamics hidden in data or elusive to us. Afterall, appropriate system simplification is one of the most important issues in science in general—as advocated by Einstein's saying paraphrased by Robinson (2018): "Everything should be made as simple as possible, but not simpler," essentially saying that simple but not too simple—and system analysis in particular (Klir 1985). Learning ROMs is explicitly dealt with in this proposed framework.

Specifically, our mission is to bring urban theory—particularly on the dynamic and complex processes—to the construction of digital twins of cities. It is of paramount importance to make digital twins urban theory-based or -informed. That is, we need to embed urban domain knowledge into digital twins so that the process and simulation results are physically meaningful and interpretable. Without urban theories, digital twins will only be technological constructs shedding very little light on our understanding of the complex evolution of cities, which is fundamental to the analysis and prediction of their dynamics and complex behavior pivotal to decision-making. With dynamics and complexity in place, we can then capitalize on the power of our information infrastructure to make more appropriate modeling, simulation, monitoring, and management of emergent urban developments in space and time.

The emphasis of this book is placed on the formulation of a general framework for the modeling of urban dynamics and complexity via digital twins of cities. The information infrastructure—which is essential and covered elsewhere in the literature will not be examined in this book. Nevertheless, a brief discussion is made on the design of sensor networks and the synchronization of models and data for building digital twins. Specifically, a view on the interoperability between models and data is given to ensure that models and data are tightly connected to form a feedback loop so that models can be made theory-based/-informed and/or data driven, and data collection can be made model-informed to optimize urban analysis and city planning. Afterall, what makes digital twins different from general models is the synergistic development of models and data in our investigations (Wright and Davidson, 2020). With historical data and streams of real time or near real time spatiotemporal data, we can update our dynamical models that describe our physical objects/systems, and with models, we can update our information infrastructure to better capture the dynamics and complexity of our physical systems through intelligent sensing and data generation/collection, particularly in real time or near real time. By leveraging real-time insights from theories and data, we can proactively simulate and manage city development to achieve liveability, resilience, and sustainability.

References

Allen PM (1997) *Cities and Regions as Self-Organizing Systems: Models of Complexity*. London: Taylor and Francis.

Allen PM, Strathern M, Baldwin J (2008) Complexity: the integrating framework for models of urban and regional systems. In: Albeverio S, Andrey D, Giordano P, Vancheri A (eds.) *The Dynamics of Complex Urban Systems: An Interdisciplinary Approach*. NY: Physica-Verlag Heidelberg, 21–42.

Allen PM (1984) Self-organization and evolution in urban systems. In Crosby R (ed.) *Cities and Regions as Non-linear Decision Systems, AAAS Selected Symposia, 77*. Boulder: Westview Press, 29–62.

Batty, M (2013) *The New Science of Cities*. Cambridge: MIT.

Forrester J W (1969) *Urban Dynamics*. Cambridge: MIT Press.

Jacobs J (1961) *The Death and Life of Great American Cities*. New York: Random House.

Klir, G. (1985) Complexity: Some General Observations. *Systems Research* 2: 131–140.

Lu K, Zhang K, Zhang H, Gu X, Jin Y, Zhao S, Fu C, Yang Y (2021) A review of model order reduction methods for large-scale structure systems. *Shock and Vibration* Volume 2021, Article ID 6631180. https://doi.org/10.1155/2021/6631180.

Lucia DJ, Beran PS, Silva WA (2004) Reduced-order modeling: new approaches for computational physics. *Progress in Aerospace Sciences* 40(1–2): 51–117.

Robinson A (2018) Did Einstein really say that? *Nature* 557(7703): 30–30.

Wilson AG (1981) *Catastrophe Theory and Bifurcation: Applications to Urban and Regional Systems*. London: Croom-Helm.

Wilson AG (2000) *Complex Spatial Systems*. Edinburgh Gate: Pearson Education.

Wright L, Davidson S (2020) How to tell the difference between a model and a digital twin. *Advanced Modeling and Simulation in Engineering Sciences 7:13*. https://doi.org/10.1186/s40323-020-00147-4.

Chapter 3
Building Digital Twins of Cities Via Governing Equations

3.1 Nonlinearity and Phase Changes in Urban Dynamics

As discussed above, to make digital twins useful to our analysis, simulation, and decision-making, the underlying complexity in city pattern evolution and formation in time and space needs to be incorporated into their construction. The key issue in system complexity is system dynamics because complex systems are generally high-dimensional nonlinear dynamical systems involving many interacting parts/units, emerging properties, and complicated states (Wiggins 1990). Dynamics, particularly those with innate nonlinearity, is what makes urban evolution and self-organization fascinating and important. Thus, nonlinearity is at the heart of complex system behaviors (Wilson 2006)—where we can have nonlinear interactions of micro diversity and macro configuration/reconfiguration (Allen 1984, 1997). Nonlinearity of interactions often gives rise to complex spatiotemporal structures and processes—such as city population growth resulting in complex urbanization, changes in the number and location of jobs, place of residence, distribution of services and facilities resulting in complex urban structures and interactions, land use transition giving rise to complex land use mix, development of transportation and communication infrastructures leading to complex urban mobility and connectedness, and even multiple stakeholder decision-making resulting in complex urban planning processes. Appropriate modeling of these intertwined dynamics and complexities is crucial to the management of city evolution toward resilience and sustainability. Through phase changes in the phase space, we can investigate structural changes of urban phenomena in space and time. Phase space depicts the states of system variables at each point in time along corresponding trajectories. Its dimension is determined by the number of defining variables of a dynamical system. By modeling the trajectories starting from some initial conditions, we may be able to predict what the urban system might develop into the future. Therefore, embedded in digital twins of cities should be linear or nonlinear dynamics giving rise to regular or peculiar urban forms—a set of states toward which an urban system tends to evolve. Specifically, we may wonder whether

Y. Leung, *Digital Twins of Cities*, Advances in Spatial Science,
https://doi.org/10.1007/978-3-032-07966-4_3

city evolution in the long run will end up at a fixed point (an equilibrium), a limit cycle (a self-sustained cyclic oscillation), a limit torus (a limit cycle in which the trajectories are bounded within the region of a ring torus), or a strange attractor. An attractor is an attracting set, a subset of the phase space, containing a dense path onto which a dissipative system will settle given some initial conditions. It characterizes the long-run or asymptotic dynamics of a system. "Strange" means the complicated geometry of the attractor, e.g. a fractal structure, in the phase space of a dissipative chaotic system. Fixed point, limit cycle, and limit torus are nonfractal attractors with predictive behaviors (Crutchfield et al. 1986).

Remark. It is worth mentioning that strange attractor does not need to be chaotic. In nonlinear dynamical systems, particularly the quasi-periodic systems, we can have strange non-chaotic attractor with complicated geometry but insensitive to initial conditions. The transition from strange non-chaotic to strange chaotic attractor occurs when the average contraction and expansion experienced by a trajectory in different regions of the phase space are balanced, and the characteristic signature of this passage to chaos is that the Lyapunov exponent passes through zero linearly from the negative side to the positive side. The Lyapunov exponent measures the sensitivity of a dynamical system to small changes in initial conditions. It renders a time scale for the divergence of nearby trajectories and the identification of chaos. If it—particularly the maximal Lyapunov exponent which measures the average rate at which initially nearby points diverge—is positive, then two trajectories with very small difference in the initial conditions diverge exponentially in time, and we have chaos. If it is zero, then the separation neither shrinks nor grows. If it is negative, then the divergence shrinks to zero. Both situations are non-chaotic. By observing the time series profile of the Lyapunov exponent, we can identify crossover points in the phase space. Relative weights of the expanding and contracting rates determine whether the asymptotic attractor is strange non-chaotic or strange chaotic. It is strange non-chaotic if the contracting rate weighs over the expanding rate, and it is strange chaotic otherwise (Lai 1996). Of course, there are other routes to chaotic attractors. So, a chaotic attractor must be a stranger attractor, but a strange attractor is not necessarily a chaotic attractor.

Conventionally, dynamics are characterized by governing equations in the form of ordinary differential equation (ODE) or partial differential equation (PDE). Therefore, I first focus on the way dynamics with governing equations can be incorporated into digital twins of cities suitable for efficient urban modeling, simulation, prediction, optimization, and control in space and time.

3.2 Dynamics and Complexity in Theory-Based Digital Twins of Cities

Without loss of generality, let us first examine the dynamics of land use change and the complexity thus arises. Land use change is an urban process whose mechanisms and dynamics pertaining to various interactions between people and places have been a key concern in urban studies over the years. Among the simulation paradigms, cellular automata (CA) (Wolfram 1986) is a flexible spatiotemporal finite-state discrete computational framework capable of simulating the complexity of urban growth from bottom up. It is a self-organized system in which complex patterns can be evolved by simple transition rules. In its simplest form, it is a cell-based idea of simulating urban evolution (Tobler 1970, 1979; Couclelis 1985). It, in a way, is an agent-based model in which agents are represented as states in a fixed geographical grid in canonical form with synchronous updating (agent-based models is further discussed in Chap. 7). Through CA, global behavior and system complexity may be understood by using simple transition rules that govern state transitions (Itami 1994). Defining appropriate CA rules is thus crucial to urban land use simulation (Batty et al. 1999; Wu and Martin 2002; Li and Yeh 2000). However, the transition rules are often ad hoc, context, and location dependent. Applying directly the same set of rules to different cities is difficult. The effectiveness of the rules often relies on intensive calibration which may result in overfitting problems. The major critique of such an approach is related to the absence of an urban economic theory underpinning most of the CA models (Batty 2008; Tsang and Leung 2011).

To achieve better generalization and interpretability, defining transition rules with a sound conceptual basis that appropriately represents the underlying mechanism governing land use transitions is thus important. In Tsang and Leung (2011), an attempt was made to formulate CA simulation of land use changes based on a land use transition theory, namely rent gap theory (Smith 1979). Rent gap theory is just used in here as a basis for discussion. Other land use transition theories can also be considered. Judging from the uncertainty involved in the dynamics and stochastic perturbations in complex land use models (Engelen and White 2008), rent gap theory is formulated as a stochastic process by Tsang and Leung (2011). Crucial to their CA simulation is the pivotal rule in the rule set that embeds the build-up value equation on a plot of land at a location at a moment in time. It is a stochastic differential equation which incorporates various dynamics concerning the change of land values in space and time. It indicates the time of appearance of rent gaps that triggers land use redevelopment and transition. Central to the rent-gap-theory-based CA simulation (Tsang and Leung 2011) is the following rule in the rule set saying that: If (build-up value < potential land value), then (rent gap appears and land use change is likely to take place). To build a digital twin for land use redevelopment and theory-based CA simulation, dynamics of the build-up value must then be incorporated. That is, the corresponding digital twin needs to respect the dynamics of such complex process. To demonstrate how to do the incorporation effectively and efficiently, I first give the land value equation and then examine the corresponding order reduction for substantiation.

By applying Ito's lemma and by rearranging the stochastic and non-stochastic terms, Tsang and Leung (2011) formulated in Eq. (3.1) the build-up value of a plot of land at a location at time t for estimating the time of appearance of a rent gap, i.e. the time for redevelopment, as follows:

$$
\begin{aligned}
&\frac{\partial H(S,g,r,t)}{\partial t} \\
&= \mu(t)S(t)\frac{\partial H(S,g,r,t)}{\partial S} + k(t)\left[\gamma(t) - r(t)\right]\frac{\partial H(S,g,r,t)}{\partial r} \\
&+ a(t)g(t)\left[\frac{G(t) - g(t)}{G(t)}\right]\frac{\partial H(S,g,r,t)}{\partial g} \\
&+ \frac{1}{2}\sigma_s^2(t)S^2(t)\frac{\partial^2 H(S,g,r,t)}{\partial S^2} + \frac{1}{2}\sigma_r^2(t)\frac{\partial^2 H(S,g,r,t)}{\partial r^2} \\
&+ \frac{1}{2}\sigma_g^2(t)g^2(t)\frac{\partial^2 H(S,g,r,t)}{\partial g^2} \\
&+ \rho_{sg}\sigma_s(t)\sigma_g(t)S(t)g(t)\frac{\partial^2 H(S,g,r,t)}{\partial S\partial g} \\
&+ \rho_{rs}\sigma_r(t)\sigma_s(t)S(t)\frac{\partial^2 H(S,g,r,t)}{\partial S\partial r} \\
&+ \rho_{rg}\sigma_r(t)\sigma_g(t)g(t)\frac{\partial^2 H(S,g,r,t)}{\partial g\partial r} - r(t)H(S,g,r,t)
\end{aligned}
\tag{3.1}
$$

Equation (3.1) is a governing equation of the land use dynamics. It shows that the rate of change of the build-up value depends on three variables: potential ground rent, S; interest rate, k; and GDP per capita, g. The first three terms are the drift terms used to describe their effects on the build-up value, respectively. The fourth to sixth terms represent volatilities of the interest rate, GDP per capita, and potential ground rent, respectively. The seventh to ninth terms are correlation effects between the three variables. Notation wise, we have $\mu(t)$ being the mean drift of potential ground rent at time t—a spatial factor which depends on the location of a site; $\sigma_s(t)$ being the volatility of potential ground rent—the noise effect due to some uncertain events; and $k(t)$ being the speed of change of the interest rate—which varies with time and depends on the economic conditions. The expected long-run interest rate, $\gamma(t)$, represents the adaptive expectation of the stable level of an interest rate in a market. The volatility of an interest rate, $\sigma_r(t)$, represents the interest rate fluctuation around its mean value. The drift speed of the GDP per capita, $a(t)$, is the speed of change, and it controls the rate of change of GDP per capita. Like the long-run interest rate, the expected long-run GDP per capita, $G(t)$, depends on the economic conditions. The volatility of GDP per capita, $\sigma_g(t)$, reflects the uncertainty in an economy. The terms ρ_{sg}, ρ_{rs}, and ρ_{rg} are the correlations between potential ground land and GDP per capita, potential ground land and interest rate, and GDP per capita and interest rate, respectively. Whether Eq. (3.1) is a parabolic or elliptic PDE depends on the magnitude of its coefficients.

It should be observed that Eq. (3.1) contains the spatial and global parameters. The spatial parameters—mean drift and volatility of land value—are affected by the location of a land parcel and its externalities, and the global parameters—mean drift and volatility of the interest rate and GDP per capita—are determined by the macroeconomic conditions. Thus, it is the interplays among the local and global variables that create the complexity of land use transition. Under complexity, we are interested in how the land use transition system evolves through self-organization (via a set of transition rules in which the build-up value plays a pivotal role), and the spontaneous emergence of global land use patterns out of local interactions of its constituent elements/parts and their interactions with the environment. It is the interactions at the macro and micro levels of the land use system that create its dynamics. These characteristics are effectively encapsulated in the build-up value, Eq. (3.1), and the other associated subrules (see Tsang and Leung [2011] for details). Therefore, such dynamics and complexity must be incorporated into the digital twin to make it theory-based and instrumental to analysis and decision-making. Furthermore, it is a means to incorporate macro dynamics into the CA microscopic behaviors with which local land use resilience can be investigated against the regional and global financial shocks or fluctuations in the multilevel context (This point is further discussed in Chap. 8).

It should be noted that Eq. (3.1) has no analytical solution, and we need to solve it by approximation methods, such as the finite difference method, with which the partial derivatives can be approximated, and the build-up value equation can be discretized into a finite difference equation as follows (Tsang 2007):

$$
\begin{aligned}
&H_{i,j,k,l+1} \\
&= h_t\left\{\frac{\mu S_i}{h_s}+\frac{1}{2}\frac{\sigma_s^2 S_i^2}{h_s^2}\right\}H_{i+1,j,k,l}+h_t\left\{\frac{k(\gamma-r_j)}{h_r}+\frac{1}{2}\frac{\sigma_r^2}{h_r^2}\right\}H_{i,j+1,k,l} \\
&+h_t\left\{\frac{a g_k}{h_g}\frac{(G-g_k)}{G}+\frac{1}{2}\frac{\sigma_g^2 g_k^2}{h_g^2}\right\}H_{i,j,k+1,l} \\
&+h_t\left\{\frac{1}{2}\frac{\sigma_s^2 S_i^2}{h_S^2}-\frac{\mu S_i}{h_S}\right\}H_{i-1,j,k,l}+h_t\left\{\frac{1}{2}\frac{\sigma_r^2}{h_r^2}-\frac{k(\gamma-r_j)}{h_r}\right\}H_{i,j-1,k,l} \\
&+h_t\left\{\frac{1}{2}\frac{\sigma_g^2 g_k^2}{h_g^2}-\frac{a g_k}{h_g}\frac{(G-g_k)}{G}\right\}H_{i,j,k-1,l}+h_t\left\{\sigma_s^2 S_i^2+\sigma_r^2+\sigma_g^2 g_k^2\right\}H_{i,j,k,l} \\
&+h_t\frac{\rho_{sg}\sigma_s\sigma_g S_i g_k}{4h_s h_g}\left\{H_{i+1,j,k+1,l}-H_{i-1,j,k+1,l}-H_{i+1,j,k-1,l}+H_{i-1,j,k-1,l}\right\} \\
&+h_t\frac{\rho_{rs}\sigma_r\sigma_s S_i}{4h_s h_r}\left\{H_{i+1,j+1,k,l}-H_{i+1,j-1,k,l}-H_{i-1,j+1,k,l}+H_{i-1,j-1,k,l}\right\} \\
&+h_t\frac{\rho_{rg}\sigma_r\sigma_g g_k}{4h_r hg}\left\{H_{i,j+1,k+1,l}-H_{i,j+1,k-1,l}-H_{i,j-1,k+1,l}+H_{i,j-1,k-1,l}\right\} \qquad (3.2)
\end{aligned}
$$

where $h_s, h_r, h_g, and\ h_t$ are the number of grid cells with respect to the potential land value, GDP per capita, interest rate, and time, respectively; and $H_{i,j,k,l} = H(S_i, r_j, g_k, t_l)$ notates a rectangular grid cell of dimension $(N_s \times N_k \times N_g \times N_t)$ in space and time, where $S_i = ih_s, r_j = jh_r, g_k = kh_g, and\ t_l = lh_t$. The integers i, j, k, l are respectively $\mathrm{i} = 1, \cdots, N_s, j = 1, \ldots, N_r, k = 1, \ldots, N_g$, and $l = 1, \ldots, N_l$. The equation is to be solved with the absorbing boundary conditions:

$$
\begin{aligned}
&\mathrm{H(S = 0, r = 0,\ g = 0) = 0\,and\,H(S = 0,\ r = 0,\ g = \infty) = 0}\\
&\mathrm{H(S = 0, r = \infty,\ g = 0) = 0\,and\,H(S = \infty,\ r = 0,\ g = 0) = 0}\\
&\mathrm{H(S = \infty, r = 0,\ g = \infty) = 0\,and\,H(S = 0,\ r = \infty,\ g = \infty) = 0}\\
&\mathrm{H(S = \infty, r = \infty,\ g = 0) = 0\,and\,H(S = \infty,\ r = \infty,\ g = \infty) = 0}
\end{aligned}
$$

Of course, other approximations—like the finite element method, finite volume method, and boundary element method—may also be employed to approximate the solutions of PDEs (Morten and Mayers 1994). As a result, we need to deal with the problem of extremely high dimensionality—it can go up to millions of degrees of freedom—and steep computational cost in solving the high-dimensional discretized model (Eq. 3.2) within the CA framework. The problem becomes exacerbating when we need to deal with multiple realizations of the stochastic PDE. Such computational complexity might prevent us from running the CA simulations and obtaining system solutions efficiently, particularly for urban simulation or control problems involving stochastic PDEs where real-time or near real-time solutions are needed. To make the corresponding digital twin efficient for urban land use simulation and prediction, we need to find a surrogate model which is much lower in dimension and yet preserves the salient dynamics of the high-dimensional system. I discuss in the following the derivation of such ROMs.

3.3 Reduced-Order Models for Digital Twins of Cities

Besides land use transition, prediction of and response to other city phenomena—such as urban climate (e.g. temperature and precipitation), air pollution, traffic flow, telecommunication, city-canyon convection, back draft, etc.—all depend on accurate and timely spatiotemporal simulations based on the high-dimensional dynamics. Therefore, digital twins of cities are often required to render off-line, real-time or near real-time simulation of complex dynamics for efficient operations and decision-making. To mitigate the curse of dimensionality and to make models/algorithms scalable, we need to capitalize on the intrinsic low dimensionality of system dynamics. The fluctuations of infectious diseases, for instance, is generally driven by low-dimensional nonlinear dynamics. Realizing that dynamics of a system is generally sparse and there usually exits a low-dimensional solution manifold for the high-dimensional PDE models, we can derive a surrogate model, a ROM, which is of lower computational complexity, much smaller (smaller degree of freedom) and faster to solve, but still possesses salient features of the high-dimensional urban land use theory—in this case, the rent gap theory. Dimension reduction targets at the search for a reduced system with sufficiently low dimension to describe the observable high-dimensional complex dynamics, and yet sufficiently large to retain the characteristics of the original complex system to obtain solutions with acceptable accuracy and low computational cost (Lu et al. 2021). Thus, ROMs can facilitate simulations, particularly real-time simulations, of complex urban systems. It also provides a means for compressing high-dimensional data generated by the simulation of high-dimensional models.

For this case, the idea is to learn the ROM of the high-dimensional model (Eq. 3.2 in this case) by projecting it onto a low-dimensional manifold—i.e. projecting the high-dimensional dynamics onto a low-dimensional subspace spanned by the dominant modes that capture the variability of the dynamical system. In brief, we learn the low-dimensional structure from the much higher-dimensional model through the low-dimensional basis via manifold learning methods such as proper orthogonal decomposition (POD) (Lumley 1967; Berkooz et al. 1993; Lu et al. 2019), or similarly classical principal component analysis (PCA) (Hotelling 1933) and its variants (Jolliffe and Cadima 2016). The purpose of POD is to identify the dominant modes of system variability embedded in the high-dimensional data to construct a low-dimensional model that captures the essential dynamics of the high-dimensional model. We project the high-dimensional system dynamics onto the reduced set of dominant modes. Such projection is structure preserving and the POD basis can extract coherent structures of the dynamics. It seeks the intrinsic modes which constitute the solution space of the dynamical system and preserve the complexity of land use dynamics stipulated in Eq. (3.1). In brief, we look for the optimal embedding space of the land use dynamics characterized by Eq. (3.1). The method, in essence, is to solve its discretized version, Eq. (3.2), to generate data—snapshots/solution vectors (Sirovich 1987)—which are representatives of the high-dimensional solutions of Eq. (3.1) for different inputs—e.g. sampling on the trajectories of the dynamical system generated by different initial conditions and/or different forcing scenarios; representatives of the parameters (in parametrized systems); and different dynamics that we would like the ROM to capture for training and prediction at many instants of time (Swischuk et at. 2019; Ghattas and Willcox 2021; Dar et al. 2023). If the snapshots are representatively chosen, say according to some appropriate time steps or cycles, we generally do not need all the solution vectors to find the POD basis—the fundamental building blocks. We can then project the sampled snapshots onto a low-dimensional space and use the projected snapshots as training data to learn the ROM. Once the ROM is learned, we can use it to simulate the dynamics at future moments in time and run it at conditions not in the training data—e.g. distinctive designs and scenarios—and get predictions and error estimates for evaluation. Digital twins thus built are interpretable, because of the embedded dynamics and complexity of the land use transition; generalizable, because of their ability to adapt to new circumstances; and efficient for near real-time and real-time simulations, optimizations, and predictions, because of its low dimensionality and simple structure. Of course, it is beneficial for long-term simulations also.

In general, the basis functions in POD are obtained from the singular value decomposition (SVD), a matrix factorization method, of the snapshot matrix. Specifically, we derive the ROM through some projection-based methods (Rowley and Dawson 2017; Lu et al. 2021) that minimize the difference between the high-dimensional solution and the reduced-order solution as follows

$$\arg\min\left\|\mathbf{H}(S, g, r, t) - \mathbf{V}\mathbf{V}_r^T\mathbf{H}(S, g, r, t)\right\| \tag{3.3}$$

where $\mathbf{H}(S, g, r, t)$, $\mathbf{H}$ (x, t) in short, is the m × n snapshot matrix containing n snapshots of the high-dimensional dynamics of the system states over time:

$$\mathbf{H}(x, t) = \begin{bmatrix} | & | & & | \\ \boldsymbol{H}_1 & \boldsymbol{H}_2 & \cdots & \boldsymbol{H}_n \\ | & | & & | \end{bmatrix} \tag{3.4}$$

where $\mathbf{H}_j$, $j = 1, \ldots,$ n, are columns containing the state solutions of the finite difference Eq. (3.2) at different points in time. Given $\mathbf{H}$ (x, t), we want to represent it through separation of variables into spatial structure (the spatial modes), and the corresponding temporal dynamics (the temporal coefficients), as follows

$$\mathbf{H}(x, t) = \sum_{k=1}^{m} u_k(x) a_k(t) \tag{3.5}$$

and low-rank factorize it into $\mathbf{H}(x, t) \approx \mathbf{U}(x)\cdot$ $\mathbf{A}$ (t) via SVD as follows

$$\mathbf{H} = \mathbf{U}\boldsymbol{\Sigma}\mathbf{V}^T \tag{3.6}$$

where $\mathbf{U} = (\boldsymbol{u}_1, \ldots, \boldsymbol{u}_m)$ is a unitary singular-vector matrix of dimension $m \times m$, with $\mathbf{U}^T\mathbf{U} = \mathbf{U}\mathbf{U}^T = \mathbf{I}$; $\mathbf{V} = (\boldsymbol{v}_1, \ldots, \boldsymbol{v}_n)$ is another unitary singular-vector matrix of dimension $n \times n$, with $\mathbf{V}^T\mathbf{V} = \mathbf{V}\mathbf{V}^T = \mathbf{I}$; and $\boldsymbol{\Sigma}$ is a rectangular diagonal matrix of dimension $m \times n$ defined as

$$\boldsymbol{\Sigma} = \begin{pmatrix} \sigma_1 & 0 & 0 & \cdots & 0 \\ 0 & \sigma_2 & 0 & \cdots & 0 \\ & & \ddots & & \\ 0 & & \cdots & & \sigma_r \\ 0 & & \cdots & & 0 \\ & & & \ddots & \end{pmatrix} \tag{3.7}$$

with $\sigma_1 \geq \sigma_2 \geq \ldots \geq \sigma_k > 0$; $\sigma_{k+1} = \ldots = \sigma_q = 0$ being the singular values—energies contained in the corresponding POD modes indicating their relative importance—of $\mathbf{H}$ arranged in descending order of importance, and the vectors $\boldsymbol{u}_1, \ldots, \boldsymbol{u}_m$

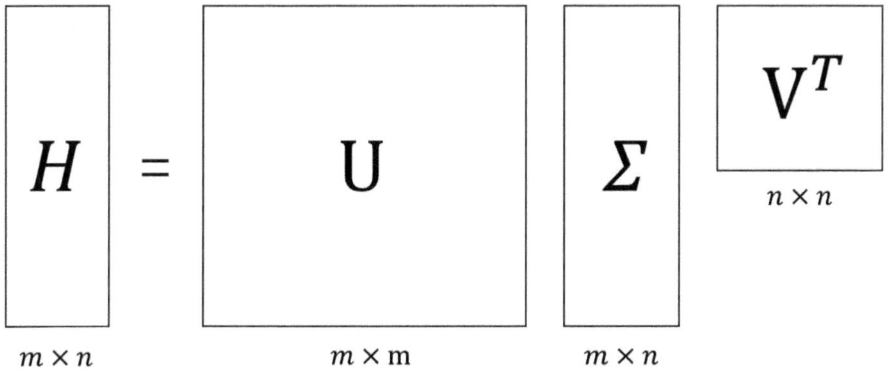

Fig. 3.1 Full singular value decomposition (SVD) of snapshot matrix H

and $\boldsymbol{v}_1, \ldots, \boldsymbol{v}_n$ are the corresponding left and right singular vectors of **H** (Fig. 3.1). The left singular vectors correspond to the dominant spatial or temporal modes, depending on the compositions of the snapshot matrix. The right singular vectors correspond to the coefficients expressing the data in terms of the dominant modes. For a historical account of SVD, see Stewart (1993).

To reduce the dimension of **H**, we can truncate the matrices **U**, **V**, and $\boldsymbol{\Sigma}$ by deleting the columns/rows of $\boldsymbol{\Sigma}$ which are of low significance via, say, the relative information content (RIC) criterion and obtain **U**, **V**, and $\boldsymbol{\Sigma}$ of usually much lower dimension. Through low-rank factorization, we obtain the following optimally truncated (reduced) SVD

$$\mathbf{H} = \mathbf{U}\boldsymbol{\Sigma}\mathbf{V}^T \approx \mathbf{U}_r\boldsymbol{\Sigma}_r\mathbf{V}_r^T = \mathbf{H}_r \tag{3.8}$$

where $r \ll n$, *and* $\mathbf{V}_r$ is the POD basis obtained through the truncation of the SVD of **H** (Fig. 3.2). It should be noted that the POD modes/basis functions intrinsic to the dynamical system form a subspace that optimally represents the data containing the dynamics. By the theorem of Eckart and Young (1936), which was generalized by Mirsky (1960), the truncated SVD gives the best low-rank approximation of the snapshot matrix **H** (St-Onge et al. 2021). It is also the rank at which emergence in a complex system will take place.

The Eckart–Young–Mirsky theorem can be briefly stated in spectral norm (L_2- norm) and Frobenius norm, respectively, as follows

$$\mathbf{H}_r = \arg\min \left\| \mathbf{H} - \mathbf{H}' \right\|_2$$
$$rank\left(\mathbf{H}'\right) = r$$

and

$$\mathbf{H}_r = \arg\min \left\| \mathbf{H} - \mathbf{H}' \right\|_F$$

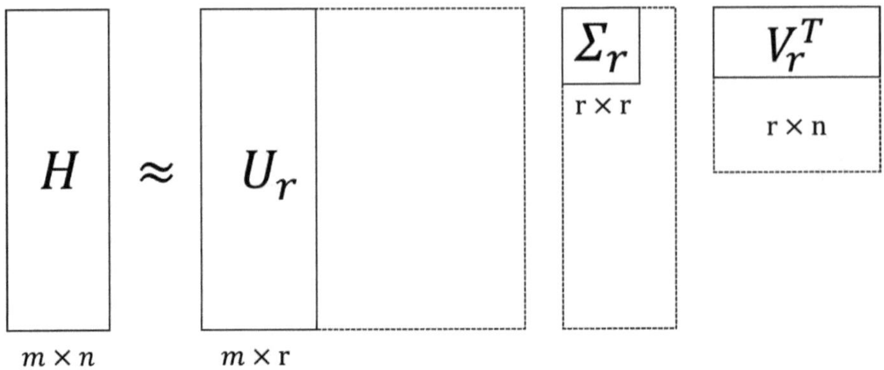

Fig. 3.2 Truncated SVD of snapshot matrix H

$$rank\left(\mathbf{H}'\right) = r$$

The basic idea behind the theorem is that given the snapshot matrix $\mathbf{H}$, we look for the matrix $\mathbf{H}'$ of rank r by means of the optimization method above. The truncated SVD matrix $\mathbf{H}_r$ turns out to be the optimal low-rank approximation of the original snapshot matrix that preserves the most important features of the high-dimensional dynamics in a lower dimensional subspace. It gives a theoretical basis for the search of the best low-rank approximation of a matrix.

It should be observed that $\mathbf{V}_r$ is the truncated $\mathbf{V}$ with r << n, and $\sigma_1 \geq \sigma_2 \geq \ldots \geq \sigma_r \geq 0$ are arranged in descending order of importance. It constitutes the orthonormal POD basis/modes of dimension r which is much smaller than n. It is the low-dimensional manifold/subspace in which the data representing the land use dynamics are embedded. That is, we obtain the POD basis through the low-rank truncation of the SVD, and it is the $\mathbf{V}_r$ that satisfies Eq. (3.8). The dimensionality of the POD depends on the dynamics occurring in the system. The truncated SVD delivers hierarchically reduced coordinates/dimensions for its representation.

It should be mentioned that the POD basis is learned from the snapshots that we sample from the land use dynamical system and can be employed to approximate $\mathbf{H}(S, g, r, t)$ by a linear expansion of the POD basis as follows

$$\hat{\mathbf{H}}(x, t) = \sum_{k=1}^{r} \sigma_k \boldsymbol{u}_k(x) \boldsymbol{v}_k^T(t) \tag{3.9}$$

where $\boldsymbol{u}_k(x)'s$ are the POD modes; $\sigma_k \boldsymbol{v}_k^T(x)$ are the corresponding POD expansion coefficients; and $\hat{\mathbf{H}}(x, t)$ is the POD approximation of $\mathbf{H}(S, g, r, t)$ at time t.

It is through the above low-dimensional manifold learning that we derive the ROM for the dynamics of land use transition. And it is through the ROM that we can model and simulate efficiently land use changes under different scenarios and make appropriate decision. The ROM provides us with a formal foundation to model complex urban dynamics and renders us a way to gain valuable insight into the dynamic behavior of the system, and efficiently evaluate, simulate, and predict complex spatiotemporal urban land use transitions. The idea of POD can be extended to dynamic mode decomposition (DMD) of time series data for the study of temporal evolution of dynamical systems (see discussion in Sect. 4.3 of Chap. 4).

Therefore, low-rank approximation plays an important role in the derivation of ROMs for high-dimensional dynamics. Snapshot matrices that need to be projected onto low-dimensional manifolds may come in with different properties. They could be sparse, symmetric, dynamic with data streams, noisy, etc. We probably need to extend the Eckart–Young–Mirsky theorem to perform low-rank approximation of such matrices. To handle high-dimensional nonlinear dynamical systems more effectively and efficiently, we might need to develop powerful nonlinear theories to do dimensionality reduction in learning dynamics resulting from nonlinear relations/interactions in urban processes.

Remark. In general, stochastic PDEs can be treated as deterministic differential equations with perturbed initial conditions or with random noise—e.g. generated by the space-time Brownian motion—introduced to the PDEs. Stochastic PDEs can commonly be expressed as the sum of deterministic and stochastic functions. In stochastic PDEs, we need to handle multiple realizations by including multiple snapshots of the system states over time. We must structure into the snapshot matrix the deterministic and stochastic components. The generated time series should represent the system states containing contributions from both components at different points in time—the deterministic trend and the stochastic fluctuations by adding noise terms or perturbations to the state variables. To derive the ROM, we can use POD when the stochasticity in the system is relatively low. When stochasticity is relatively high, POD may not be able to capture the great temporal variability, and we may want to use other dimension reduction methods like DMD or POD that can incorporate the temporal evolution of the modes. Thus, a POD-based or DMD-based ROM with very low degrees of freedom renders a means to explore the behavior of large ensembles of PDE solutions efficiently. It gives a good approximation of the expected value of the stochastic PDE solution. As discussed above, the success of POD projection relies entirely on the information in the snapshot set. So, deriving an appropriate snapshot set from the solutions of the high-dimensional stochastic PDEs with high diversity and multiple realizations is pivotal to the learning of a good ROM which we can use to reconstruct and efficiently simulate system behavior under various stochastic conditions. The POD approach can be generalized to the embedding of dynamics in the noisy discrete and continuous spatiotemporal domains with stochastic perturbations (Burkardt et al. 2007; Nouy 2009). For directly dealing with the projection of stochastic PDEs, we can use Karhunen–Loeve transform (Maccone 2009) which, similar in spirit to PCA, decomposes a stochastic process into a set of orthogonal functions/eigenfunctions that captures the dominant modes of variability of the high-dimensional stochastic dynamics in the low-dimensional subspace via SVD. However, practical applications of the transform of huge dataset relies on a powerful numerical algorithm to be efficient. In the presence of stochasticity, we may need to utilize probabilistic methods to analyze the convergence behavior of ROMs.

3.4 Digital Twins of Cities Through Parametric Reduced-Order Models

We generally model the behavior of a dynamical system as a function of space, time, and its parameters. Dynamical urban systems that depend on parameters may exhibit drastic qualitative changes in the dynamics known as bifurcations—can be viewed as topological changes of the attractors—as parameters are slightly varied (Wilson 1981), or chaotic behaviors (Dendrinos and Sonis 1990; Nijkamp and Reggiani 1992). Though a universal definition of chaos does not exist, chaos is generally considered aperiodic long-term behavior in a deterministic dynamical system which is sensitive to initial conditions. They render models of transition or instability when the associated parameters are varied. Chaotic systems may contain just a few units/variables whose interactions, however, generate intricate dynamics in their evolutions. Sensitivity to initial conditions often makes it difficult to accurately predict the evolution of a system because of different trajectories it might follow given the initial conditions. However, the statistical behavior—signified by hyperbolicity, autocorrelation functions, power spectra, etc. (Anishchenko et al. 2004; Araujo et al. 2014)—of such systems is simpler and often predictable. If the parameters are control parameters, it will shed light on the appropriate control of dynamical systems. The basic idea is to stabilize unstable periodic orbits inside a chaotic attractor by slightly adjusting certain control parameters. By tuning the control parameters, we can guide a dynamical system to pass through a phase transition at appropriate time. We can also learn under what critical values the system will experience abrupt qualitative changes. It should be aware that chaotic systems are not necessarily complex, and complex systems are not necessarily chaotic. However, under certain conditions—e.g. certain values of the parameters or variables—a system can be both chaotic and complex.

3.4.1 Reduced-Order Models for Logistic Urban Population Growth

To build a digital twin for urban population growth, for instance, we need to model its dynamics. The most basic model without capacity constraint is the exponential growth model of population

$$P = P_0 e^{rt} \tag{3.10}$$

where P is the population size at time t; P_0 is the population size at the initial time; and r is the intrinsic rate of natural increase, i.e. the birth rate minus the death rate. To be more realistic and general, we can write

$$\frac{dP}{dt} = Pf(P) \tag{3.11}$$

where $f(P) = a - bP$, $(a, b > 0)$—a linear assumption saying that the larger the population, the greater the inhibition of further growth due to carrying capacity.

Thus, we have the Verhulst-Pearl equation for logistic urban population growth (Pielou 1969)

$$\frac{dP}{dt} = P(a - bP) \tag{3.12}$$

where aP is the potential rate of increase of a population of size P, and a is the intrinsic rate of natural increase. Then, the deterministic equation for the population dynamics is

$$dP = \left(aP - bP^2\right)dt \tag{3.13}$$

All complicated dynamics is embedded in the parameter a (May 1976). By changing its value, it generates a large variety of dynamic behaviors. The logistic equation exhibits a cascade of bifurcations that leads to complicated trajectories. It is a strange non-chaotic attractor at the values of a where an accumulation of infinite number of period doublings exists (Feigenbaum 1978). The bifurcations become more frequent when the value of a increases.

The evolution of other urban phenomena like zonal employment can also be represented by the logistic model as follows (Allen and Sangher 1981)

$$\frac{dx_j}{dt} = a\left(1 - \frac{x_j}{N}\right)x_j \tag{3.14}$$

where x_j is the number of employments in zone j; and a is a parameter indicating the speed of adjustment of x_j to its potential value—carrying capacity N—which varies with respect to the position of zone j in relation to activities in other zones.

The logistic equation only describes the dynamics of population growth of a place, e.g. a zone or a city. It does not consider simultaneously the propagation/diffusion of people that structures the population landscape of the interconnected systems. To incorporate population growth and diffusion into digital twins of cities, we need the governing equations of such dynamics. The Fisher-KPP (Kolmogorov-Petrovsky-Piskunov) equation is an appropriate model that captures the interaction between the logistic growth and wave-like diffusion of population in city systems. It takes on the following general reaction-diffusion form

$$\frac{\partial u}{\partial t} = \mu\frac{\partial^2 u}{\partial x^2} + f(u, a) \tag{3.15}$$

i.e.

$$\frac{\partial u}{\partial t} - \mu\frac{\partial^2 u}{\partial x^2} = f(u, a) \tag{3.16}$$

where $u(x, t)$ is the size/concentration/density of population; μ is the diffusion coefficient (the larger it is, the faster the diffusion); and $f(u, a)$ is the reaction term parameterized by the reaction rate a. Both Eqs. (3.15) and (3.16) satisfy the following conditions

$$f(0) = f(1) = 0$$
$$f(u) > 0, \quad for\, 0 < u < 1$$
$$f'(0) = a > 0, \; f'(u) < a, \quad for\, 0 < u < 1$$

The LHS and RHS of Eq. (3.16) depicts the diffusion and reaction parts of the spatiotemporal population dynamics, respectively. For $f(u, x, t) = au(1-u)$, we have the Fisher's equation (Fisher 1937)

$$\frac{\partial u}{\partial t} - \frac{\partial^2 u}{\partial x^2} = au(1-u) \tag{3.17}$$

where μ is removed by nondimensionalization, and the RHS is just the logistic Eq. (3.13). Equation (3.17) depicts the evolution of a population that satisfies logistic dynamics at each point of a city together with diffusion into other parts of the city. There are two equilibrium states in Eq. (3.17): $u = 0$ and $u = 1$, with the former being unstable and the latter being stable fixed points. Depending on the choice of the location-dependent parameter value, we will have phase transition of different dynamical spatiotemporal behaviors in the city population systems.

Sometimes, we may want to incorporate population migration, e.g. periodic migration, into the diffusion process as follows

$$\frac{\partial u}{\partial t} = \mu \frac{\partial^2 u}{\partial x^2} - \omega \frac{\partial u}{\partial x} \tag{3.18}$$

where, with respect to migration alone, we have

$$\frac{\partial u}{\partial t} = -bc\cos(ct)\frac{\partial u}{\partial x} \tag{3.19}$$

for $u(x, t) = u_0(x - b\sin(ct))$ depicts periodic migration waves. For certain parameter values, the system may have chaotic evolutions.

3.4.2 Global Basis for Parameterized Reduced-Order Models

As discussed in Sect. 3.2, for a given snapshot matrix, we can derive a ROM for the dynamics of an urban process, like land use transition discussed above. Reduced-order models such derived can then be used for efficient computation and simulation. The capability of the POD basis in approximating the system states depends on the completeness and quality of the snapshot set. The basic assumption is that the parameter is kept constant. A potential problem is that if another snapshot set is obtained which is drastically different from the previous one that we used for learning because of the change in parameter values, the POD basis previously derived may no longer be appropriate for deriving the ROM for the new snapshot matrix. For example, if the differential equation governing the dynamics of the system is parameterized like the above urban population growth and propagation models, we may need different POD bases to derive the ROM to approximate the corresponding dynamics with respect to different values of the parameter in the parametric space. In general, parameters may represent initial and boundary conditions, system geometry and configuration, land use transition conditions, urban design constraints, Reynolds number for turbulent dynamics, etc. This is especially so in nonlinear dynamics characterized by bifurcations and chaos. It is worth noting that the curse of dimensionality arises when the number of parameters of a chaotic system increases. Under this situation, we need to decide which POD basis is most appropriate for a given snapshot matrix representing a dynamical regime, and ultimately whether we have a global basis for the ROM that captures all the dynamical regimes reflecting the parametrized governing equations over the whole parameter space. That is, such a ROM should possess similar parametric dependence of the original high-dimensional parameterized model and ideally captures the system behaviors at all points of the parameter space so that different plausible realizations of the system can be efficiently simulated. Therefore, instead of one single high-dimensional solution, we may need a family of solutions based on different initial and/or boundary conditions and/or additional parameters to be estimated. The success of order reduction hinges on our ability to generate snapshot sets that capture a wide spectrum of dynamical system behaviors over the time and parameter domains. For this, we need to devise appropriate sampling schemes to obtain representative snapshot sets for the construction of the local or global basis. We can draw samples in the time and parameter spaces and apply the projection operations accordingly. One way to obtain the global basis is to sample on the parameter space and obtain the corresponding snapshots on which we perform the SVD on all the snapshots to obtain a single global basis. Whichever method we use, the idea is to derive a stable and accurate global basis across the parameter space of the underlying dynamics. This may require us to be able to identify the dynamic regimes and then perform the POD on them and subsequently derive the global basis.

To learn the most appropriate ROM, which may be a combination of several parametrized ROMs, we can build a library of POD bases augmented by sparse sampling from which we can choose the global basis that matters most through machine learning by leveraging sparsity with regularization (Kutz et al. 2017). The objective of sparsity promotion is to search for the smallest number of most predictive variables in the high-dimensional dataset, and the purpose of regularization is to encourage models to learn more general patterns in data without overfitting.

In brief, for a particular value of the parameter μ, we have $\mathbf{V}_r^{\mu}$ such that

$$\mathbf{H}^{\mu} = \mathbf{V}_r^{\mu} \boldsymbol{\Sigma} \mathbf{U}^T \tag{3.20}$$

For all plausible value of μ we build a library $\mathbf{V}_L$, a matrix $\{\mathbf{V}_r^{\mu}\}$ for all μ, i.e. we store the POD modes with respect to μ into column blocks of $\mathbf{V}_L$. Then, we can approximate $\mathbf{H}$ as follows

$$\hat{\mathbf{H}} = \mathbf{P}\mathbf{V}_L\alpha \tag{3.21}$$

where $\mathbf{P}$ is a $\{0, 1\}$—measurement matrix, with measurement locations taking the value of 1, which defines a projection onto the measurement space $\hat{\mathbf{H}}$ that is employed to approximate $\mathbf{H}$. For certain conditions, a sparse solution of $\hat{\mathbf{H}}$—i.e. using the sparsest vector α—can be obtained as follows (Kutz et al. 2017)

$$\begin{aligned} &\arg\min_{\boldsymbol{\alpha}'} \left\|\boldsymbol{\alpha}'\right\|_1 \\ &\text{s.t. } \hat{\mathbf{H}} = \mathbf{P}\mathbf{V}_L\boldsymbol{\alpha} \end{aligned} \tag{3.22}$$

where $\left\|\boldsymbol{\alpha}'\right\|_1$ is the l_1—norm that promotes sparsity of $\boldsymbol{\alpha}'$.

However, in the above global basis procedure, if the solution manifold has slow decaying Kolmogorov n-width, we most likely need to obtain snapshots at many parameter values for systems with complex dynamics, resulting in prohibitively high computational cost and the truncated global basis might not contain enough POD modes—i.e. the low-rank ROM is not global enough—for accurate simulation and prediction. Under this situation, we might need to obtain the global basis as a concatenation of the local bases derived from projections with respect to different parameter values.

Instead of directly deriving the global basis—which may not be feasible under certain circumstances—we can obtain an interpolated basis by interpolating the local bases of different parameter values. Each local basis corresponding to a particular parameter value is obtained by the POD method discussed above. By transforming each POD-precomputed ROM into a consistent set of generalized coordinates, and by interpolating the associated linear operators on their appropriate matrix manifold, the robust ROM can then be used for efficient simulation and prediction with respect to designated or unseen parameter values (Amsallem and Farhat 2011). It should be noted that if inappropriate interpolation methods are used, the interpolated basis may lose essential properties such as orthogonality. Therefore, property preserving interpolation techniques need to be used to obtain the global basis. It does not matter which method we use to obtain the global basis, obtaining the most appropriate snapshots that capture the multistability properties (see Sect. 9.5 of Chap. 9 for a discussion) of the underlying dynamical complex systems is of paramount importance.

Remark. The projection-based ROM might need a large basis to be faithful to the original high-dimensional dynamics. It has been experimentally observed that the truncated POD modes may be unstable and prone to modeling error, particularly for evolving the dynamics of complex systems. The modes being truncated away at the early stage may partially or entirely lie outside the learned POD-spanned space, but they are significant in accounting for the evolution of the system dynamics, particularly the subtle effects in the high-dimensional data. Hybridization of the POD method with the data-driven approach have been attempted to alleviate instability and to enhance the accuracy of the POD ROM (see citations in Rahman et al. (2018); see also Guan et al. (2020) for the use of SINDy). However, such hybridization may increase the computational overhead. A discussion is given in Chap. 4 on incorporating dynamics and complexity into digital twins of cities by the hybridization of projection-based methods and data-driven methods.

Since urban systems are ever evolving, the underlying dynamics themselves may change over time. To be in tone with such time-varying/time-dependent system behavior, dynamic updating of the basis through adaptive basis selection and construction methods may need to be developed to derive time-adaptive ROMs of urban dynamics across various temporal regimes. Adaptive projection methods—such as dynamic POD that captures time evolving modes for low-dimensional manifold learning—will be resourceful for such undertaking. The Bayesian approach to data assimilation (discussed in Chap. 9) and the error propagation methods (discussed in Chap. 10) will be useful for the updating of system parameters, initial conditions, boundary conditions, and ROMs with observed data embedded with noise or errors.

To handle high-dimensional nonlinear dynamical systems more effectively and efficiently, we might need to develop nonlinear theories to do dimensionality reduction in learning dynamics due to nonlinear relations/interactions in urban processes. To improve computational efficiency, we might employ parallel computing or novel nonlinear model order reduction techniques tailored particularly for high-dimensional systems.

Figure 3.3 summarizes our discussion in this Chapter.

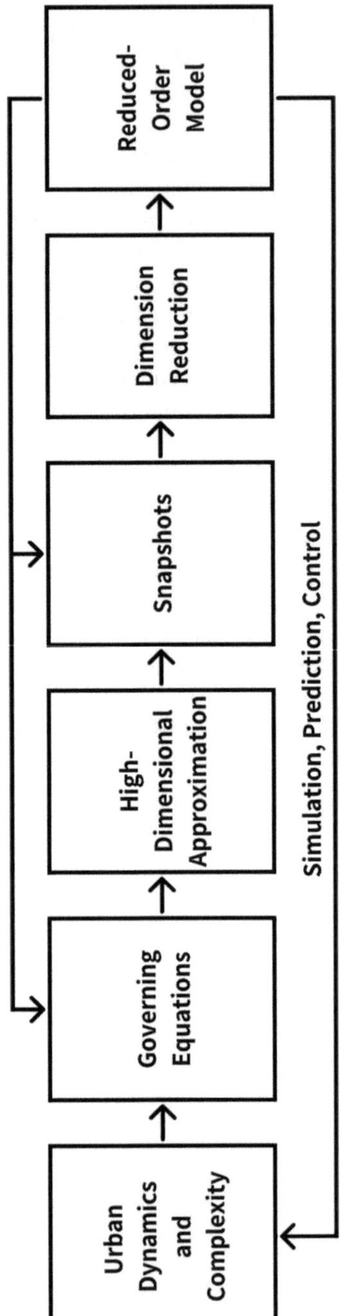

Fig. 3.3 Deriving reduced-order models for digital twins of cities from urban dynamics via governing equations

References

Allen PM (1984) Self-organization and evolution in urban systems. In Crosby R(ed.) *Cities and Regions as Non-linear Decision Systems, AAAS Selected Symposia, 77*. Boulder: Westview Press, 29–62.

Allen PM (1997) *Cities and Regions as Self-Organizing Systems: Models of Complexity*. London: Taylor and Francis.

Allen PM, Sangher M (1981) Urban evolution, self-organization and decision Making. *Environment and Planning* 13: 169–183.

Amsallem D, Farhat C (2011) An online method for interpolating linear parametric reduced-order models. *SIAM Journal on Scientific Computing* 33.5: 2169–2198.

Anishchenko VS, Vadivasova TE, Strelkova GI, Okrokvertskhov GA (2004) Statistical properties of dynamical chaos. *Mathematical Biosciences and Engineering* 1(1): 161–184.

Araujo V, Galatolo S, Pacifico MJ (2014) Statistical properties of Lorenz-like flows, recent developments and perspectives. *International Journal of Bifurcation and Chaos* 24 (10): 1430028. https://doi.org/10.1142/S0218127414300286.

Batty M (2008) Fifty years of urban modeling: macro-statics to micro-dynamics. In: Albeverio S, Andrey D, Giordano P, Vancheri A (eds.) *The Dynamics of Complex Urban Systems: An Interdisciplinary Approach*. NY: Physica-Verlag Heidelberg, 1–22.

Batty M, Xie Y, Sun Z (1999) Modeling urban dynamics through GIS-based cellular automata. *Computers, Environment and Urban Systems* 23: 205–233.

Berkooz G, Holmes P, Lumley J L (1993) The proper orthogonal decomposition in the analysis of turbulent flows. *Annual Review of Fluid Mechanics* 25(1): 539–575.

Burkardt J, Gunzberger MD, Webster C (2007) Reduced order modeling of some nonlinear stochastic differential equations. *International Journal of Numerical Analysis and Modeling* 4(3): 368–391.

Couclelis H. (1985) Cellular worlds: a framework for modelling micro - macro dynamics. *Environment & planning A* 17: 585–596.

Crutchfield JP, Farmer JD, Packard NH, Shaw RS (1986) Chaos. *Scientific American* 254: 46–57.

Dar Z, Baiges J, Codina R (2023) Reduced order modelling. In Hong H (ed.) *Machine Learning and Deep Learning in Computational Toxicology*, 297–339. Gwerbestrasse: Springer Nature. https://doi.org/10.1007/978-3-031-36644-4_8.

Dendrinos DS, Sonis M (1990) *Chaos and Socio-Spatial Dynamics*. NY: Springer.

Eckart C, Young G (1936) The approximation of one matrix by another of lower rank. *Psychometrika* 1.3: 211–218.

Engelen G, White R (2008) Validating and calibrating integrated cellular automata-based models of land use change. In Albeverio S, Andrey D, Giordaño P, Vancheri A (eds.) *The Dynamics of Complex Urban Systems: An Interdisciplinary Approach*. NY: Physica-Verlag Heidelberg, 164–184.

Feigenbaum MJ (1978) Quantitative universality for a class of nonlinear transformations. *Journal of Statistical Physics* 19 (1): 25–52.

Fisher RA (1937) The wave of advance of advantageous genes. *Annals of Eugenics* 7(4): 353–369.

Ghattas O, Willcox K (2021) Learning physics-based models from data: perspectives from inverse problems and model reduction. *Acta Numerica*:445–554. https://doi.org/10.1017/S09624929 21000064

Guan Y, Brunton SL, Novosselov I (2020) Sparse nonlinear models of chaotic electroconvection. *Royal Society Open Science* 24 8(8): 202367. https://doi.org/10.1098/rsos.202367.

Hotelling H (1933). Analysis of a complex of statistical variables into principal components. *Journal of Educational Psychology 24*(6): 417–441. https://doi.org/10.1037/h0071325

Itami RM (1994) Simulating spatial dynamics: cellular automata theory. *Landscape and Urban Planning* 30(1–2): 27–47.

Jolliffe IT, Cadima J (2016) Principal component analysis: a review and recent developments. *Philosophical Transaction A* 374: 20150202. https://doi.org/10.1098/rsta.2015.0202.

Kolmogorov A, Petrovskii I, Piskunov N (1937) Study of a diffusion equation that is related to the growth of a quality of matter, and its application to a biological problem. *Moscow University Mathematics Bulletin*: 1(1–26).

Kutz JN, Sargsyan S, Brunton SL (2017) Leveraging sparsity and compressive sensing for reduced order modelling. In Benner P, Ohlberger M, Patera A, Rozza G, Urban K (eds.) *Model Reduction of Parametrized Systems*. Gewerbestrasse: Springer, 301–315.

Lai YC (1996) Transition from strange nonchaotic to strange chaotic attractors. *Physical Review E* 53(1): 57–65.

Li X, Yeh AGO (2000) Modeling sustainable urban development by the integration of constrained cellular automata and GIS. *International Journal of Geographical Information Science* 14:131–152.

Lu K, Jin Y, Chen Y, Yang Y, Hou L, Zhang Z, Li Z, Fu C (2019) Review for order reduction based on proper orthogonal decomposition and outlooks of applications in mechanical systems. *Mechanical Systems and Signal Processing* 123: 264–297.

Lu K, Zhang K, Zhang H, Gu X, Jin Y, Zhao S, Fu C, Yang Y (2021) A review of model order reduction methods for large-scale structure systems. *Shock and Vibration* Volume 2021, Article ID 6631180. https://doi.org/10.1155/2021/6631180.

Lumley JL (1967) The structure of inhomogeneous turbulent flows. Atmospheric turbulence and radio wave propagation. In Yaglom AM, Tartarsky VI (eds.) *Atmospheric Turbulence and Radio Wave Propagation*, Nauka, Moscow, 166–177.

Maccone C (2009) A simple introduction to the KLT (Karhunen—Loève Transform). In *Deep Space Flight and Communications,* Chichester: Praxis. https://doi.org/10.1007/978-3-540-72943-3_10.

May R (1976) Simple mathematical models with very complicated dynamics. *Nature* 261: 459–467.

Mirsky L (1960) Symmetric gauge functions and unitarily invariant norms. *Quarterly Journal of Mathematics* 11: 50–59. https://doi.org/10.1093/qmath/11.1.50.

Morten KW, Mayers DF (1994) *Numerical Solution of Partial Differential Equations: An Introduction.* NY: Cambridge University Press.

Nijkamp P, Reggiani A (1992) Interaction*, Evolution and Chaos in Space.* Berlin: Springer-Verlag.

Nouy A (2009) Recent developments in spectral stochastic methods for the numerical solution of stochastic partial differential equations. *Archives of Computational Methods in Engineering* 16: 251–285.

Pielou EC (1969) *An Introduction to Mathematical Ecology*. NY: Wiley.

Rahman S, San O, Rasheed A (2018) A hybrid approach for model order reduction of barotropic quasi-geostrophic turbulence. *Fluids 3*(4): 86. https://doi.org/10.3390/fluids3040086.

Rowley CW, Dawson STM (2017) Model reduction for flow analysis and control. *Annual Review of Fluid Mechanics* 49: 387–417.

Sirovich L (1987) Turbulence and the dynamics of coherent structures. I. Coherent structures. *Quarterly of Applied Mathematics 45 (3): 561–571.*

Smith N (1979) Toward a theory of gentrification, a back to the city movement by capital, not people. *Journal of the American Planning Association 45: 538 –549.*

St-Onge G, Thibeault V, Allard A, Dube LJ, Hebert-Dufresne L (2021) Master equation analysis of mesoscopic localization in contagion dynamics on higher-order networks. *Physical Review E* 103, 032301. https://doi.org/10.1103/PhysRevE.103.032301.

Stewart GW (1993) On the early history of the singular value decomposition. SIAM Review, 35 (4): 551–566.

Swischuk R, Mainini L, Peherstorfer B, Willcox K (2019) Projection-based model reduction: formulations for physics-based machine learning. *Computers and Fluids* 179: 704–717.

Tobler, WR (1970) A Computer Model Simulation of Urban Growth in the Detroit Region. *Economic Geography* 46: 234–240.

Tobler WR (1979) Cellular geography. In Gale S, Olsson G (eds.) *Philosophy in Geography.* Dordrecht: D Reidel, 279–386.

Tsang SW (2007) *A Rent-gap-theory-based Cellular Automata Approach to Urban Land Use Simulation.* PhD dissertation. Department of Geography and Resource Management, The Chinese University of Hong Kong. UMI Number: 3295104.

Tsang SW, Leung Y (2011) A theory-based cellular automata for the simulation of land-use change. *Geographical Analysis* 43:142–171.

Wiggins S (1990) *Introduction to nonlinear applied dynamical systems and chaos.* Berlin: Springer.

Wilson AG (1981) *Catastrophe Theory and Bifurcation: Applications to Urban and Regional Systems.* London: Croom-Helm.

Wilson AG (2006) Ecological and urban systems models: some explorations of similarities in the context of complexity theory. *Environment and Planning A* 38: 633–646.

Wolfram S. (1986) *Theory and Applications of Cellular Automata.* Singapore: World Scientific.

Wu F, Martin D (2002) Urban expansion simulation of southeast England using population surface modeling and cellular automata. *Environment and Planning A* 34:1855–1876.

Chapter 4
Data-Driven Approach to the Construction of Digital Twins of Cities

4.1 The Necessity of Enabling Digital Twins of Cities with Data-Driven Learning

In the above discussion, reduced-order models are urban theory-based models whose derivation requires the knowledge of the equations governing complex system dynamics. However, for highly complex urban systems, we may not know which variables will be present, and we may not be able to explicitly describe the underlying dynamics, or we may not even know the governing equations of the structural evolution (Allen et al. 2008). For instance, the backdraft phenomenon in building fires—the abrupt burning of superheated gases—is highly complex with nonlinear dynamics. It depends on hot smoke components, temperature, energy balance, oxygen supply, building layout, and various environmental conditions. To build a digital twin for building backdraft, we need to be able to represent and simulate the phenomenon for its complicated dynamics and abrupt changes and predict the onsets of severe fire events and backdraft explosions. Though the stages of development of backdraft are generally known, its exact dynamics is difficult to characterize, albeit we may model it as a volatile phenomenon via catastrophe theory (Zeeman 1976) exhibiting, for example, the cusp catastrophe as parameters change (Bishop et al. 1993). Under these situations, we may need to unravel the hidden macroscopic dynamics directly from observations/data and construct an efficient model for real-time simulation of such fast dynamics. Besides these fast dynamics, we may not have a clear knowledge about the governing equations of many slower or long-term urban dynamics and spatial interactions. We need to rely on data to unravel and formally represent these hidden dynamics. Therefore, urban dynamical analysis and complexity modeling via digital twins of cities need to be made data-driven under these circumstances.

Sparse regression methods, Gaussian processes, and neural network models are common approaches to the data-driven discovery of equations governing the dynamics of complex systems. The first approach employs sparse regression methods that take advantage of the sparsity of nonlinear terms constituting the underlying

Y. Leung, *Digital Twins of Cities*, Advances in Spatial Science,
https://doi.org/10.1007/978-3-032-07966-4_4

governing equations to learn parsimonious models of city evolution. Sparse identification of nonlinear dynamics can be extended to model learning in a noisy environment with stochastic perturbations and controls. It can also be combined with neural networks to find the right coordinates of dynamical systems. The second approach is the Gaussian process with mixture distributions. It is the statistical learning of hidden dynamics with complete or incomplete observations in the phase space. Neural networks constitute the third approach in which black box methods are employed to uncover nonlinear mappings between system inputs and outputs. These approaches are respectively discussed in the sections to follow.

4.2 Discovering Governing Equations of Urban Dynamics via Sparse Identification

Inspired by the genetic programming approach to the discovery of nonlinear differential equations governing dynamical systems (Schmidt and Lipson 2009), Brunton et al. (2016a) proposed a method for the sparse identification of nonlinear dynamical systems (SINDy) in which no assumptions are made on the forms of the equations governing the underlying dynamics. By observing that most dynamical systems have relatively few nonlinear terms out of a family of possible terms constituting the governing equations, and by leveraging on sparsity, SINDy targets the discovery of a model out of many candidate models that balance sparsity and accuracy along the Pareto front—the trade-off frontier between sparsity and accuracy. It attempts to find the most relevant few terms by penalizing the number of terms in the dynamics through a regularization procedure that scale well to large problems. So, it attempts to recover the dynamics we may have some knowledge about in a parsimonious form and hopefully discover dynamics that are elusive to us. In short, it is a data-driven method for the identification of a sparse set of nonlinear terms that can best describe the underlying dynamics. It unravels the parsimonious governing equations through a linear combination of some basic functions/terms selected from a pre-constructed function library representing the functional space.

4.2.1 Deriving Reduced-Order Model by Sparse Identification of Nonlinear Dynamical Systems

Taking the stance that the dynamics f in many dynamical systems

$$\dot{\mathbf{x}}(t) = \frac{d}{dt}\mathbf{x}(t) = f(\mathbf{x}(t)) \tag{4.1}$$

are nonlinear and sparse in the space of the RHS function, where the vector

$$\mathbf{x}(t) = [x_1(t)\ x_2(t) \cdots x_n(t)]^T \tag{4.2}$$

is the state of the system variables with respect to time t, and $\dot{\mathbf{x}}(t)$ is the corresponding time derivatives. To determine the form of the function, we can obtain the time series of observational data about the state along the trajectories of the vector field and construct them as a snapshot matrix $\mathbf{X}$ along with the matrix of the corresponding derivatives $\dot{\mathbf{X}}$ as

$$X = \begin{bmatrix} \mathbf{X}^{\mathrm{T}}(t_1) \\ \mathbf{X}^{\mathrm{T}}(t_2) \\ \vdots \\ \mathbf{X}^{\mathrm{T}}(t_m) \end{bmatrix} = \begin{bmatrix} x_1(t_1) & x_2(t_2) & \ldots & x_n(t_n) \\ x_1(t_2) & x_2(t_2) & \ldots & x_n(t_n) \\ \vdots & \vdots & & \vdots \\ x_1(t_m) & x_2(t_m) & \cdots & x_n(t_m) \end{bmatrix} \tag{4.3}$$

$$\dot{\mathbf{X}} = \begin{bmatrix} \dot{\mathbf{X}}^{\mathrm{T}}(t_1) \\ \dot{\mathbf{X}}^{\mathrm{T}}(t_2) \\ \vdots \\ \dot{\mathbf{X}}^{\mathrm{T}}(t_m) \end{bmatrix} = \begin{bmatrix} \dot{x}_1(t_1) & \dot{x}_2(t_2) & \ldots & \dot{x}_n(t_n) \\ \dot{x}_1(t_2) & \dot{x}_2(t_2) & \ldots & \dot{x}_n(t_n) \\ \vdots & \vdots & & \vdots \\ \dot{x}_1(t_m) & \dot{x}_2(t_m) & \cdots & \dot{x}_n(t_m) \end{bmatrix} \tag{4.4}$$

where each column of the corresponding matrix is the time series of x_i, i =1, 2, …, n, taken at time instants 1,2, …, m.

Based on matrix $\mathbf{X}$, we can construct a library of candidate nonlinear functions, $\theta(\mathbf{X})$, that may describe the observed dynamics as

$$\theta(\mathbf{X}) = \begin{bmatrix} | & | & | & & | & & | & | & \\ 1 & \mathbf{X} & \mathbf{X}^2 & \cdots & \mathbf{X}^{\mathrm{d}} & \cdots & \sin(\mathbf{X}) & \cos(\mathbf{X}) & \cdots \\ | & | & | & & | & & | & | & \end{bmatrix} \tag{4.5}$$

where $\theta(\mathbf{X})$ denotes a matrix with column vectors being all possible time series of polynomials of degree d in the state $\mathbf{x}$, and the rest may be trigonometric functions or any functions that may plausibly account for the dynamics. For example,

$$\mathbf{X}^2 = \begin{bmatrix} x_1^2(t_1) & x_1(t_1)x_2(t_1)\ldots & x_1(t_1)x_n(t_1)\ldots & x_2^2(t_1)\ldots & x_n^2(t_1) \\ x_1^2(t_2) & x_1(t_2)x_2(t_2)\ldots & x_1(t_2)x_n(t_2)\ldots & x_2^2(t_2)\ldots & x_n^2(t_2) \\ \vdots & \vdots & \vdots & \vdots & \vdots \\ x_1^2(t_m) & x_1(t_m)x_2(t_m)\ldots & x_1(t_m)x_n(t_m)\ldots & x_2^2(t_m)\ldots & x_n^2(t_m) \end{bmatrix} \tag{4.6}$$

Since we suspect that only a few of these nonlinearities are relevant to the dynamics, we may represent $\dot{\mathbf{x}}(t) = f(\mathbf{x}(t))$ as a sparse regression problem (Loiseau and Brunton 2018)

$$\dot{\mathbf{X}} = \theta(\mathbf{X})\boldsymbol{\xi} \tag{4.7}$$

where each column $\boldsymbol{\xi}_k$ in the matrix $\boldsymbol{\xi} = (\boldsymbol{\xi}_1 \boldsymbol{\xi}_2 \ldots \boldsymbol{\xi}_n)$ is a sparse vector of coefficients determining which terms are active in each row of f. We would like to have as few terms as possible in $\boldsymbol{\xi}$. Such a parsimonious model may be obtained by performing a convex l_1—regularized sparse regression—such as the least absolute shrinkage and selection operator (LASSO) (Tibshirani 1996). Therefore, $\boldsymbol{\xi}_k$ is obtained as

$$\boldsymbol{\xi}_k = arg \min_{\boldsymbol{\xi}_k} \left\| \dot{\mathbf{X}}_k - \theta(\mathbf{X})\boldsymbol{\xi}_k \right\|_2 + \lambda \left\| \boldsymbol{\xi}_k \right\|_1 \tag{4.8}$$

where $\dot{\mathbf{X}}_k$ stands for the k-th row of $\dot{\mathbf{X}}$; or more efficiently, using the sequential thresholded least-square algorithm (Brunton et al. 2016a) for very large datasets. The sparsity parameter λ—that controls the amount of sparsity—is chosen to strike a good trade-off between complexity and model accuracy while avoiding overfitting. The $\boldsymbol{\xi}$ such determined allows us to construct a model of each row of the governing equation as follows:

$$\dot{x}_k = f_k(\boldsymbol{x}) = \theta\left(\boldsymbol{x}^T\right)\boldsymbol{\xi}_k \tag{4.9}$$

where $\theta\left(\boldsymbol{x}^T\right)$ is a vector of symbolic functions of elements of $\boldsymbol{x}$. The overall model becomes

$$\dot{\boldsymbol{x}} = f(\boldsymbol{x}) = \boldsymbol{\xi}^T \left(\theta\left(\boldsymbol{x}^T\right)\right)^T \tag{4.10}$$

Therefore, we can recover through SINDy the known dynamics of a complex system, and we may discover elusive dynamics hidden in the system. It is useful to note that we can impose constraints on the entries of $\boldsymbol{\xi}$ so that prior knowledge reflecting physical properties of the problem can be incorporated (see relevant discussion in Chap. 5).

4.2.2 *Sparse Identification of Chaotic Urban Dynamics*

The above approach, for instance, can be employed to study the dynamics of population size, employment rate, and immigration rate of cities based on the classical Lorenz equations describing a dissipative dynamical system (Lorenz 1963; Sparrow 1982)

$$\begin{aligned} \frac{\mathrm{d}x}{\mathrm{d}t} &= \sigma(y - x) \\ \frac{\mathrm{d}y}{\mathrm{d}t} &= x(\rho - z) - y \\ \frac{\mathrm{d}z}{\mathrm{d}t} &= xy - \beta z \end{aligned} \tag{4.11}$$

where σ, ρ, and $\beta > 0$ are parameters representing respectively the Prandtl number, the Rayleigh number, and a nameless number (e.g. it can be used to characterize the aspect ratio of the convection cell in thermal convection). The system is defined in three dimensions with the Lyapunov spectrum containing three Lyapunov exponents. The signs of the three exponents indicate the continuous expansion and contraction of trajectories along the three dimensions/axes, respectively. The sum of all Lyapunov exponents is the rate of expansion or contraction of the phase space. The coexistence of both positive and negative Lyapunov exponents is indicative of strangeness. When $\sigma = 10$, $\rho = 28$ and $\beta = 8/3$, the famous butterfly shape—a fractal—appears (Lorenz 1963). The system is chaotic in that two trajectories starting with adjacent initial conditions diverge exponentially in time, but each converges to the attracting set, leading to completely different futures that are difficult to predict. So, the Lorenz attractor is both chaotic and strange in general sense. However, it has been shown that the chaotic behavior of the classical Lorenz system and its variants appears only for certain combinations of their parameter values (Sparrow 1982; Algaba et al. 2018).

Based on Eq. (4.11), Nijkamp and Reggiani (1992) modeled the evolution of a city during a certain phase of its development characterized by a structural decline via the Lorenz-based equations as follows:

$$\begin{aligned}
\frac{\mathrm{d}x}{\mathrm{d}t} &= \sigma_1 y - \sigma_2 \\
\frac{\mathrm{d}y}{\mathrm{d}t} &= -\delta_1 y - \delta_2 xz + \delta_3 x \\
\frac{\mathrm{d}z}{\mathrm{d}t} &= -\beta_1 z + \beta_2 xy
\end{aligned} \tag{4.12}$$

where x, y, and z are the population size, employment rate, and immigration rates, respectively; σ_1 and σ_2 are the growth and decline rates, respectively; $-\delta_1$ is the negative growth rate of the employment potential of a structurally declining city, δ_2 is the influence of the city size, and δ_3 is the positive influence by a rise in city size, respectively; β_1 is the growth rate of the immigration rate and β_2 is the influence of agglomeration economies emerging from city size.

Specifically, to discover the dynamics with respect to the classical Lorenz model in Eq. (4.11) which has seven terms, we may structure Eq. (4.7) as

$$\underbrace{\begin{bmatrix} \dot{x} & \dot{y} & \dot{z} \\ | & | & | \end{bmatrix}}_{\dot{X}} = \underbrace{\begin{bmatrix} \mathbf{1} & x & y & z & x^2 & xy & xz & y^2 & \dots & z^2 \\ | & | & | & | & | & | & | & | & \dots & | \end{bmatrix}}_{\theta(\mathbf{X})} \underbrace{\begin{bmatrix} \xi_1 & \xi_2 & \xi_3 \\ | & | & | \end{bmatrix}}_{\xi} \tag{4.13}$$

Here, $\dot{x} = dx/dt$, $\dot{y} = dy/dt$, $\dot{z} = dz/dt$. And the unknown model takes the following general form

$$\begin{aligned}
\dot{x} &= a_0 + a_1x + a_2y + a_3z + a_4x^2 + a_5xy + a_6xz + a_7y^2 + \ldots + a_kz^2 \\
\dot{y} &= b_0 + b_1x + b_2y + b_3z + b_4x^2 + b_5xy + b_6xz + b_7y^2 + \ldots + b_kz^2 \\
\dot{z} &= c_0 + c_1x + c_2y + c_3z + c_4x^2 + c_5xy + c_6xz + c_7y^2 + \ldots + c_kz^2
\end{aligned} \tag{4.14}$$

where k is an integer depending on the number of coefficients (number of candidate terms in the library) to be identified. The low-dimensional Lorenz model with fewer terms than the classical model can then be learned according to the procedure described above (Fig. 4.1). Similar procedure can also be employed to learn other Lorenz-like systems.

Remark. Since the Lorenz-like systems—including the classical Lorenz system—are polynomial differential system with nonlinearity coming from the cross product of variables like xy and xz, we can define a more general Lorenz-like system as follows (Messias and Silva 2022).

$$\begin{aligned}
\dot{x} &= a_1x + b_1y + c_1z + d_1yz \\
\dot{y} &= a_2x + b_2y + c_2z + d_2xz \\
\dot{z} &= a_3x + b_3y + c_3z + d_3xy
\end{aligned} \tag{4.15}$$

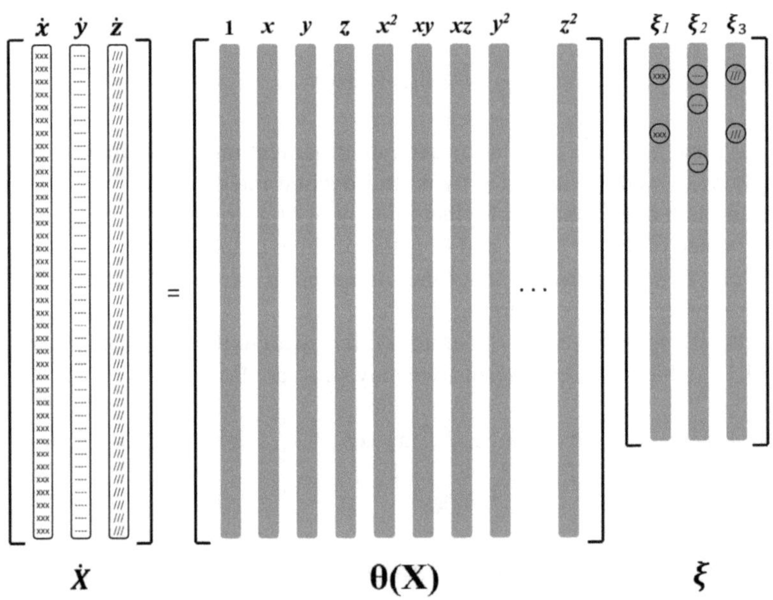

Fig. 4.1 Unraveling Lorenz Equations by sparse identification of nonlinear dynamical systems (SINDy) (Based on Brunton et al. (2016a))

With a suitable choice of the parameters a_i, b_i, c_i, and $d_i \in \mathbb{R}$, $i = 1, 2, 3$, we can obtain various kinds of Lorenz-like systems. As stated above, these systems are chaotic only for certain combinations of the parameter values. Then it is logical to ask under what conditions on the parameters are these systems non-chaotic, and under what manipulations will there be a transition in behavior from non-chaotic to chaotic. Based on the integrability theory (Dumortier et al. 2006), Messias and Silva (2022) gave the sufficient conditions on the parameters which can ensure the non-chaotic behavior of the general Lorenz-like system in Eq. (4.15). They also showed that these non-chaotic differential systems have invariant algebraic surfaces containing the stable (or unstable) invariant manifolds of their equilibrium points. Slightly perturbing the parameter values can destroy the invariant algebraic surface and subsequently deforms these invariant manifolds and reorganizes the global structure of the phase space, leading to a transition from non-chaotic to chaotic behavior of such differential systems. Perhaps the transient dynamics capturing the system transition from one distinct region to another separate region of the phase space makes urban dynamics more interesting and important.

4.3 Sparse Identification of Underlying Urban Dynamics in a Noisy Environment

Since measurements obtained from observations, especially from sensors, may contain noise, the data matrix $\mathbf{X}$ and the corresponding derivatives $\dot{\mathbf{X}}$ may be contaminated with noise, which in turn makes it difficult to obtain an accurate and robust model with, for example, the sparse regression procedure. Under this situation, the snapshot matrix of the state variables needs to contain noise in the measurements. The library matrix $\theta(\mathbf{X})$ should contain candidate functions that represent the noise terms/functions and/or interactions between state variables and noise in order to discern true system dynamics and noisy outliers/artifacts. Brunton et al. (2016b) proposed to solve the following extended version of the sparse regression problem

$$\dot{\mathbf{X}} = \theta(\mathbf{X})\boldsymbol{\xi} + \eta\mathbf{Z} \tag{4.16}$$

where $\mathbf{Z}$ is a matrix of independent and identically distributed (i.i.d.) Gaussian noise (random perturbations) with zero mean, and η is the noise magnitude. To simultaneously denoise the data and parsimoniously learn the underlying dynamical system from noisy time series data, Kaheman et al. (2020) constructed a modified SINDy algorithm that solves the following optimization problem

$$\begin{aligned} &\arg\min_{\xi,\hat{N}} L(\boldsymbol{\xi}, \hat{\mathbf{N}}) \\ &s.t.(|\boldsymbol{\xi}| < \lambda) = 0 \end{aligned} \tag{4.17}$$

where $\widehat{\mathbf{N}} = [\widehat{\mathbf{n}}(t_1); \widehat{\mathbf{n}}(t_2); \ldots; \widehat{\mathbf{n}}(t_m)] \in \mathbb{R}^{m \times n}$ is the estimated noise matrix in which $\widehat{\mathbf{n}}(t) \in \mathbb{R}^{1 \times n}$ is a hyperparameter indicating the estimated noise; L is the loss function involving the sparsity parameters $\boldsymbol{\xi}$ and the noise parameters $\widehat{\mathbf{N}}$; and λ is the value of the sparsity parameter that varies based on the noise added.

If we treat birth and death as chance occurrences, the urban population dynamics in Eq. (3.13) can be expressed as the following stochastic equation (Bartlett 1960):

$$dP = (aP - bP^2)dt + dZ \tag{4.18}$$

where dZ is the chance fluctuation (a stochastic forcing) with $E[dZ] = 0$ and $E\left[(dZ)^2\right] = var[dZ]$. By sampling the stochastic system at ten parameter values of a, and subject it to the SINDY algorithm discussed in Sect. 4.2, Brunton et al. (2016a) correctly identified the underlying parameterized dynamics characterized by parametric governing equations with noise like Eq. (4.16).

However, in realistic data collection settings in cities, particularly those with multi-view sensors, the i.i.d. assumption may be too simple for practical applications. Noise is generally complex and may be non-independent and non-identically distributed. In each view/from each sensor, data noise is often complex that goes beyond the simple Gaussian or Laplacian configuration. Furthermore, the noise distributions of different views are non-identical and distinctive, and noises among different views are usually non-independent but correlated. Under this situation, the data matrix becomes $\mathbf{X} = (\mathbf{X}^v, v = 1, \ldots, V)$, where $\mathbf{X}^v \epsilon \mathbb{R}^{d \times n}$ is the v-th view of the data, and n and d are the number of data samples and the dimensionality in each view, respectively. By considering a generative model, Yue et al. (2020) proposed a novel multi-view subspace learning—which aims to obtain a low-dimensional subspace from multi-view data—by decomposing the observed data from each view into

$$\mathbf{X}^v = \mathbf{S}^v + \mathbf{E}^v \tag{4.19}$$

where $\mathbf{S}^v \epsilon \mathbb{R}^{d \times n}$ is the expected data located on the latent subspace, and $\mathbf{E}^v = \left\{e_{ij}^v\right\}_{d \times n}$ is the noise (residual sum), with e_{ij}^v being modeled as a hierarchical Dirichlet Process Gaussian mixture distribution that accommodates various types of noises going beyond the conventionally assumed i.i.d. noise. The multi-view subspace learning is then carried out by applying the variational Bayes algorithm to solve the integrated graphics model thus constructed (see Yue et al. (2020) for details). This novel approach sheds light on deriving data-driven ROMs to incorporate dynamics and complexity into digital twins of cities in environments contaminated by highly complex noises.

Remark. It should be realized that the dynamics that we attempt to uncover may involve observations collected at m points in time and n locations in space. Under this situation, we first stack the spatiotemporal time series into one column in the data matrix. We then subject it to the sparse regression procedure discussed above to identify the parsimonious governing equations (Rudy et al. 2017).

4.4 Uncovering Underlying Dynamics with Control for Digital Twins of Cities

Feedback control is important in the management of complex urban systems that put some measures in place so that urban development can be made responsive to designated policies. Though government intervention might reduce the efficiency of the free market, it is arguably justifiable under market failure or unexpected externally generated extreme shocks. Governmental mediation might, for example, stabilize housing market by eliminating instability of the chaotic system at a critical state. In the rent-gap-theory-based CA simulation in Tsang and Leung (2011) discussed in Sect. 3.2 of Chap. 3, external interpositions—such as government's development plans at various points in time with or without location preferences, land reclamation policies, and sudden change in development plans—were factored into the CA rule set to accommodate exogenously induced repercussive impacts. As another example, outbreaks and spreads of infectious diseases in cities have spatial and temporal components whose dynamics we would like to change with preventive or intervention measures such as a vaccination campaign (Leung et al. 2011; Ge et al. 2012). We can think of many other urban phenomena—such as traffic congestion due to huge volume of traffic flows involving different transportation modes, varying travel patterns, and road carrying capacities in space and time, etc.—whose dynamics we might want to control, say driving the dynamical system from a chaotic state to a periodic or equilibrium state. Through appropriate controls, we can regulate the robustness and resilience of systems to perturbations and exogeneous influences.

4.4.1 Dynamic Mode Decomposition of Urban Dynamics With Control

Chaos in general is an undesirable state of urban development, and chaos control can redirect the system to the desirable or orderly state—e.g. switching from one attractor to another—with as minimal perturbation as possible. By changing a control parameter, we change the properties of an attractor. Under these situations, we need to extend the learning algorithm to identify an input–output model appropriate for the management of these urban phenomena. The input can be current state of the system and the exogeneous forcings we might want to instill into the system. If we do not have the governing equations of such a high-dimensional control problem, then we can employ the data-driven approach to collect snapshots

$$\boldsymbol{x}_k = \boldsymbol{x}(k\Delta t) \in \mathbb{R}^n \tag{4.20}$$

where n denotes the number of spatial measurements. Using dynamic mode decomposition (DMD) (Schmid and Sesterhenn 2008; Tu et al. 2014), Proctor et al. (2016) proposed to seek a linear operator to form the following approximation.

$$\boldsymbol{x}_{k+1} \approx \mathbf{A}\boldsymbol{x}_k \tag{4.21}$$

Remark. DMD is an equation-free method which only relies on data but not on knowledge of the governing equations. It is a dimensionality reduction algorithm that decomposes complex and nonlinear systems into a set of dynamically invariant and often nonorthogonal modes revealing underlying dynamics of the evolution of coherent structures through spectral analysis. It gives insight into the dynamic system behavior with which we can derive ROMs.

By arranging $m + 1$ snapshots into the current state snapshot matrix $\mathbf{X}$ and the future state snapshot matrix $\mathbf{X}'$ as follows

$$\mathbf{X} = [\boldsymbol{x}_1\boldsymbol{x}_2 \ldots \boldsymbol{x}_m]; \qquad \mathbf{X}' = \left[\boldsymbol{x}_1\boldsymbol{x}_2 \ldots \boldsymbol{x}_{m+1}\right] \tag{4.22}$$

we can relate them by finding an operator $\mathbf{A}$—which is a DMD approximation of the Koopman operator—such that

$$\mathbf{X}' \approx \mathbf{A}\,\mathbf{X} \tag{4.23}$$

The Koopman operator (Koopman 1931) is a linear composition operator that embeds a high-dimensional nonlinear system of finite dimension into an infinite-dimensional linear framework so that methods of linear analysis and control can be efficiently applied.

In brief, for a nonlinear dynamical system

$$\begin{aligned} \dot{\boldsymbol{x}}(t) &= f(\boldsymbol{x}(t)) \\ \boldsymbol{x}_{k+1} &= F(\boldsymbol{x}_k) \end{aligned} \tag{4.24}$$

whose dynamics is unknown to us. If we have data that can be collected and organized into $\mathbf{X}$ and $\mathbf{X}'$, then the linear approximation using the Koopman operator can be expressed in Eq. (4.23) in which $\mathbf{A}$ is used to capture approximately the dynamics in terms of the flow of data under F, which can be measured by measurement g, such that

$$\begin{aligned} \mathbf{y} &= \left[g_1(\boldsymbol{x}_k), g_2(\boldsymbol{x}_k), \ldots, g_q(\boldsymbol{x}_k)\right] \\ \mathbf{y}_{k+1} &= K(\mathbf{y}_k) \end{aligned} \tag{4.25}$$

where K is an infinite-dimensional linear operator that advances measurement functions g, $\mathbf{y} = g(\boldsymbol{x})$, as follows

$$K_g = g \circ F;\ Kg(\boldsymbol{x}_k) = g(\boldsymbol{x}_{k+1}) \tag{4.26}$$

From Eq. (4.23), we can find the approximated linear dynamics $\boldsymbol{A} \approx \mathbf{X}'\boldsymbol{X}^{+}$, where $\boldsymbol{X}^{+}$ is the pseudoinverse. Based on Williams et al. (2015), for dimension reduction, we can employ POD via Eq. (3.6) to parsimoniously approximate $\mathbf{X}$ as

$$\mathbf{X} = \mathbf{U}\boldsymbol{\Sigma}\mathbf{V}^T \tag{4.27}$$

That is, $\mathbf{X}' = \mathbf{A}\mathbf{U}\boldsymbol{\Sigma}\mathbf{V}^T$. Since $\mathbf{A}$ is high-dimensional, we can project the least-square solution $A = \mathbf{X}'\boldsymbol{X}^+$, where $\boldsymbol{X}^+ = \boldsymbol{V}\boldsymbol{\Sigma}^{-1}\boldsymbol{U}^T$, onto the POD modes to obtain a ROM for $\mathbf{A}$ (Proctor et al. 2016) as

$$\tilde{\boldsymbol{A}} = \boldsymbol{U}^T\mathbf{X}'\boldsymbol{V}\boldsymbol{\Sigma}^{-1} \tag{4.28}$$

Now, $\tilde{\boldsymbol{A}}$ is of much lower dimension than $\mathbf{A}$. Subsequently, we can eigen-decompose $\tilde{\boldsymbol{A}}$

$$\tilde{\boldsymbol{A}}\boldsymbol{W} = \boldsymbol{W}\boldsymbol{\Lambda} \tag{4.29}$$

where $\boldsymbol{\Lambda}$ is the eigenvalue matrix containing DMD eigenvalues, and $\boldsymbol{W}$ is the corresponding eigenvector matrix of $\tilde{\boldsymbol{A}}$. Based on Tu et al. (2014), we can obtain the eigenvector matrix of $\mathbf{A}$ as

$$\boldsymbol{\phi} = \mathbf{X}'\boldsymbol{V}\boldsymbol{\Sigma}^{-1}\boldsymbol{W} \tag{4.30}$$

With that we can predict the future states at the k-th time step as

$$\mathbf{X}(k\Delta t) = \boldsymbol{\phi}\boldsymbol{\Lambda}^t\mathbf{d}_0 \tag{4.31}$$

where $\mathbf{d}_0$ are the amplitudes of the DMD modes computed by using the initial conditions.

To cast the whole input–output model in the classical control framework in discrete time, it can be stated as

$$\boldsymbol{x}_{k+1} \approx \mathbf{A}\boldsymbol{x}_k + \mathbf{B}\mathbf{u}_k \tag{4.32}$$

where k is time; $\mathbf{A}$ is an operator on the system – state dynamics; $\mathbf{B}$ is the operator on the impact of the inputs on the state of the system dynamics; and $\mathbf{u}_k$ is the control input. Now in addition to the data matrices $\mathbf{X}$ and $\mathbf{X}'$ in Eq. (4.22), we need to collect another snapshot matrix

$$\boldsymbol{\gamma} = \begin{bmatrix} | & | & & | \\ \mathbf{u}_1 & \mathbf{u}_2 & \dots & \mathbf{u}_n \\ | & | & & | \end{bmatrix} \tag{4.33}$$

for the control from observations in its vector field.

From the DMD with control, $\mathbf{A}$ and $\mathbf{B}$ are approximated from data by

$$\mathbf{X}' = \boldsymbol{A}\boldsymbol{X} + \boldsymbol{B}\boldsymbol{\gamma} \tag{4.34}$$

If $\boldsymbol{B}$ is known, then we can easily solve for $\boldsymbol{A}$ with

$$(\mathbf{X}' - \boldsymbol{B}\boldsymbol{\gamma}) = \boldsymbol{A}\boldsymbol{X} \tag{4.35}$$

If $\boldsymbol{B}$ is unknown, then according to Proctor et al. (2016), we can simultaneously solve for $\boldsymbol{A}$ and $\boldsymbol{B}$ via the application of DMD on the following augmented problem

$$\mathbf{X}' = (\mathbf{A}\,\mathbf{B})\begin{pmatrix} \boldsymbol{X} \\ \boldsymbol{\gamma} \end{pmatrix} \tag{4.36}$$

by taking SVD/truncated SVD on the augmented column matrix on the RHS of Eq. (4.36) and obtaining its pseudoinverse and then using data-driven regression to do the estimation.

4.4.2 *Sparse Identification of Nonlinear Dynamics with Control*

As an alternative, SINDy can be generalized to the identification of nonlinear dynamics with control (Brunton et al. 2016b). From the SINDy perspective for urban management, we may want to use our urban knowledge to instill into city dynamical systems actuations—inputs or feedback controls based on some urban policies—to produce desirable behavior. Our dynamical system becomes

$$\dot{\mathbf{x}}(t) = f(\mathbf{x}(t), \mathbf{u}(t)) \tag{4.37}$$

where $\mathbf{u}(t)$ are the control inputs. Along the line of reasoning of SINDy, we need to build an extended library of functions $\theta(\mathbf{X}, \mathbf{u})$ that incorporates $\mathbf{u}$ and the cross terms of $\mathbf{x}$ and $\mathbf{u}$. If the signal corresponds to an external forcing, then we can solve for the sparse coefficients $\boldsymbol{\xi}$ as follows

$$\dot{\mathbf{X}} = \theta(\mathbf{X}, \mathbf{U})\boldsymbol{\xi} \tag{4.38}$$

where $\mathbf{u}$ is a function of the state $\mathbf{U}$ via sparse regression as above (Brunton et al. 2016b). The augmented snapshot matrix contains the state variables and control inputs. On the other hand, if the signal $\mathbf{u}$ corresponds to a feedback signal, i.e. $\mathbf{u} = k(\mathbf{x})$, then the control $\mathbf{u}$ can be identified as a function of the state as follows

$$\mathbf{U} = \theta(\mathbf{X})\boldsymbol{\xi}_u \tag{4.39}$$

And the sparse coefficients $\boldsymbol{\xi}_u$ can be identified by perturbing $\mathbf{u}$ with a sufficiently large white noise signal so that it can be discerned from the $k(\mathbf{x})$ terms (Brunton et al. 2016b).

Chaotic dynamics may lead to instabilities and unacceptable system irregular vibrations, making long-term prediction impossible because of this exponential amplification of small changes in initial conditions or uncertainties. Chaos control is thus instrumental in preventing a system from entering an undesirable state with minimal perturbation. From the urban planning perspective, effective methods for chaos control are essential for mitigating undesirable urban chaotic behavior. Transforming chaotic oscillations into desirable behaviors or stable solutions via slight perturbations may be a means to the optimal control of city development. To regulate traffic congestion in cities, for example, transport planners may want to have traffic signal timing control or traffic diversion control in response to irregular traffic time dynamics (Kachroo and Sastry 2016). To mitigate the impact of structural decline of a city, policy makers may want to place policy to interfere its decline. Using the Lorenz-equation-based model of Nijkamp and Reggiani (1992) discussed in Sect. 4.2 as an example, mathematically we are placing external forcing on the system as a feedback control by adding a perturbation signal to the input as follows:

$$\begin{aligned}\frac{dx}{dt} &= \sigma_1 y - \sigma_2 x + f(u)\\ \frac{dy}{dt} &= -\delta_1 y - \sigma_2 xz + \delta_3 x\\ \frac{dz}{dt} &= -\beta_1 z + \beta_2 xy\end{aligned} \tag{4.40}$$

For numerical demonstration, Brunton et al. (2016b) used a periodic signal $u(t) = 50sin(10t)$ with $f(u) = u^3$ for the forcing and the system was subjected to SINDy with control for simulation. The algorithm correctly identified the model and predicted the system behavior in response to a new forcing that was not used in the training data.

Similarly, for the logistic model describing the dynamics of urban population growth in Eq. (3.14), we can introduce slight perturbation for its chaotic control as follows

$$\frac{dx_j}{dt} = (a + \delta a)\left(1 - \frac{x_j}{N}\right)x_j \tag{4.41}$$

or,

$$\frac{dx_j}{dt} = a\left(1 - \frac{x_j}{N}\right)x_j + \delta a \tag{4.42}$$

4.4.3 Other Methods for Discovering Underlying Dynamics With Control

Based on the idea of small perturbation, Lin and Jou (1999) formulated a temporal-difference and genetic-algorithm-based reinforcement learning neural network for the control of chaotic systems (See Sect. 4.7 for a discussion on neural networks). The scheme contains two integrated neural networks with the critic network helps to learn the action network which determines the output (control actions) of the learning system. The critic network is a two-layer feedforward neural network with inputs being the states of the environment and the output being the evaluation of the state that generates the internal reinforcement signal—serving as a fitness measure of the action network that produces control actions. Genetic algorithm (GA), see Sect. 5.5 in Chap. 5 for a brief note, is employed to train the action network by using the internal reinforcement signal—indicating the goodness of the current action network—from the critic network as the fitness function.

Al-Kaff et al. (2024), on the other hand, employed the method (Ott et al. 1990) which controls a chaotic system by stabilizing one of the many unstable periodic orbits embedded in an attractor with slight perturbations in some parameters to study bifurcations—changes in the properties of an attractor when the control parameter is changed—and control of chaos observed in the reduced Lorenz model. Klus et al. (2020) proposed a general data-driven framework to compute a matrix approximation of the Koopman generator for finding the governing equations of deterministic dynamical systems and identifying the drift and diffusion terms in stochastic systems. It also gives schemes for open- and closed-loop controls.

4.5 Finding the Right Coordinates for Discovering the Dynamics of Complex Urban Systems

Given a high-dimensional dataset, sometimes we do not know whether the coordinates are right to describe the dynamics observed in the high-dimensional data, and whether we can discover the intrinsic coordinates for a parsimonious representation of the high-dimensional data from which we can learn the governing equations of the dynamics. The POD and DMD methods discussed above find modes for the approximation of a linear subspace that may fall short of capturing the full dynamics of a nonlinear dynamical system. Even if they can aptly catch the nonlinear dynamics, we may need a larger number of reduced coordinates to accomplish the task with acceptable accuracy. Under such circumstances, a nonlinear mapping may better achieve the mission in finding the right coordinates.

4.5.1 Finding Coordinates by Sparse Identification With Autoencoder

Champion et al. (2019) proposed to use an autoencoder (Boulard and Kamp 1988), a special type of neural network in the form of a tuple of two functions (φ, ψ)—i.e. two neural network components—to find the low-dimensional reduced coordinates and then learn the dynamics with SINDy from the reduced data all together (A more detailed exposition of the neural network approach is given in Sect. 4.7). In brief, the encoder network—it can be a deep feedforward neural network—takes the original input and transforms it into a lower dimensional representation via φ. The decoder network—it can be a deep feedforward neural network—then takes the deduced input—with certain information loss from the original input—and reconstructs the original input through ψ. Therefore, the two networks need to work together as a whole to minimize the reconstruction loss through dimension reduction. The deep autoencoder targets at finding the best learning process to achieve dimension reduction of the input with least information loss. It is a method for nonlinear dimensinality reduction. Therefore, Champion et al. (2019) capitalized on the power of autoencoder in obtaining the best reduced coordinates for the data and learn the parsimonious model of the underlying dynamics via the capability of SINDy in the reduced space.

To learn the hidden dynamics with reduced coordinates, their method promotes low dimensionality and sparsity in learning the dynamics embedded in data. Specifically, given the high-dimensional data $\boldsymbol{x}_i$, the autoencoder first encodes the data into a lower dimensional representation in terms of the intrinsic latent coordinates $\mathbf{z}_i$ through a mapping φ—the encoder—and the results can then be decoded back to the high-dimensional data $\tilde{\boldsymbol{x}}_i$ via the mapping ψ—the decoder—as system outputs. The latent representation with autoencoder weights is subjected to SINDy to learn the hidden dynamics via the latent coordinates. The whole process involves the following loss function

$$\frac{1}{N}\sum_{i=1}^{N}\|\boldsymbol{x}_i-\tilde{\boldsymbol{x}}_i\|_2^2 \tag{4.43}$$

with the loss due to SINDy being

$$\frac{1}{N}\sum_{i=1}^{N}\|\dot{\mathbf{z}}_i-\theta\left(\mathbf{z}_i^T\right)\boldsymbol{\xi}\|_2^2 \tag{4.44}$$

where $\dot{\mathbf{z}}_i = \nabla_x\varphi(\boldsymbol{x}_i)\dot{\boldsymbol{x}}_i$, and $\theta\left(\mathbf{z}_i^T\right) = \theta\left(\varphi(\boldsymbol{x}_i)^T\right)$. By incorporating SINDy into the autoencoder, and by considering it together with the regularization on $\boldsymbol{\xi}$, the dynamics is learned by minimizing the following composite loss function

$$\mathcal{L} = \frac{1}{N}\sum_{i=1}^{N}\|\boldsymbol{x}_i - \psi(\varphi(\boldsymbol{x}_i))\|_2^2 + \lambda_1\frac{1}{N}\sum_{i=1}^{N}\left\|\nabla_x\varphi(\boldsymbol{x}_i)\dot{\boldsymbol{x}}_i - \theta\left(\varphi(\boldsymbol{x}_i)^T\right)\xi\right\|_2^2$$
$$+ \lambda_2\frac{1}{N}\left\|\dot{\boldsymbol{x}}_i - \left(\nabla_{\mathbf{z}}\psi(\varphi(\boldsymbol{x}_i))\theta\left(\varphi(\boldsymbol{x}_i)^T\right)\xi\right\|_2^2 - \lambda_3\|\xi\|_1 \quad (4.45)$$

where the first term on the RHS is the autoencoder loss (the reconstruction loss); the second term is the SINDy loss; the third term is the consistency loss to ensure the matching of the time derivatives of the network output and input; the fourth is the regularization term to promote the sparsity in $\boldsymbol{\xi}$—i.e. to have as few terms as possible in the governing equation; and λ_1, λ_2, and λ_3 are hyperparameters which weigh the contributions of each of the corresponding terms, respectively. It is thus an approach for achieving simultaneously dimensionality reduction and complex dynamical system identification with as few terms as possible (Fig. 4.2).

Building on the work of Champion et al. (2019), Bakarji et al. (2023) employed the autoencoder with SINDy discussed in Sect. 4.2 to learn from time delay embedding (see Sect. 4.6 for a discussion of delay embedding) of partial observations—transforming a time series into a matrix of time-dependent chunks of data—the ROM of the Lorenz system, e.g. the urban evolution Eq. (4.12), Rossler and Lotka–Volterra systems discussed in Sect. 7.2 in Chap. 7, in a sparse and closed form.

4.5.2 *Finding Coordinates for Dynamical Systems with Bifurcation and Chaos*

As discussed in Sect. 3.4 in Chap. 3, complex urban systems often exhibit bifurcation and chaotic behaviors. The underlying dynamics are then parameterized. Within the SINDy framework, we can append a bifurcation parameter μ to the dynamics as follows

$$\begin{aligned}\dot{\mathbf{x}} &= f(\mathbf{x}, \mu)\\ \dot{\mu} &= 0\end{aligned} \quad (4.46)$$

We can then identify the RHS as a sparse combination of functions of the components in $\mathbf{x}$ and the bifurcation parameter μ. By collecting the time histories of $\mathbf{x}$ and $\dot{\mathbf{x}}$ for different values of the bifurcation parameter μ, we can identify instabilities and bifurcations which might occur in the latent dynamics that lead to macroscopic behavioral changes of the physical system within the autoencoder + SINDy framework discussed above. Hence, it is crucial to estimate at what parameter configurations these regime transitions might occur. For example, variations of input parameters can result in the development of vorticity in fluids or resonance phenomena in mechanical structures. Conti et al. (2023) proposed a reduced-order modeling method for parameterized systems by incorporating into the autoencoder + SINDy framework

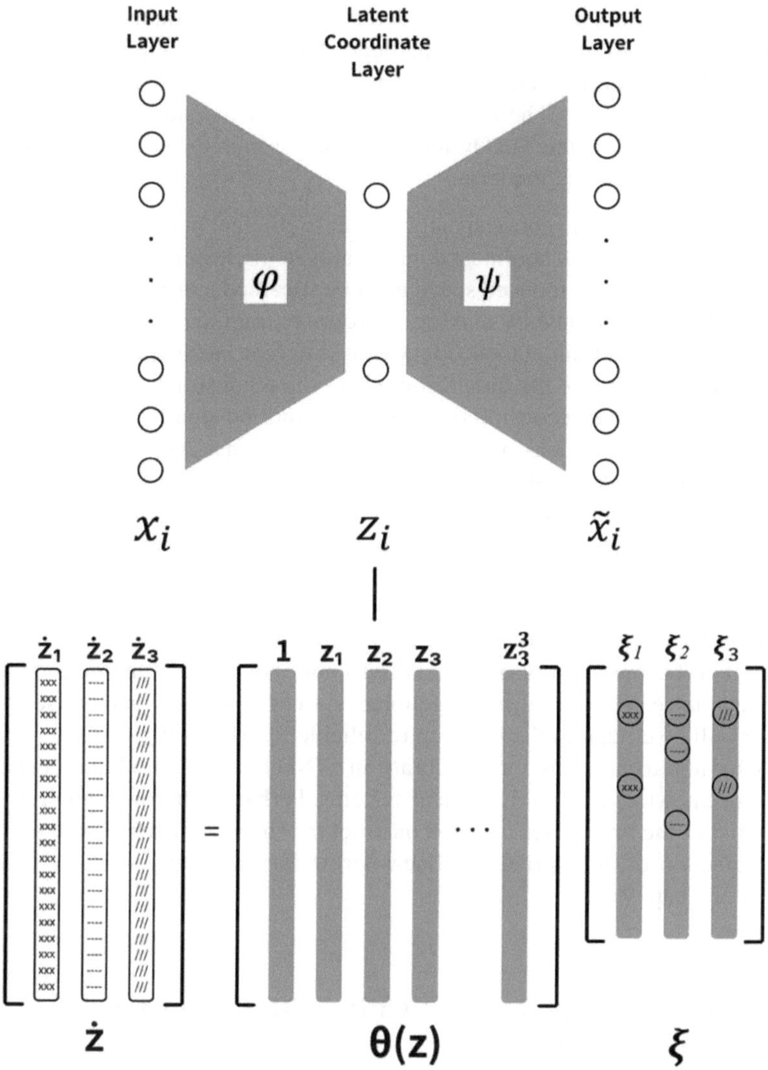

Fig. 4.2 Learning underlying dynamics with autoencoder + SINDy

the POD procedure to construct ROMs for more efficient simulation of parameterized dynamical systems. The solution to the problem involves the minimization of the following composite loss function in matrix form

$$L = \left\|\tilde{\mathbf{X}} - \psi\left(\varphi\left(\tilde{\mathbf{X}}\right)\right)\right\|_2^2 + \lambda_1 \left\|\dot{\mathbf{Z}} - \theta(\mathbf{Z}, \mu)\boldsymbol{\xi}\right\|_2^2 + \lambda_2 \left\|\dot{\mathbf{X}} - \nabla_2 \psi(\mathbf{Z})\theta(\mathbf{Z}, \mu)\boldsymbol{\xi}\right\|_2^2 + \lambda_3 \|\boldsymbol{\xi}\|_1 \tag{4.47}$$

where $\tilde{\mathbf{X}} = \mathbf{X}\mathbf{U}$ is the state matrix expanded by the POD coordinates $\mathbf{U}$; $\mathbf{Z}$ are latent variables; $\theta(\mathbf{Z}, \mu)$ is the library of candidate functions including the bifurcation parameter μ for the description of the dynamics of the data; and the others are same as those described above. The first term of the right-hand side is the autoencoder loss, the second term is the SINDy loss, the third term is the consistency loss, and the fourth is the regularization term.

Remark. Though the conventional autoencoder is efficient in learning latent coordinates for high-dimensional nonlinear dynamical systems, it suffers from the drawback that the dimension of the reduced space must be specified a priori. Fortunately, such a problem can be overcome by making appropriate training of the neural network. For example, we can train autoencoders with different latent space dimensions by trial and error and choose the dimension where the reconstruction error reaches its height—indicating that reconstruction quality cannot be significantly improved by further increasing the dimension. Alternatively, we can use AIC to evaluate autoencoders with different latent space dimensions and select the one with the lowest AIC value that balance reconstruction accuracy and model complexity. Formal methods—such as variational autoencoder (Kingma and Welling 2022)—allow the latent space dimension to be learned by data-driven dimensionality reduction methods leveraging, for example, regularization during training.

With respect to the SINDy approach, as mentioned in Sect. 4.3, we still need to improve its robustness to noise, especially to non-independent and non-identically distributed noise. How to discern genuine system dynamics and noise-induced behavior will be crucial to the building of reliable ROMs for digital twins of cities. Identifying nonlinear terms for the library in SINDy is kind of ad hoc or relies on some prior knowledge about dynamical systems. Perhaps a thorough analysis of the characteristics the time series used to construct the snapshot matrix could shed light on the selection of appropriate nonlinear terms for the library (see discussion in Sect. 9.5 of Chap. 9).

4.6 Building Digital Twins of Cities with Parametric Mixture Distributions

In our discussion on the incorporation of dynamics and complexity into digital twins of cities in the previous sections of this chapter, it is assumed that we have access to the full state space of the dynamical system and calculate the relevant derivatives and perform various decomposition methods to derive ROMs. In certain situations, however, we may not have complete knowledge about the underlying dynamics of a system so that we can write down the governing equations. Even though we know the underlying dynamics, we sometimes may not have complete observations/measurements of the dynamics of all system variables for us to construct the phase space. That is, we may not have access to the time series for all system variables. Under such circumstances, we need to reconstruct the phase space of a system with partial information—say a single variable—and develop methods to uncover the underlying dynamics—such as attractors and bifurcations on the manifold—and perhaps control them by steering the system to a desirable trajectory.

4.6.1 Learning System Dynamics from Reconstructed Phase Space

From differential topology, we can map any smooth manifold to the Euclidean space of sufficiently high dimension and unfold it completely. Whitney (1936), for example, gave an embedding theorem proving that any smooth compact n-dimensional manifold can be embedded into a Euclidean space of dimension 2n + 1. Such a generic map is an embedding. The phase space is reconstructed in such a way that each state can be uniquely identified by a vector of 2n + 1 measurements. Therefore, we can embed a dynamical system into a high-dimensional Euclidean space to better understand its geometric properties and analyze its behavior. If M is a smooth manifold and f is a generic invertible smooth map, then M and f (M) are diffeomorphic—two manifolds are said to be diffeomorphic if there is a diffeomorphism (an isomorphism of space equipped with a differentiable manifolds) from one to the other. If A is an attractor on M, then the embedding of A is a smooth diffeomorphism, a one-to-one mapping, from A to its image f(A).

Therefore, Whitney's embedding theorem gives the general condition under which smooth manifolds can be embedded into a Euclidean space of sufficiently high dimension. By embedding the phase space of a dynamical system, we can explicate the dynamics and make the underlying structure easier to identify, more comprehensible and interpretable. Thus, it renders a theoretical foundation for phase space reconstruction. However, Whitney's theorem does not say how one can do it experimentally, particularly when the full state space of a dynamical system is inaccessible. Building on Whitney's general theory, Takens (1981) gave the condition under which a smooth attractor can be reconstructed from the observations made with a generic function in his delay embedding theorem stated as follows.

Let M be a compact manifold of dimension m. For pairs (φ, y), $\varphi : M \to M$ a smooth diffeomorphism and y: $M \to \mathbb{R}$ a smooth function, it is a generic property that the map $\boldsymbol{\phi}_{(\varphi,y)} : M \to \mathbb{R}^{2m+1}$, defined by

$$\boldsymbol{\phi}_{(\varphi,y)}(x) = (y(x), y(\varphi(x)), \ldots, y\big(\varphi^{2m}(x)\big)$$

is an embedding; by "smooth" we mean at least C^2.

This is complemented by a more intuitive theorem given by Takens (1981) in the context of vector field as follows.

Let M be a compact manifold of dimension m. For pairs (**X**, y), **X** a smooth (i.e. C^2) vector field and y a smooth function on M, it is a generic property that $\boldsymbol{\phi}_{X,y} : M \to \mathbb{R}^{2m+1}$, defined by

$$\boldsymbol{\phi}_{X,y} = \{y(x), y(\varphi_1(y)), \ldots, y(\varphi_{2m}(x))$$

is an embedding, where φ_t is the flow of **X**.

Takens' theorem is important for constructing the underlying behaviors and properties of nonlinear dynamical systems with incomplete observations by time delay embedding. We can reconstruct the phase space from the observation of a single variable—a single observed time series—of a multivariable dynamical system. We can then embed the time series in a higher-dimensional space via time delay embedding. That is, for a sufficiently high-dimensional space, an attractor of a dynamical system can be reconstructed from a single observed time series. By choosing the appropriate embedding dimension—i.e. the number of axes in the reconstructed state space—and time delay, we can reconstruct an attractor of a dynamical system in the embedded space with which we can gain insight into the behavior, which may be chaotic, of the system because the embedding preserves the topology (the morphology) but not the geometry (geometric shape) of the original manifold. The Lyapunov exponent, for example, is invariant under the delay-coordinate embedding. This in fact makes it easier to interpret the time series by plotting the associated trajectory in the phase space via time delay coordinates. Since the embedding is diffeomorphic—i.e. the mapping from one to the other is differentiable and has a differentiable inverse—we can project the embedded manifold back to the individual coordinates/dimensions of the original system to obtain the corresponding individual time series (Fig. 4.3).

For instance, with an appropriate choice of the embedding dimension and time delay, we can reconstruct the attractor of the Lorenz system in the embedded space. Furthermore, we can compute dynamical invariants, such as the Lyapunov exponent, in the embedded space which theoretically should hold true in the unobserved dynamics in the original state space.

Given a time series: $x = x_n$, $n = 1, \ldots, N$, sampled from the state variable of a dynamical system, we can form a reconstructed phase space (RPS) matrix **X** of dimension d and time lag τ defined by its row vector—a point in the RPS—as follows

$$\mathbf{x}_n = [x_{n-(d-1)\tau} \ x_{n-(d-2)\tau} \cdots x_{n-\tau} \ x_n] \tag{4.48}$$

where d is the embedding dimension of the matrix; τ is the time lag; and $n = (1 + (d-1)\tau) \ldots N$. The parameters d and τ must be appropriately chosen—e.g. d must be greater than twice the box-counting dimension of the underlying dynamics to preserve the global properties of the dynamical system, and τ should provide low correlation between adjacent elements in the embedded vector and must be large enough to unfold the dynamics—to ensure topological conjugacy between the original dynamics and the RPS. For example, if τ is too small, there is no difference between the delay vectors in the embedded space, leading to strongly correlated phase space vectors, and if it is too large, we may lose information or unnecessarily complicate the underlying attractor which is intrinsically simple. The RPS dimension can be reduced by selecting appropriately the time lag in the construction of the RPS.

We can arrange the time delay embedding into a Hankle matrix taking the following form

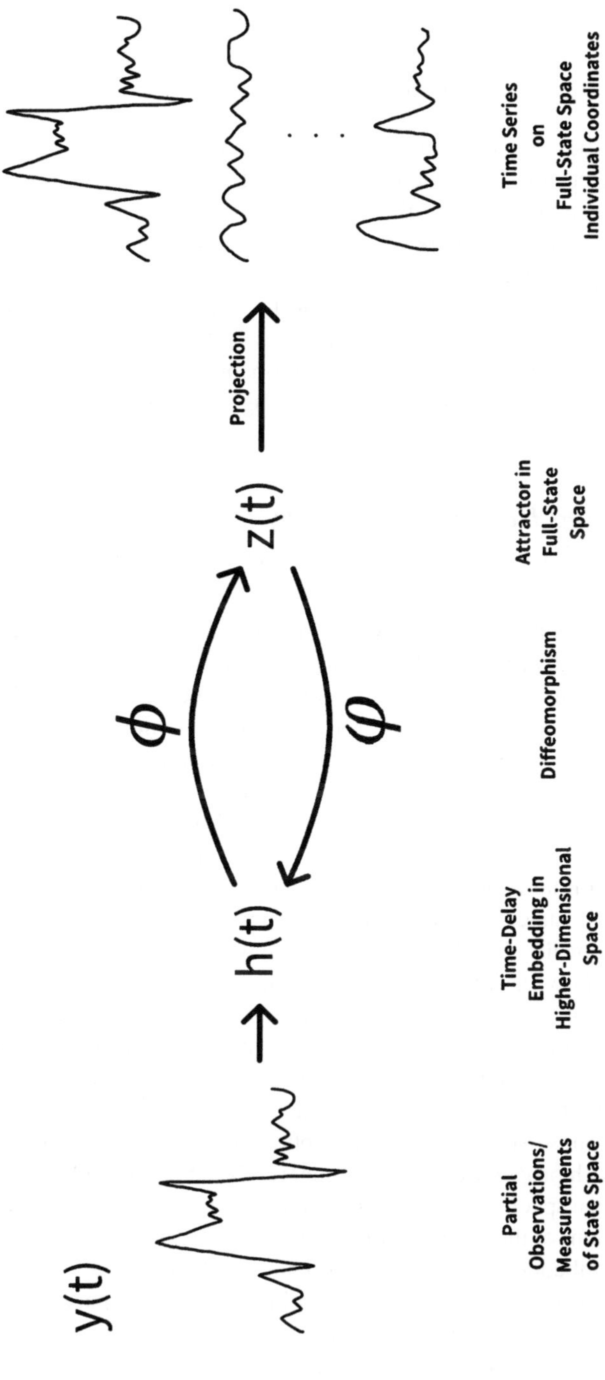

Fig. 4.3 Illustration of Takens's delay embedding theorem

$$\begin{bmatrix} y(t_1) & y(t_2) & \dots & y(t_k) \\ y(t_2) & y(t_3) & \dots & y(t_{k+1}) \\ \vdots & \vdots & \vdots & \vdots \\ y(t_n) & y(t_{n+1}) & \dots & y(t_{n+k+1}) \end{bmatrix}$$

where k is the number of data points, and each column is one data point in the delay coordinates. If we perform truncated SVD on the Hankle matrix constructed from a single time series and determine the number of significant modes/dimensions, it gives us a rough idea about its rank which implies the number of variables possibly involved in the original dynamical system.

Takens's theorem essentially builds a bridge between nonlinear dynamical systems and experimental time series analysis. Sauer et al. (1991) generalized Takens's theorem by replacing generic with probability one and the manifold by a possibly fractal set with non-integer box-counting dimension.

4.6.2 Unraveling Hidden Dynamics by Regression-Class Mixture Decomposition—The Gaussian Approach

Urban processes are generally complex, exhibiting chaotic dynamics with the presence of mixing. The distribution of city air pollution, for instance, is characterized by the mixing of point source and non-point source gas emission and diffusion. Such distribution is chaotic with a background distribution interspersed with plumes occurring haphazardly in space and time, creating turbulence in air flow and along building corridors with intermittent concentrations and transition boundaries over the cities. Such gas mixing can be appropriately modeled by parametric mixture distributions. In general, different attractors may coexist in a nonlinear dynamical system. Depending on the initial conditions, for the same set of parameters the system may have multiple stable states/attractors (see a discussion on multistability in Sect. 9. 5 of Chap. 9). From the distribution point of view, we may represent the mixing by parametric mixture distribution. Because of the complexity of these dynamical systems, we may not have complete knowledge or measurements about the underlying dynamics. Therefore, instead of manifold learning through projection discussed in Chap. 3, statistical learning from data is another way to learn and incorporate parametric dynamical systems—particularly chaotic systems—into digital twins of cities via reconstructed phase space (RPS) that captures the dynamics of the underlying physical system with properly chosen parameters. Based on the embedding theorem (Takens 1981) which specifies the conditions under which a delay embedding formed by the lagged versions of the observed variables can ensure the existence of governing equations in the embedded space, we can obtain a RPS such that each state of the dynamical system is uniquely specified by a point in the phase space. Appropriately constructed, the attractor of a dynamical system is equivalently mapped to the RPS via delay coordinates. Based on Takens' work, Povinelli et al. (2004) showed that a time series of observations sampled on a single state variable of a system can be employed to reconstruct a space topologically equivalent to the original system. They built a Gaussian mixture model (GMM), because of its robustness (McLachlan and Basford 1988), of signal trajectory densities in a RPS and differentiate signals employing a Bayesian classifier. Using only the number of mixtures, the signals and their class labels as inputs, the method calculates the parameters to form a suitable RPS.

Observing that chaotic systems exhibit random-like behavior in the time domain but are ordered in the state space having a specific topology taking usually the form of strange attractor, the attractor resulting from a series of bifurcations of a dynamical system (Ruelle and Takens (1971), Shekofteh et al. (2015) followed the line of reasoning of Povinelli et al. (2004) and proposed GMM as a parametric model of the strange attractor in a physical system. Since state space can appropriately represent chaotic and nonlinear behavior of a dynamical system, GMM can capture the attractor topology and nonlinearity from the distribution of observed vectors, i.e. points, in the state space. Starting from an initial point and with $t \to \pm\infty$, it produces a corresponding attractor in the state space. So, state space is an appropriate domain to represent chaotic and nonlinear behaviors of complex dynamical systems. In Shekofteh et al. (2015), a GMM is employed to learn the probability distribution of the strange attractor of the physical system. Given a set of differential equations with unknown parameters describing a chaotic system, a GMM is first fitted to the pretrained data for the attractor of the physical system to identify the parameters using maximum likelihood estimation, and the best set of parameters of the model is selected from the search space formed by a set of acceptable values of the model parameters by minimizing a cost function based on the similarity indicating the closeness of the chaotic time series obtained by the parametrized model and that obtained from the physical system. The minimum point of the cost surface determines the parameters of the best model. Though Shekofteh et al. (2015) showed that the method is not sensitive to initial conditions (it is worth mentioning that chaotic systems are sensitive to initial conditions and changes in parameters), it still suffers from the inability in determining analytically the number of mixtures/components needed in the GMM because of the complexity of the data set, the inefficiency of the expectation maximization algorithm in the maximum likelihood estimation, and the limited capability in resisting a high level of noise in data that impact the search for the global minimum of the cost function.

Treating a large data set as a mixture population, Leung et al. (2001) proposed a robust and effective regression-class mixture decomposition (RCMD) method to unravel hidden functions—linear and/or nonlinear—in small, medium, and large data sets. The method does not require a priori specification of the number of regression classes (mixtures) in the GMM, and it can resist a very high level of data contamination. It should be noted that the performance of the RPS method depends on the appropriate sampling of the dynamics and the resistance to noise. For accurate prediction in chaotic systems, for example, appropriate handling of noise is particularly important. We should also differentiate between noise due to external forcing and noise intrinsic to nonlinearity of complex dynamical systems. The RCMD is also equipped with a highly efficient genetic algorithm—a multi-point stochastic search algorithm (Holland 1975, 1992)—for the optimization of the objective function for parameter estimation (see a short discussion of genetic algorithm in Chap. 5). The method only involves parameters of a regression class at each time of the data mining process. It can be employed to learn parametric dynamical systems—particularly chaotic dynamics (meaning the presence of mixing)—in which the number and types of dynamics as well as the locations of the attractors may be unknown, and the data are limited but noise level is high.

In a nutshell, the RCMD method assumes that there are m regression classes representing the number of individual mixture components constituting the dynamics hidden in a dataset, and m is known in advance—actually, under the RCMD method, m does not need to be specified in advance; it can be automatically determined at the end of the learning process when all plausible regression classes have been identified. We insert all signals of a particular class into the RPS. The number of regression classes is possibly related to the underlying distribution of the RPS density. The objective is to find all distinguished regression classes (sub-dynamics), to identify the parameter vectors, and to make interpretation by the mixture model. The method is briefly summarized as follows.

For a fixed integer, a regression class (a mixture) is defined by

$$G_i : Y = f_i(\mathbf{X}, \boldsymbol{\beta}_i) + e_i \tag{4.49}$$

where G_i, i = 1, ..., m, is a regression class; Y is the response variable; $\mathbf{X}$ is a random vector with a probability density function $p(.)$; the error term e_i is a random variable with a probability density function $\psi(u; \sigma_i)$ having a parameter σ_i, E $e_i = 0$; and $\mathbf{X}$ and e_i are independent. The regression function $f_i(., .)$ is known and $\boldsymbol{\beta}_i$ is an unknown regression vector. A random vector ($\mathbf{X}$, Y) belongs to a regression class G_i if it is distributed according to the regression model G_i. This implies that the vector has a probability density function

$$p_i(\boldsymbol{x}, y; \boldsymbol{\theta}_i) = p(\boldsymbol{x})\psi\left(r_i(\boldsymbol{x}, y; \boldsymbol{\beta}_i); \sigma_i\right), \boldsymbol{\theta}_i = \left(\boldsymbol{\beta}_i^T, \sigma_i\right)^T \tag{4.50}$$

That is, $G_i = G(\boldsymbol{\theta}_i) = \{(\boldsymbol{x}, y) : p_i(\boldsymbol{x}, y; \boldsymbol{\theta}_i) \geq b_i\}$ with $b_i > 0$ being determined by $P\left[p_i(\boldsymbol{x}, y; \boldsymbol{\theta}_i) \geq b_i\right] = a$, a is a probability threshold specified a priori and approaches 1.

To be efficient, we take a random sample of size n on the dataset and obtain n i.i.d. random vectors (x_1, y_1), ..., (x_n, y_n) with a common mixture distribution population

$$p(\boldsymbol{x}, y; \theta) = \sum_{i=1}^{m} \pi_i p_i(\boldsymbol{x}, y; \boldsymbol{\theta}_i) \tag{4.51}$$

i.e. they consist of random observations from regression classes with prior probabilities $\pi_1, \ldots, \pi_m (\pi_1 + \cdots + \pi_m = 1, \pi_i \geq 0, 1 \leq \mathrm{i} \leq m)$, $\boldsymbol{\theta}^T = \left(\boldsymbol{\theta}_1^T, \ldots, \boldsymbol{\theta}_m^T\right)$.

Under noise contamination, there is a considerable number of outliers in the dataset. To unravel the m regression classes, we need to be able to differentiate between inliers—vectors that belong to a particular regression class—and outliers—vectors that do not belong. With high level of noise, the number of outliers may exceed the number of inliers with respect to each regression class. This makes many algorithms fail to identify the mixtures/regression classes from the highly contaminated dataset (most of the robust methods tolerate only less than 50% of outliers). Among other things, the RCMD method is formulated to solve this problem that can tolerate more than 50% of outliers.

When $\pi_1, \ldots, \pi_m$ are known and the true parameters $\boldsymbol{\theta}^T = \left(\boldsymbol{\theta}_1^T, \ldots, \boldsymbol{\theta}_m^T\right)$ are known a priori and the outliers/noise are absent ($\varepsilon_i = 0, 1 \leq \mathrm{i} \leq m$), then the posterior probability that $\left(\boldsymbol{x}_j, y_j\right)$ belongs to G_i is given by

$$\tau_i\left(\boldsymbol{x}_j, y_j; \boldsymbol{\theta}_i\right) = \frac{\pi_i p_i\left(\boldsymbol{x}_j, y_j; \boldsymbol{\theta}_i\right)}{\sum_{k=1}^{m} \pi_k p_k\left(\boldsymbol{x}_j, y_j; \boldsymbol{\theta}_k\right)}, 1 \leq i \leq m \tag{4.52}$$

The partitioning of the sample $Z = \{(\boldsymbol{x}_1, y_1), \ldots, (\boldsymbol{x}_n, y_n)\}$ into m regression classes can be made by the Bayesian decision rule which assigns each to the population to which it has the highest estimated posterior probability of belonging to G_i if

$$\tau_i\left(\boldsymbol{x}_j, y_j; \boldsymbol{\theta}_i\right) > \tau_k\left(\boldsymbol{x}_j, y_j; \boldsymbol{\theta}_k\right), 1 \leq k \leq m, k \neq i \tag{4.53}$$

If the parameters $\boldsymbol{\theta}^T = \left(\boldsymbol{\theta}_1^T, \ldots, \boldsymbol{\theta}_m^T\right)$ are unknown, then $\boldsymbol{\theta}$ is replaced by the maximum likelihood estimator (MLE) $\widehat{\boldsymbol{\theta}}$ constructed by the sample from the mixture population as follows

$$\widehat{\boldsymbol{\theta}} = arg \max_{\theta \in \boldsymbol{\theta}^*} l(\boldsymbol{\theta}) \tag{4.54}$$

$$l(\boldsymbol{\theta}) = ln \prod_{j=1}^{n} p\left(\boldsymbol{x}_j, y_j; \boldsymbol{\theta}\right) = \sum_{j=1}^{n} ln\, p\left(\boldsymbol{x}_j, y_j; \boldsymbol{\theta}\right) \tag{4.55}$$

where $\boldsymbol{\theta}^*$ is a parameter space.

Now, if $p_i(\boldsymbol{x}, y; \boldsymbol{\theta}_i)$ is contaminated, we have the contaminated neighborhood as follows

$$U(\varepsilon_i) = \left\{p_i^{\varepsilon}(\boldsymbol{x}, y; \boldsymbol{\theta}_i) : p_i^{\varepsilon}(\boldsymbol{x}, y; \boldsymbol{\theta}_i) = (1 - \varepsilon_i)p_i(\boldsymbol{x}, y; \boldsymbol{\theta}_i) + \varepsilon_i h_i(\boldsymbol{x}, y)\right\} \tag{4.56}$$

where $h_i(\boldsymbol{x}, y)$ is a probability density function of outliers in G_i, and ε_i is an unknown fraction of outliners present in G_i. So, Z becomes the random sample from the following mixture probability density function

$$p_\varepsilon(\boldsymbol{x}, y; \boldsymbol{\theta}) = \sum_{i=1}^{m} \pi_i p_i^\varepsilon(\boldsymbol{x}, y; \boldsymbol{\theta}_i) \tag{4.57}$$

When $\pi_1, \ldots, \pi_m$ are unknown, let $\boldsymbol{\pi} = (\pi_1, \ldots, \pi_m)^T$, $\boldsymbol{\varphi} = \left(\boldsymbol{\pi}^T, \boldsymbol{\theta}^T\right)^T$, $L(\boldsymbol{\varphi}) = ln \prod_{j=1}^{n} p_\varepsilon\left(\boldsymbol{x}_j, y_{j;} \boldsymbol{\theta}\right)$, and

$$\eta_i\left(\boldsymbol{x}_j, y_j; \boldsymbol{\varphi}\right) = \frac{\pi_i p_i^\varepsilon\left(\boldsymbol{x}_j, y_j; \boldsymbol{\theta}_i\right)}{\sum_{k=1}^{m} \pi_k p_k^\varepsilon\left(\boldsymbol{x}_j, y_j; \boldsymbol{\theta}_k\right)}, 1 \le i \le m \tag{4.58}$$

Without further elaboration, we can find the MLE of $\boldsymbol{\varphi}$, $\widehat{\boldsymbol{\varphi}} = \left(\widehat{\boldsymbol{\pi}}^T, \widehat{\boldsymbol{\theta}}^T\right)^T$ (see Leung et al. (2001) for details). It is worthy pointing out that when m is large—i.e. many parameters are involved in a dynamical system—it is difficult to obtain the parameters $\widehat{\boldsymbol{\varphi}}$ by directly estimating the parameters of the mixture densities via MLE, even with the help of the expectation maximization algorithm which is often slow in convergence. The RCMD method with a GA was shown to be effective in accomplishing such a task (Leung et al. 2001).

In brief, a mixture density is treated as a contaminated density with respect to each cluster in the mixture. The mixture probability density function in Eq. (4.57) with respect to G_i can be rewritten as

$$p_\varepsilon(\boldsymbol{x}, y; \boldsymbol{\theta}) = \pi_i(1 - \varepsilon_i)p_i(\boldsymbol{x}, y; \boldsymbol{\theta}_i) + \pi_i\varepsilon_i h_i(\boldsymbol{x}, y) + \sum_{j \ne i}^{m} \pi_j p_j^\varepsilon\left(\boldsymbol{x}, y; \boldsymbol{\theta}_j\right)$$

$$= \pi_i(1 - \varepsilon_i)p_i(\boldsymbol{x}, y; \boldsymbol{\theta}_i) + [1 - \pi_i(1 - \varepsilon_i)]g_i(\boldsymbol{x}, y) \tag{4.59}$$

So, the dataset comes from the above mixture probability density function $p_\varepsilon(\boldsymbol{x}, y; \boldsymbol{\theta})$ with probability $\pi_i(1 - \varepsilon_i)$, together with an unknown outlier with probability $[1 - \pi_i(1 - \varepsilon_i)]$. That is, a sample point from the above mixture probability density function is classified as inlier if it is realized from $p_i(\boldsymbol{x}, y; \boldsymbol{\theta}_i)$, or as an outlier if it comes from $g_i(\boldsymbol{x}, y)$.

By assuming that $g_i\left(\boldsymbol{x}_1, y_1\right) = \cdots = g_i\left(\boldsymbol{x}_n, y_n\right) = \delta_i$ (an appropriately chosen value, see Leung et al. (2001) for justification), Eq. (4.59) becomes

$$p_\varepsilon(\boldsymbol{x}, y; \boldsymbol{\theta}) = \pi_i(1 - \varepsilon_i)p_i(\boldsymbol{x}, y; \boldsymbol{\theta}_i) + (1 - \pi_i + \pi_i\varepsilon_i)\delta_i \tag{4.60}$$

The log-likelihood function of observing Z corresponding to Eq. (4.55) becomes

$$l(\boldsymbol{\theta}_i) = n\ ln[\pi_i(1 - \varepsilon_i)] + \sum_{j=1}^{n} \ln\left[p_i\left(\boldsymbol{x}_j, y_j; \boldsymbol{\theta}_i\right) + \frac{1 - \pi_i + \pi_i\varepsilon_i}{\pi_i(1 - \varepsilon_i)}\delta_i\right] \tag{4.61}$$

To estimate the parameters $\boldsymbol{\theta}_i$ from Z, we need to maximize $l(\boldsymbol{\theta}_i)$ with each δ_i subject to $\sigma_i > 0$. Because the maximization of $l(\boldsymbol{\theta}_i)$ at δ_i with respect to $\boldsymbol{\theta}_i$ is equivalent to maximizing the model-fitting function

$$l_i(\boldsymbol{\theta}_i; t_i) = \sum_{j=1}^{n} ln\left[p_i\left(\boldsymbol{x}_j, y_{j;} \boldsymbol{\theta}_i\right) + t_i\right] \tag{4.62}$$

at t_i with respect to $\boldsymbol{\theta}_i$, provided that $t_i = (1 - \pi_i + \pi_i\varepsilon_i)\delta_i/[\pi_i(1 - \varepsilon_i)] - t_i$ corresponds to a value δ_i of the outliner distribution $g_i(\boldsymbol{x}, y)$, we only employ the partial information about the model without the knowledge of the whole shape of $g_i(\boldsymbol{x}, y)$— we can investigate the problem of maximizing $l(\boldsymbol{\theta}_i)$ subject to $\sigma_i > 0$. We call each $t_i(\geq 0)$ a partial model.

So, for a regression class G_i and the dataset Z, the t-level set of G_i is defined by

$$G_i(\boldsymbol{\theta}_i; t) = \left\{\left(\boldsymbol{x}_j, y_j\right) : p_i\left(\boldsymbol{x}_j, y_j; \boldsymbol{\theta}_i\right) > t\right\} \tag{4.63}$$

and the t-level support set of an estimator $\widehat{\boldsymbol{\theta}}_i$ for $\boldsymbol{\theta}_i$ is defined as the subset of all inliers with respect to G_i at a partial model t. It indicates the extent to which the dataset supports the estimator at partial model level t. The RCMD estimator of the parametric vector $\boldsymbol{\theta}_i$ for a regression class G_i is defined by

$$\hat{\theta}_i^t = \arg\max_{\boldsymbol{\theta}_i} l_i\left(\boldsymbol{\theta}_{i;} t_i\right), \boldsymbol{\theta}_i = \left(\boldsymbol{\beta}_i^T, \sigma_i\right)^T, \sigma_i > 0 \tag{4.64}$$

If $\mathbf{X}$ is uniformly distributed and $e_i \sim N\left(0, \sigma_i^2\right)$, the maximization of $l_i(\boldsymbol{\theta}_i; t_i)$ is equivalent to

$$l_i(\boldsymbol{\theta}_i; t_i) \equiv \sum_{j=1}^{n} \ln\left(\psi\left[y_j - f_i\left(\boldsymbol{x}_j, \boldsymbol{\beta}_i\right); \sigma_i\right] + t_i\right) \tag{4.65}$$

Therefore, Eq. (4.63) becomes

$$G\left(\boldsymbol{\theta}_{i;} t_i\right) = \left\{\left(\boldsymbol{x}_j, y_j\right) : \psi\left[r_i\left(\boldsymbol{x}_j, y_j; \boldsymbol{\beta}_i\right)\sigma_i\right] > t_i\right\}. \tag{4.66}$$

And

$$G_i(\boldsymbol{\theta}_i) = \left\{(\boldsymbol{x}, y) : \left|\left(\boldsymbol{x}, y; \boldsymbol{\beta}_i\right)\right| \leq 3\sigma_i\right\} \tag{4.67}$$

which is based on the three σ-criterion of the normal distribution. The corresponding RCMD method can be summarized as follows (Fig. 4.4).

At each selected partial model $t_i^{(s)}$, s = 1,..., S, we maximize $l_i\left(\boldsymbol{\theta}_i; t_i^{(s)}\right)$ with respect to $\boldsymbol{\beta}_i$ and σ_i by using a GA that employs $l_i(\boldsymbol{\theta}_i; t_i)$ as the fitness function and $\boldsymbol{\theta}_i$ as

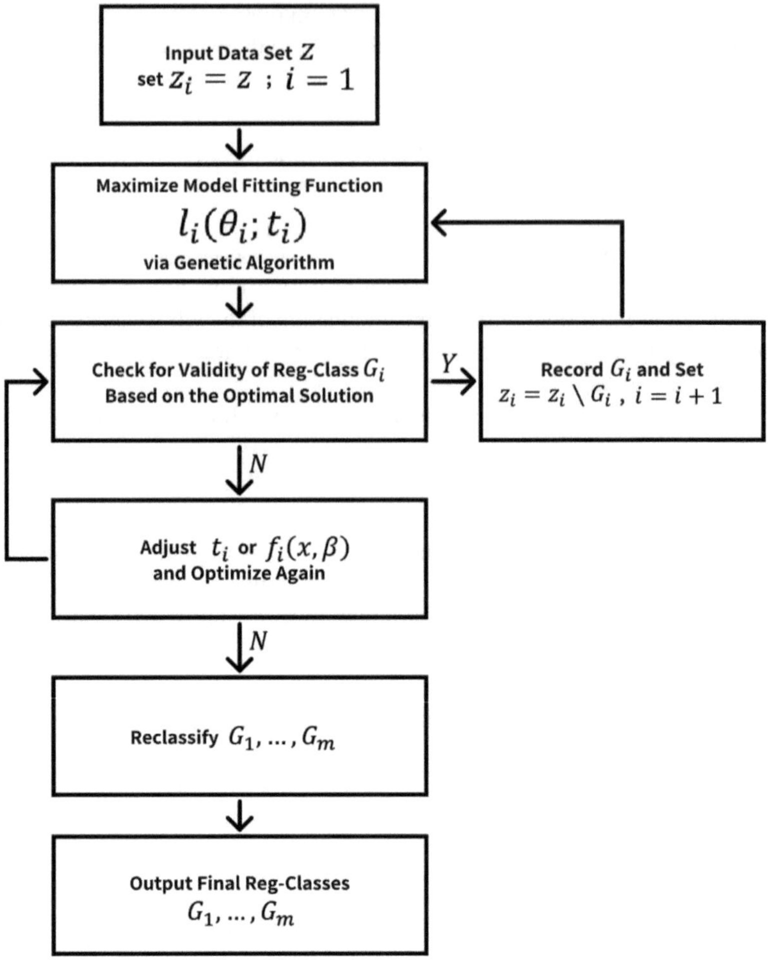

Fig. 4.4 Flowchart of the regression-class mixture decomposition (RCMD) method (based on Leung et al. (2001))

the chromosome to represent the parametric estimation. Having solved $\max_{\boldsymbol{\beta}_i \sigma_i} l_i\left(\theta_i; t_i^{(s)}\right)$ for $\hat{\boldsymbol{\beta}}_i\left(t_i^{(s)}\right)$ and $\hat{\sigma}_i\left(t_i^{(s)}\right)$, we calculate the possible reg-class $G_i\left(\hat{\boldsymbol{\theta}}_i\left(t_i^{(s)}\right)\right)$ followed by the test of normality on $G_i\left(\hat{\boldsymbol{\theta}}_i\left(t_i^{(s)}\right)\right)$. If the test statistic is not significant at a prespecified level of significance, then the respective distribution is normal and a valid reg-class, $G_i\left(\hat{\boldsymbol{\theta}}_i\left(t_i^{(s)}\right)\right)$, has been determined. Otherwise, we proceed to the next partial model if the upper bound $t_i^{(s)}$ has not been reached. It can be said that the identity of each $G_i\left(\hat{\boldsymbol{\theta}}_i\left(t_i^{(s)}\right)\right)$ is based on its t -level set. After a valid reg-class has been detected, it is extracted from the current dataset, and the next regression class will be identified in the new size-reduced dataset. Individual regression classes continue to be estimated recursively until there are no more valid reg-classes, or until the size of the new dataset gets to be too small for estimation.

Thus, the proposed method can handle an arbitrary number of regression-class models with single regression-class extraction. That is, the parameters of each regression class can be estimated progressively, and the data points are partitioned into inliers and outliers with respect to that regression class. The RCMD method should be efficient in learning the parametric dynamical systems and the strange attractors of the parametric chaotic systems under high-level noise contamination.

The RCMD method can in a way be treated as a generalization of the Gaussian-process regression for learning nonlinear PDEs in which the dynamics are only captured by a single Gaussian regression (Raissi et al. 2018). Since the computation time is very high in simulating the dynamics via the Gaussian-process regression, Raissi et al. (2018) proposed to obtain the ROM of the regression by making the prior assumption that the high-fidelity model is the linear combination of the ROM and noise, both are Gaussian processes. Another approach to derive a ROM can be via the deep autoencoding GMM method that employs a deep autoencoder (discussed in Sect. 4.5) to generate a low-dimensional representation of an input sample by concatenating reduced low-dimensional features from encoding and reconstruction error from decoding and then subject it to GMM for mixture estimation in the end-to-end training. The method optimizes the parameters of the deep autoencoder and the GMM simultaneously (Zong et al. 2018). For RCMD, computational complexity and indirect dimension reduction is in a way accomplished by the sequential unraveling of the individual mixture components. Dynamical system identification can be treated as the discovery of attractors from a long sequence of sub-dynamics one after another. In each round of the RCMD unraveling, we are essentially narrowing our search space—i.e. using a reduced input set—and lowering the learning errors and computational complexity. Without pre-specification, the number and types of attractors are automatically determined in the end by the RCMD procedure. The RCMD method is essentially a data-driven approach to learn the dynamics and complexity of dynamical systems with multiple equilibrium points as a regression problem involving mixture distributions. This may be used to identify the dynamic regimes across the parameter space of complex dynamics for the search a global basis via the projection methods discussed in Sect. 3.4 of Chap. 3. It should be noted that the RCMD method is not only applicable to RPS, but it can also be applied to the full state space with complete observations/time series of the dynamics of all variables.

Remark. Though Takens's theorem is powerful for embedding manifold in the Euclidean space, there are issues that need further investigations or extensions. (1) Determination of the optimal embedding dimension and time delay via means discussed in Sect. 9.4 to faithfully reconstruct the phase space of high-dimensional dynamics of a system from a given time series. (2) Phase space reconstruction with non-uniform sampling of data in time to break from the restriction of uniform sampling (This becomes more complicated if delay embedding is to be carried out in space as well as in space and time). (3) Embedding dynamics with noisy data to avoid inaccurate phase space reconstruction. (4) Handling nonlinearity and non-stationarity in underlying dynamics to relax the deterministic and stationarity assumptions. (5) Parallel to time delay embedding of manifolds based on time series for the unraveling of dynamical processes discussed in Sect. 3.4, we may wonder whether we can perform space-delay embedding based on the observed distribution of one single variable when we do not have access to the full state space of a spatial process. To unravel spatial relationships and structures—which may be chaotic—with partial observations, we need to develop a spatial embedding scheme with appropriate spatial embedding dimension and spatial lags/delays. Spatial embedding will involve embedding spatial data—for instance, in the form of images or spatial distributions—into a higher-dimensional space by incorporating spatial lags/delays and dependencies between neighboring regions. Here, concepts such as spatial autocorrelation, spatial non-stationarity, and fractals will play a role in its construction. (6) Considering spatial and temporal dimensions simultaneously, we again may not have full access to the full spatiotemporal state space of a dynamical system and most likely need to develop space–time embedding that can map one spatiotemporal region to another. By considering both temporal delays and spatial delays, we may be able to reconstruct and unfold spatiotemporal dynamics of a system in a higher-dimensional space. And, by projecting it back to the spatial and temporal dimensions, we may uncover individually the spatial and temporal dynamics. These undertakings are by no means straightforward, and they impose a significant challenge that requires rigorous theoretical underpinning, efficient computational algorithms, and empirical validations. This, however, will be a worthy attempt to advance the interoperability between dynamical spatiotemporal models and spatiotemporal data in building digital twins of cities for the analysis, simulation, monitoring, and prediction of a large variety of dynamical behaviors over space and time.

4.7 Neural Network Approach to the Building of Digital Twins of Cities from Data

As discussed above, to unravel PDEs governing the dynamics of complex systems from data, we need to compute derivatives with respect to the space and time coordinates. Compared to other methods such as finite element, finite difference, etc., the neural network approach (Arbib 2002) appears to be less sensitive to noise in data and renders good functional approximation. It serves as a data-driven method that can be used to discover dynamics whose governing equations are unknown or hidden in the complex dynamical process of a system. Without loss of generality, let the general form of the nonlinear second-order PDE be

$$\begin{aligned} u_t &= \gamma_1 + \gamma_2 u + \gamma_3 u^2 + \gamma_4 u_x + \gamma_5 u_x^2 + \gamma_6 u u_x \\ &\quad + \gamma_7 u_{xx} + \gamma_8 u_{xx}^2 + \gamma_9 u u_{xx} + \gamma_{10} u_x u_{xx} \end{aligned} \tag{4.68}$$

According to Schaeffer (2017), it can be expressed as the product of the terms with fixed coefficients as follows

$$u_t = F\left(1, u, u^2, u_x, u_x^2, uu_x, u_{xx}, u_{xx}^2, uu_{xx}, u_x u_{xx}\right).\boldsymbol{\gamma} \tag{4.69}$$

where F is a nonlinear function of space x, time t, solution u and its derivatives, each of the terms is a plausible feature that depicts the dynamics of the observed data, and $\boldsymbol{\gamma}$ are the coefficients to be determined. For each term, the subscripts denote the partial differentiation with respect to x or t. Specifically, $u_x = \frac{\partial u}{\partial x}$, $u_{xx} = \frac{\partial^2 u}{\partial x^2}$, $uu_x = u\frac{\partial u}{\partial x}$, $uu_{xx} = u\frac{\partial^2 u}{\partial x^2}$. What we want to discover from data is the PDE taking the following general form

$$u_t = F(u) \cdot \boldsymbol{\gamma} \tag{4.70}$$

For instance, we may want to predict some urban phenomena/variables of interest with respect to the spatial coordinates and time. While we do not have the exact form of the governing equation, what we have are observational data, $\{u(x_i, t_i), i = 1, \ldots, n\}$. Here, $F(u)$ is the library of the plausible terms/features constituting the PDE. Since the PDE should hold at each data point in the spatiotemporal domain, we can re-express u_t as

$$\mathbf{U}_t = \phi(\mathbf{U}) \cdot \boldsymbol{\gamma} \tag{4.71}$$

taking the following expanded form

$$\begin{bmatrix} \mathrm{u_t(x_1, t_1)} \\ \mathrm{u_t(x_2, t_2)} \\ \vdots \\ \mathrm{u_t(x_n, t_n)} \end{bmatrix} = \begin{bmatrix} 1 & \mathrm{u(x_1, t_1)} & \ldots & \mathrm{uu_x(x_1, t_1)} & \cdots & \mathrm{uu_{xx}(x_1, t_1)} & \cdots \\ 1 & \mathrm{u(x_2, t_2)} & & \mathrm{uu_x(x_2, t_2)} & & \mathrm{uu_{xx}(x_2, t_2)} & \cdots \\ \vdots & \vdots & \cdots & \vdots & \cdots & \vdots & \\ 1 & \mathrm{u(x_n, t_n)} & \cdots & \mathrm{uu_x(x_n, t_n)} & \ldots & \mathrm{uu_{xx}(x_n, t_n)} & \cdots \end{bmatrix} .\boldsymbol{\gamma} \tag{4.72}$$

where $\phi(\mathbf{U})$ is the discretized library with each column being a feature vector in the library.

To unravel the PDEs governing the dynamics of a system, we need to calculate the derivatives in $\mathbf{U}_t$ and $\phi(\mathbf{U})$ to learn $\boldsymbol{\gamma}$. To better handle the impact of noisy data, we can employ appropriate neural networks to approximate the dynamics and obtain the required derivatives through automatic differentiation (Baydin et al. 2018). Since a multilayer feedforward neural network is an universal approximator of any function (Scarselli and Tsoi 1998), it can serve as a good candidate to accomplish the task.

4.7.1 Learning Urban Dynamics by Multilayer Feedforward Neural Networks

By conventional neural network learning, the solution of the dynamical system, $u(x, t)$, is obtained by minimizing the following loss function

$$L(\boldsymbol{\theta}) = \frac{1}{n}\sum_{i=1}^{n}(u(x_i, t_i) - N(x_i, t_i; \boldsymbol{\theta}))^2 \tag{4.73}$$

where $u(x_i, t_i), i = 1, \ldots, n$, is the observation at the colocation point i in the spatiotemporal domain, and $N(x_i, t_i; \boldsymbol{\theta})$ is the value approximated by the neural network N with parameters $\boldsymbol{\theta}$. If N is a deep fully connected feedforward neural network with one input layer, one output layer, and several (can be numerous) hidden layers in-between (Fig. 4.5), then the connection of two adjacent layers can be expressed as follows

$$y_j^l = \sigma^{l-1}\left(\sum_k \omega_{jk}^l y_k^{l-1}\right) + b_j^l, l = 1, \ldots, L-1 \tag{4.74}$$

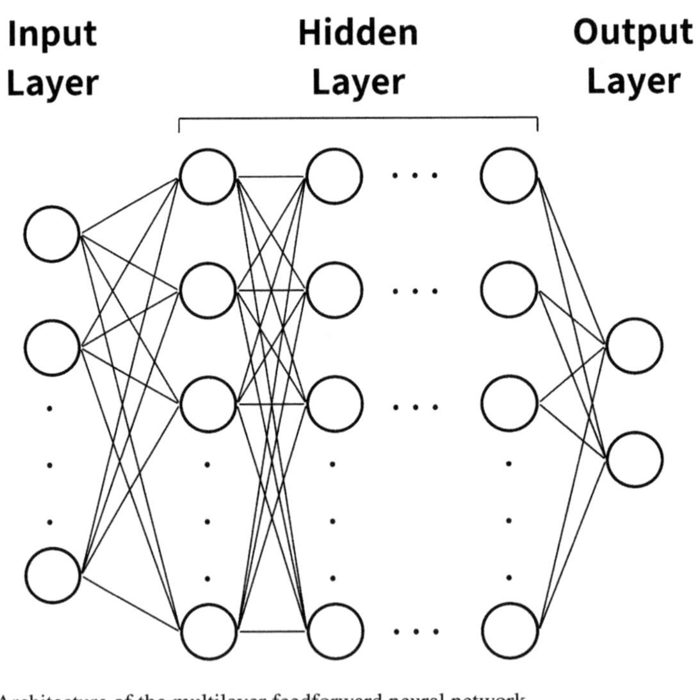

Fig. 4.5 Architecture of the multilayer feedforward neural network

where l denotes layer, $\boldsymbol{\omega}$ denotes the connection weights between neurons, $\boldsymbol{b}$ denotes bias, and σ denotes the activation function which is generally nonlinear. We can simplify the above expression in vector form as.

$$\mathbf{y}^l = \sigma^{l-1}\left(\mathbf{W}^l\mathbf{y}^{l-1} + \mathbf{b}^l\right), l = 1, \cdots, L-1 \tag{4.75}$$

By the idea of a multilayer feedforward neural network, we can express the mapping from the input vector containing the spatial and temporal coordinates to the output $u(x, t)$ in the network N via a concatenation of piecewise linear or nonlinear functions

$$\mathbf{y}^L = N(\mathbf{y}_0; \boldsymbol{\theta}) = \mathbf{W}^L\sigma^{l-1}\left(\cdots\sigma\left(\mathbf{W}^2\sigma^0\left(\mathbf{W}^1\mathbf{y}_0 + \mathbf{b}^1\right) + \mathbf{b}^2\right)\right) + \mathbf{b}^L \tag{4.76}$$

where $\boldsymbol{\theta} = \left\{\mathbf{w}^1, \mathbf{b}^1, \mathbf{w}^2, \mathbf{b}^2, \ldots, \mathbf{w}^L, \mathbf{b}^L\right\}$ are the coefficients to be learned through the training of the neural network. The corresponding neural network becomes

$$N(\boldsymbol{x}, t; \boldsymbol{\theta}) = \mathbf{W}^L\sigma^{l-1}\left(\cdots\sigma\left(\mathbf{W}^2\sigma^0\left(\mathbf{W}^1\mathbf{y}_0 + \mathbf{b}^1\right) + \mathbf{b}^2\right)\right) + \mathbf{b}^L \tag{4.77}$$

If the number of hidden layers L is large, then the neural network is said to be deep, and it can be trained via deep learning, an approach in machine learning (LeCun et al. 2015). After the neural network has been trained, the required derivatives can simply be obtained by applying automatic differentiation through backpropagation.

To learn the nonlinear differential operator F in Eq. (4.70), we can minimize the following loss function

$$L(\boldsymbol{\theta}; \boldsymbol{\gamma}) = \frac{1}{n}\sum_{i=1}^{n}(f(x_i, t_i) - F[N(x_i, t_i; \boldsymbol{\theta})])^2 \tag{4.78}$$

A more detailed discussion is given in Chap. 5 about the learning of governing equations with respect to the setup of the loss function based on losses due to theory, initial/boundary conditions, and data.

To have a parsimonious representation, we can apply regularization via sparse regression to trim down the number of constituent terms so that only a few significant terms will be selected to construct the governing equations. Furthermore, noisy observations/data will also affect the numerical approximation of derivatives, making the result of the learning problem unstable and ill-conditioned/posed. Instead of using a neural network to calculate the derivatives of the observed data and then use sparse regression to approximate the PDEs (Berg and Nyström 2019), Xu et al. (2021) used the trained neural network to generate meta data to complement the observational data to enhance the accuracy in the unraveling of the PDEs with limited and noisy data. Using the sparse regression technique (Rudy et al. 2017), $\mathbf{U}_t = \phi(\mathbf{U}) \cdot \boldsymbol{\gamma}$ can be solved as

$$\hat{\gamma} = arg \min_{\gamma} \|\phi\gamma - \mathbf{U}_t\|_2^2 + \lambda\|\gamma\|_1 \tag{4.79}$$

where coefficients whose values are larger than a prespecified threshold will be selected. The $l_1 - norm$ is used to encourage sparsity of the feature vectors by key-feature learning, and $\lambda > 0$ is the coefficient that balances model complexity with accuracy. Therefore, the hidden equations governing the dynamics of a complex system can be unraveled via neural network learning from data and regularization.

4.7.2 The Long Short-Term Memory for Learning Urban Dynamics with Sequential Memories

High-dimensional nonlinear complex systems may exhibit memory effect which needs to be effectively captured for accurate prediction. A basic agenda of ROM is to use the POD basis that capture the spatiotemporal dynamics of complex systems and then evolve the basis—rather than the original high-dimensional model—to predict the states at future moments in time. However, POD basis such derived may not be quite robust to changing conditions, particularly in non-stationary and chaotic systems. Under this situation, the data-driven approach, like neural networks, can be employed to learn spatiotemporal dynamics from high-dimensional data and generate from them a ROM for the prediction of future states. The explicit handling of sequential memories makes long short-term memory (LSTM) an effective approach for modeling dynamics of complex systems, sequence-to-sequence learning and prediction without the vanishing gradient problem (Hochreiter and Schmidhuber 1997).

Differing from recurrent neural networks, LSTM in addition has cells carrying a self-loop as internal recurrence. In brief, the LSTM models the transmission of cell states by controlling information flow into the network from previous time steps of the time series through a number of gates. A standard LSTM unit contains a memory cell, an input gate, a forget gate, and an output gate (Fig. 4.6). The memory cell, c_t, whose state is controlled by three gates which can add or remove information: namely the input gate i_t, the forget gate f_t, and the output gate o_t. The LSTM cell changes the flow of information via these gates. The input gate controls the flow of the input information into the LSTM cell. At every single time when the input gate is activated, the information of the new input will be accumulated in the memory cell. The forget gate filters the incoming information from the previous time steps and decides on the retention or abandonment of information. If the forget gate is activated, the past cell status will be forgotten. The output gate controls the output flow of the LSTM cell and the propagation of the latest cell state to the final state. The memory cell is basically an accumulator of state information used to ensure the information flow along the sequence unchanged.

Formally, we can specify various cell states and various gates as follow

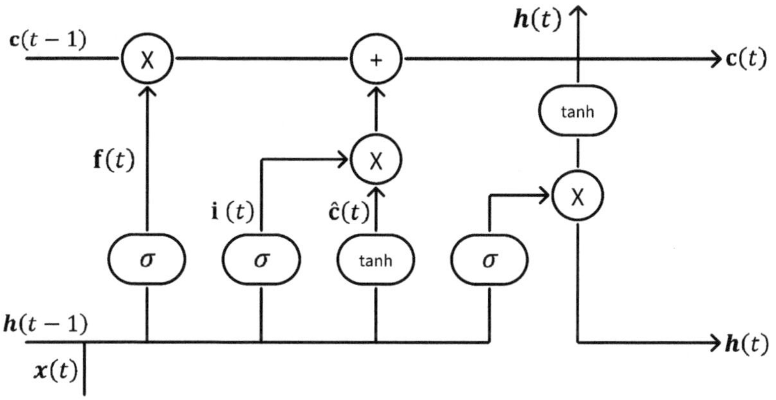

Fig. 4.6 The long short-term memory (LSTM) unit

$$
\begin{aligned}
\mathbf{i}(t) &= \sigma(\mathbf{W}_i[\mathbf{h}(t-1), C(t)] + \mathbf{b}_i)\\
\mathbf{f}(t) &= \sigma\left(\mathbf{W}_f[\mathbf{h}(t-1), C(t)] + \mathbf{b}_f\right)\\
\mathbf{o}(t) &= \sigma(\mathbf{W}_O[\mathbf{h}(t-1), C(t)] + \mathbf{b}_O)
\end{aligned}
\tag{4.80}
$$

where $\mathbf{h}(t-1)$ is the previous hidden state, and $C(t)$ is the current input. The parameters are the respective connection weights $\mathbf{W}_i, \mathbf{W}_f, \mathbf{W}_O$, and the bias vectors $\mathbf{b}_i, \mathbf{b}_f, \mathbf{b}_O$. The cell state $\mathbf{c}(t)$ can be updated by composing the previous state $\mathbf{c}(t-1)$ and the newly generated state $\hat{\mathbf{c}}(t)$ through the forget gate and the input gate as follows

$$
\begin{aligned}
\hat{\mathbf{c}}(t) &= \tanh(\mathbf{W}_c[\mathbf{h}(t-1), C(t)] + \mathbf{b}_c)\\
\mathbf{c}(t) &= \mathbf{f}(t) \circ \mathbf{c}(t-1) + \mathbf{i}(t) \circ \hat{\mathbf{c}}(t)
\end{aligned}
\tag{4.81}
$$

where $\circ$ means elementwise multiplication, and tanh is the hyperbolic tangent activation function. The updated cell state can be used to generate the new hidden state through the output gate as follows

$$
\mathbf{h}(t) = \mathbf{o}(t) \circ \tanh(\mathbf{c}(t)) \tag{4.82}
$$

Figure 4.7 depicts the cell connections in LSTM along the sequence.

The LSTM has been found to be the data-driven approach instrumental to the discovery of dynamics in spatiotemporal data, particularly those involving time series (Siami-Namini et al. 2018). The main idea of combining ROM and LSTM to model spatiotemporal dynamics is to construct a ROM based on the POD modes and employ LSTM to evolve the corresponding time coefficients to predict the state at the next moment in time. Given snapshots of the field obtained from the simulations of the discretized high-dimensional model, we apply the procedure discussed in Sect. 3.3 of Chap. 3 to derive the POD basis and the respective time coefficients. The time

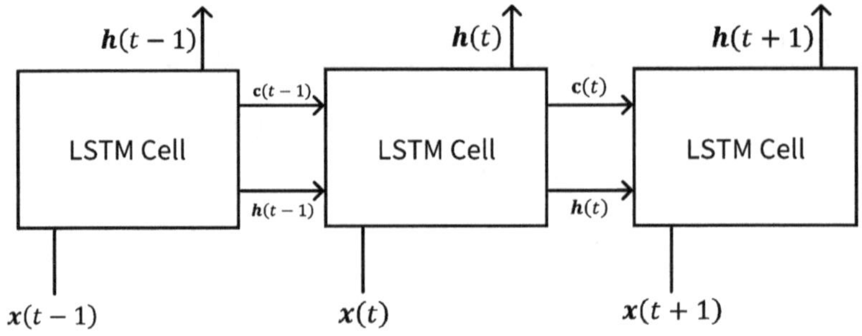

Fig. 4.7 Cell connections in LSTM unit

coefficients are then employed as inputs for the LSTM training. Specifically, the evolution of the time coefficients can be expressed as (Wang et al. 2018a, b):

$$a_k(t+1) = f(a_k(t)), k \in \{1, 2, \ldots, r\} \tag{4.83}$$

for r POD modes. The time coefficients $a_k(t+1)$'s are then used to predict the state at the next step in time. The function f is constructed via a deep LSTM which maps the input x (a sequence) to the output y (a sequence) through several gates in the network. The LSTM is effective in learning the temporal dependence in data without complicated initial and boundary conditions using long-term and short-term memories (Fig. 4.8).

The combined use of LSTM and ROM, called LSTM-ROM, has been demonstrated to be useful in unraveling and predicting the dynamics of complex systems in low-dimensional space (Wang et al. 2018a; Mohan and Gaitonde 2018; Rahman et al. 2018; Yousif and Lim 2022). It has been shown that LSTM is more appropriate for the modeling of time series without long-range correlation. It is useful to model chaotic behavior in time series having a fractal structure that exhibits self-similarity (Vlachas et at. 2018). To predict chaotic time series that conform to the classical Lorenz model, Eq. (4.11) for instance, the input to the LSTM is the state variable vector $[x(t), y(t), z(t)]$ based on the current values of the chaotic time series at time t, and the output vector $[x(t+\delta t), y(t+\delta t), z(t+\delta t)]$ is the future values of the time series at time $t+\delta t$. However, LSTM has low capability in modeling time series with long-range dependence. Bidirectional LSTM (Graves and Schmidhuber 2005)—in which inputs are presented forwards and backwards to two separate recurrent networks with both connected to the same output layer—are shown to be useful in training with time series data having long-range correlation (Yousif and Lim 2022). It can also be combined with ROM to perform prediction in low-dimensional space.

By introducing exponential gating with appropriate normalization and stabilization techniques and by modifying the memory structures, Beck et al. (2024) formulated xLSTM and showed that it can boost the capability of LSTM to perform favorably well both in performance and scaling in comparison to state-of-the-art Transformers and state-space models. It might be worthy to explore the use of xLSTM to

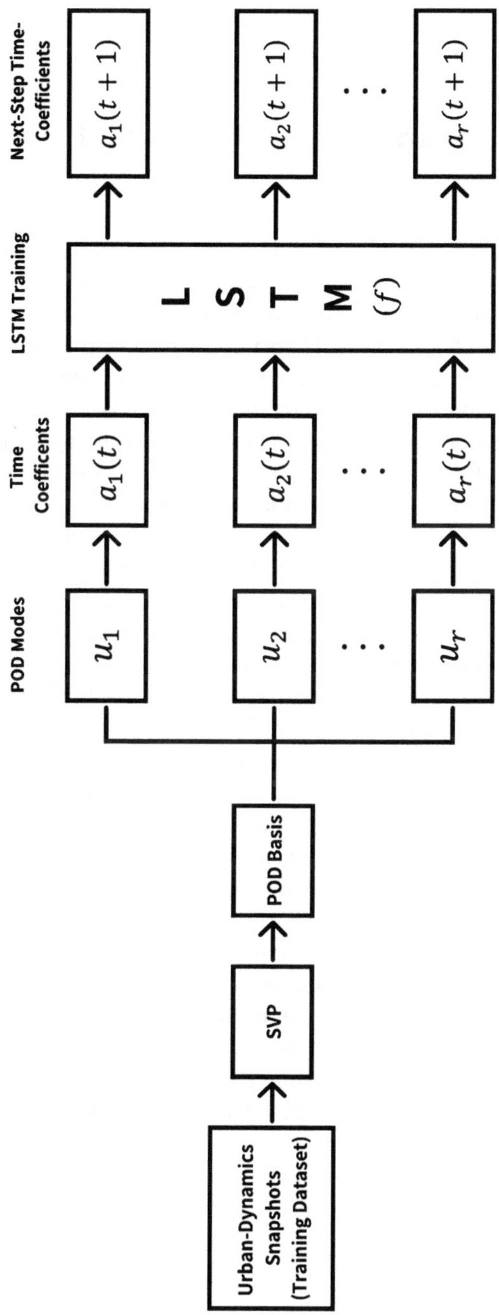

Fig. 4.8 The LSTM-ROM for the discovery and modeling of urban dynamics

incorporate dynamics and complexity into digital twins of cities. A further discussion on the use of time series data and LSTM to build digital twins of cities is given in Chap. 9.

4.8 Theory-Based Neural Network for Digital Twins of Cities

The data-driven approach is data hungry. Its universality in approximation is handicapped by its inadequacy in interpretability, particularly from the urban science point of view. Therefore, making the data-driven models urban theory-informed is a plausible way to get the best of both worlds. Theory-informed data-driven digital twins of cities may be able to accomplish such objective. Take neural network as an example, can we make neural-network-based urban dynamical models theory-based or theory-informed? Under certain circumstances, it is in fact possible by carefully building into the neural network the urban theory involved. Below, I use spatial interaction modeling as a concrete example to substantiate our discussion.

Spatial interaction has been a main concern in urban analysis. Regardless of whether we are dealing with movement of people, commodities, financial transactions, daily commuting, information and communication flows via traditional means or IoT, etc., we generally need to estimate interpoint (points can be subway stations, telecommunication nodes, neighborhoods, urban districts, cities, regions, etc.) flow patterns and their changes in time and space. Parametric estimation has been employed to obtain a least-squares solution through a feedforward neural network (Fischer 1998; Fischer and Leung 1998; Fischer et al. 1999). However, such data-driven method is a black box with low interpretability in terms of urban theory, and the results may not optimize the objective and satisfy the inflow and outflow conditions stipulated by the interaction model. Spatial interactions can be overly complex exhibiting linear or nonlinear dynamics. Developing digital twins for spatial interactions thus needs to take into consideration the complexity and dynamics of such urban structures and processes. Entropy maximization (EM) has been demonstrated to be a powerful model for spatial interaction analysis. In what follows, I give a discussion on how spatial interaction can be modeled as a dynamical system beneficial to the embedding of complexity into digital twins of cities.

Since its inception, entropy maximization (Wilson 1967, 1970, 2010) has been a pilar of spatial interaction research. The classical entropy-maximization model can be formulated as follows

$$\begin{aligned}
&\max\ W = \frac{T!}{\prod_{i,j} T_{i,j}!} \\
&\approx \min \sum_{i,j} T_{ij} \ln T_{ij} \\
&\text{s.t.} \\
&\sum_{j} T_{ij} = O_i, \qquad i = 1, 2, \ldots, m \\
&\sum_{i} T_{ij} = D_j, \qquad j = 1, 2, \cdots, n \\
&\sum_{i,j} c_{ij} T_{ij} \le c \\
&T_{ij} \ge 0, \qquad i = 1, 2, \ldots, m;\ j = 1, 2, \ldots, n.
\end{aligned} \tag{4.84}$$

It should be noted that the equality cost constraint in the classical model is a special case of the inequality cost function in Eq. (4.84), which is guaranteed by the necessary and sufficient conditions stipulated in Leung et al. (2004).

The curiosity is: could we solve the high-dimensional entropy-maximization problem with dense structure through a theory-based data-driven approach and yet manage to embed all the salient features of the classical model into it? For efficient simulations and predictions, could we solve the EM model in near real-time or real time? Can we make it scalable? To provide an answer to these questions, Leung et al. (2004) formulated a dual neural network to solve a family of EM models efficiently. With respect to the classical EM model stated above, the Wolfe dual problem of Eq. (4.84) is first formulated via the duality theory, and a neural network is then constructed to solve the dual problem in real time. It turns out that the Wolf dual problem can be formulated as a much simpler convex optimization problem as follows

$$\begin{aligned}
&\max\ \overline{\mathcal{L}}(\boldsymbol{T}, \boldsymbol{\lambda}, \boldsymbol{\mu}, y) \\
&\text{s.t. } \nabla_{\boldsymbol{T}}\ \overline{\mathcal{L}}(\boldsymbol{T}, \boldsymbol{\lambda}, \boldsymbol{\mu}, y) = 0 \\
&y \ge 0
\end{aligned} \tag{4.85}$$

where

$$\boldsymbol{T} = \left(T_{11}, T_{12}, \ldots, T_{1n,} T_{21}, T_{22}, \ldots, T_{2n,} T_{m1}, T_{m2}, \ldots, T_{mn}\right) \in R^{m \times n}$$

$$\boldsymbol{\lambda} = \left(\lambda_{1,} \lambda_2, \ldots, \lambda_m\right)^T \in R^m$$

$$\boldsymbol{\mu} = \left(\mu_{1,} \mu_{2,\ldots,} \mu_n\right)^T \in R^n$$

$$\overline{\mathcal{L}}(\boldsymbol{T}, \boldsymbol{\lambda}, \boldsymbol{\mu}, y) = \sum_{i,j} T_{ij} \ln T_{ij} - \sum_{i} \lambda_i \left(\sum_{j} T_{ij} - O_i \right) - \sum_{j} \mu_j \left(\sum_{i} (T_{ij} - D_j \right) - y \left(c - \sum_{ij} c_{ij} T_{ij} \right)$$

$$T_{ij} = exp\left(\lambda_i + \mu_j - yc_{ij} - 1\right) > 0, i = 1,2, \ldots, m; j = 1,2, \ldots, n$$

By substituting T_{ij} into the objective function $\overline{\mathcal{L}}(\boldsymbol{T}, \boldsymbol{\lambda}, \boldsymbol{\mu}, y)$, the dual problem is effectively reduced to

$$\begin{gathered} \max \overline{\mathcal{L}}(\boldsymbol{\lambda}, \boldsymbol{\mu}, y) \\ \text{s.t. } y \geq 0 \end{gathered} \tag{4.86}$$

where

$$\overline{\mathcal{L}}(\boldsymbol{\lambda}, \boldsymbol{\mu}, y) = \sum_{i} \lambda_i O_i + \sum_{j} \mu_j D_j - yc - \sum_{i,j} exp\left(\lambda_i + \mu_j - yc_{ij} - 1\right)$$

Leung et al. (2004) showed that the dual problem can be solved by the following well-defined neural network model which is constructed by the necessary and sufficient conditions for an optimal solution to the EM problem as follows

$$\begin{aligned} \frac{\mathrm{d}\lambda_i}{\mathrm{d}t} &= O_i - \sum_{j} exp\left(\lambda_i + \mu_j - yc_{ij} - 1\right), \quad i = 1, 2, \ldots, m \\ \frac{\mathrm{d}\mu_j}{\mathrm{d}t} &= D_j - \sum_{i} exp\left(\lambda_i + \mu_j - yc_{ij} - 1\right), \quad j = 1, 2, \ldots, n \\ \frac{\mathrm{dy}}{\mathrm{dt}} &= \left[y - C + \sum_{i,j} C_{ij} exp\left(\lambda_i + \mu_j - yc_{ij} - 1\right) \right]^{+} - y \end{aligned} \tag{4.87}$$

The RHS of the neural network is Lipschitz continuous, and thus the initial value problem of the network has a unique continuous solution. Therefore, the solution to the dual problem is equivalent to finding an equilibrium point of the neural network. By Lyapunov stability theory and LaSalle invariance principle, Leung et al. (2004) proved that the dual neural network is Lyapunov stable, and its every trajectory can be guaranteed to converge asymptotically to an exact solution of the dual problem. It should be noted that the neural network has a very simple structure and is much lower in dimension. Unlike the conventional EM calibration methods which are greatly affected by the complexity and scale of the problem as well as the iterative procedure and complicated conditioning of the variables involved, calibration of the dual neural network is not affected by the variation of scale at all. It can also be implemented in hardware for even more efficient real-time simulation (Leung et al. 2004). This tremendously enhances the practicality of the EM method, and the digital twin thus constructed. Furthermore, the proposed neural network approach can solve a large variety of entropy-maximization problems efficiently (see Leung et al. 2004 for details), including the transportation problem in Evans (1973), an extended entropy model with probabilistic underpinning (Snickars and Weibull 1977), the generalized link traffic count EM models in Wu (1997), a schedule-based transit network model in Wong and Tong (1998), the EM interaction model in Senior (1979), and the gravity-opportunity model in Gonçalves and Ulysséa-Neto (1993). Besides being efficient, these neural network formulations, unlike neural networks which are black box in general, are interpretable and retain the corresponding objectives and constraints of the original EM models.

What makes the above data-driven approach different from the purely data-driven digital twins is that it is not a black box because all the EM features, including objective and constraints, are explicitly incorporated into the dual neural network. It is in fact a theory-based digital twin!

Remark. In general, we may not be able to turn an urban model into a data-driven neural network model and retain all its salient features for subsequent interpretations, like what we have done for the EM problem above. Nevertheless, we can make a neural network model respect the dynamical theory of a process. The main idea is to use a neural network to learn the underlying dynamics of an urban process from high-fidelity simulated datasets and use the learned network to predict the dynamics at future moments in time. If we suspect that the high-fidelity dynamics has an intrinsic low-dimensional manifold, we can use the learned network to generate a ROM first and use it for future simulations and predictions, or to learn new dynamical models that have never been noticed or specified for a dynamical system. A discussion on building intelligible neural networks is given in the section to follow.

4.9 On Intelligibility of Data-Driven Learning

Data-driven learning is considered black box learning in which accuracy comes at the expense of intelligibility. Learning results of neural networks, for example, are often difficult to interpret. In response to this comes the so-called glass-box learning which attempts to enhance the intelligibility of such type of machine learning so that the learning process and result are interpretable, accurate, editable, and re-trainable. It tries to improve accuracy and interpretability by striking a balance between feature sparsity, data fidelity, and accuracy. Ideally, we want to use sufficiently sparse features to accurately learn an input–output mapping that truly reflects the characteristics of data, including the nuances and anomalies.

4.9.1 The Generalized Additive Models—The Glass-Box Approach

Along this line of thought, the generalized additive model (GAM) targets the learning of the relationship, particularly nonlinear relationship, between the dependent/response variable and multiple independent/predictor variables. It can be considered a statistical model specified as follows

$$g(E[y]) = \beta_0 + f_1(x_1) + f_2(x_2) + \cdots + f_m(x_m) \tag{4.88}$$

where y is the dependent variable; x_i, $i = 1,2, \ldots, m$, are the independent variables; g is the link function; and f_i is the univariate shape function, usually a smooth function like a spline. Interaction terms can also be built into the model to evaluate the impact of interactions between independent variables on the dependent variable. Traditional GAMs are trained with splines and are later developed into variants which better handle sharp drops and more complex relationships through some trend-filtering methods (Chang et al. 2021). The generalized additive neural network (GANN) employs neural networks with one hidden layer and a few hidden nodes to learn the input–output mapping. It might require up to millions of shallow bagged trees to learn the shape function. It is computationally costly and possibly an overkill!

The advantages of GAMs are that they are flexible in using prior knowledge to choose smooth functions to capture nonlinear relationships and the results can be visualized and interpretable. Because of the smoothness of the function, they are, to a certain extent, robust to noise and outliers. However, when relationships are highly nonlinear and there are high-dimensional interaction terms to handle, visualize and interpret, GAMs may not perform and scale well. Building on GANNs, neural additive model (NAM) combines the expressivity of deep neural networks and the interpretability of GAMs to form a family of glass-box models through a combination of deep neural networks, each attending to a single input feature (Argarwal et al. 2021). This makes more complex shape functions easier to learn. Again, would it be an overkill for such a learning task? What about the visualization and interpretability of the high-dimensional interaction terms and the impact on computational cost?

To improve accuracy, explainable boosting machine (EBM) combines the strength of GAMs and the gradient boosting machine to make the data-driven learning human-interpretable and accurate simultaneously and allows for model editing based on visualization (Chang et al. 2021). It emphasizes the importance of decomposing a multiple-feature link function into individual features and study and interpret their behaviors individually to facilitate post-learning model editing. It is accomplished by employing a set of simple and interpretable rules, e.g. piecewise constant functions, to learn the input–output map, and combine them additively to form the final model for prediction. Interactions are implicitly handled by multidimensional boosting that learns a separate set of simple rules for each interaction of features. Again, would this scale well under high nonlinearity and complex interactions. Again, would this be an overkill?

To sum up, the above GAM-based models aim at making data-driven learning intelligible and accurate. It attempts to make the learning process feature-sparse and yet interpretable and accurate. Feature sparsity will not compromise data fidelity and prediction accuracy. For each feature in a graph, we visually look for jumps from one regime to another and perform model editing by adjusting for anomaly with monotonicity forced locally within a chosen neighborhood via domain-specific knowledge.

4.9.2 Issues of the Generalized Additive Models

There are, however, issues about the GAM-based methods which need further investigations. First, jumps and nuances of data are deciphered from the visualization of the feature graphs depicting the relationships between the dependent variable and each of the independent variables. This process is not automatic and involves human intervention and subjective judgment. From a purely data-driven point of view, this task can actually be accomplished by applying advanced non-stationary and nonlinear time series analysis such as detrended fluctuation analysis (DFA) and multifractal detrended fluctuation analysis (MFDFA)—briefly discussed in Sect. 9.4 of Chap. 9. Though the objectives of GAM and DFA/MFDFA are different, using techniques in DFA and MFDFA can help us identify crossover time scales/jumps that separate different behavioral regimes in the shape functions—local trends exhibiting monotonicity within individual regimes—and long-range correlation in data. This information can be visualized and is useful for subsequent model editing if unreasonable irregularities need to be adjusted. Furthermore, we do not need to worry about the selection of shape functions (see related discussion on model-data interoperability in Sect. 9.4 of Chap. 9). With denoising, the process will be robust. Figure 4.9 shows the identification of crossover time scales by MFDFA that separate rainfall regimes exhibiting local trends for the corresponding time series depicted in Fig. 4.10. Apparently, they are very intelligible. Accurate identification of rainfall regimes will shed light on urban planning for climate resilient cities.

Cointegration of time series of the dependent and independent variables will indicate how closely the two are related. In the multivariate case, we can use multivariate empirical mode decomposition (MEMD) (Rehman and Mandic 2010; see a brief discussion in Sect. 9.4 of Chap. 9) which adopts the concept of multivariate joint oscillation, and processes the multivariate time series in the multidimensional domain to obtain the multidimensional envelop by projecting along different directions in the multidimensional space to find common oscillatory modes. This appears to be more natural and informative for uncovering patterns of urban dynamics and complexity.

Second, though there are some measures to alleviate the pressure of high-dimensional interaction between features in some of the GAM-based methods, the impact of high-dimensional interaction can be severe in complex situations. GAM-based methods face the scalability problem when we have high-order interactions. It may still work well in problems with a few features. Does it scale well if the

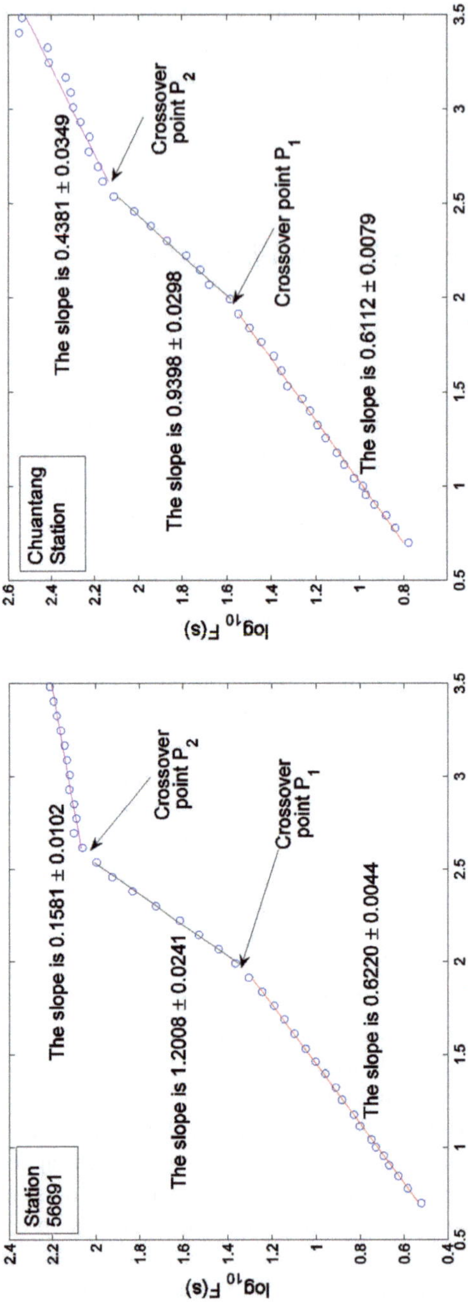

Fig. 4.9 Log–log plots of $F_q(s)$ versus s for the daily rainfall time series of station 56,691 in Pearl River basin (left) and Station Chuantang in East River basin (right) with $q = 2$ (derived from Yu et al. (2014))

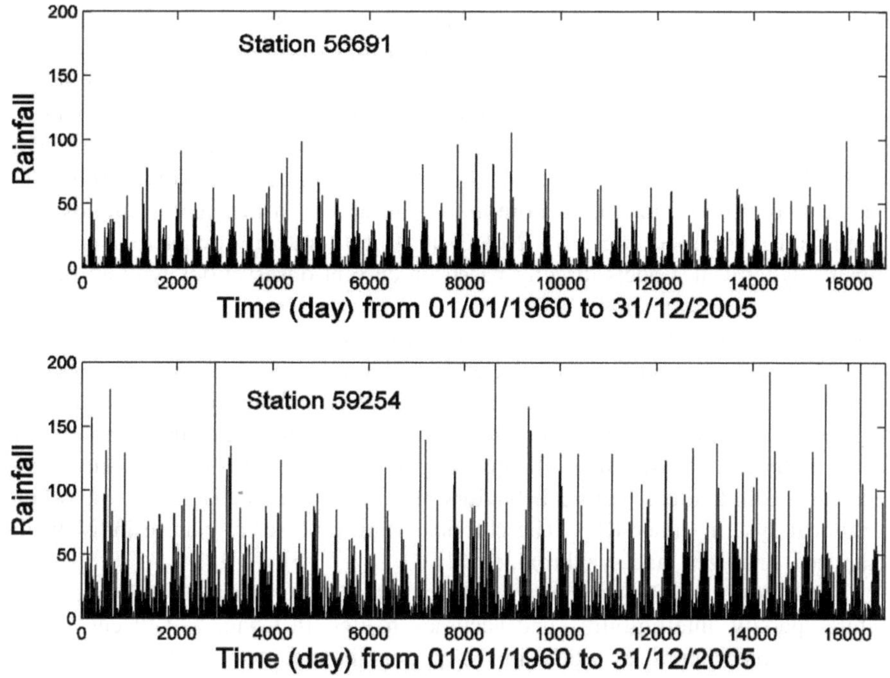

Fig. 4.10 Daily rainfall data of two stations in Pearl River basin of China (adopted from Yu et al. (2014))

number of features is large, say hundreds or thousands. Under these circumstances, we need to study, visualize, differentiate, and make sense of hundreds or thousands of graphs. A very challenging task. Furthermore, if we need to take all possible interactions—though boosting can eliminate some of the interactions—between features into account, we may still face the combinatorial explosion problem in computation, visualization (It's difficult to visualize in 3-D and we cannot visualize beyond 3-D), and interpretation. If we really need to do it, perhaps one way to deal with the problem is to project the high-dimensional model/data onto a low-dimensional subspace to derive a reduced-order model/data (like what is discussed in Chap. 3) and use the empirical mode decomposition (EMD) method—briefly discussed in Sect. 9. 4 of Chap. 9—to identify the most relevant modes, and then study the resulting features individually via GAM-based methods or methods such as DFA, MFDFA, etc., whichever deems appropriate. With the EMDs, DFA, and MFDFA, we can automatically extract useful structure and semantics information about the shape functions which in turn can greatly assist us to do model editing or recalibration to improve predictions/estimations.

Third, the post-learning model editing with GAM requires domain-specific knowledge. However, domain experts, say a medical doctor, may not have sufficient machine-learning knowledge to differentiate whether the parts of the model that need editing is a result of noise or genuine outliers (a peculiar occurrence with significant implications). On the other hand, an AI expert may not have the knowledge (say medical knowledge) to tell whether the parts that need editing are due to noise or genuine peculiar behavior/an outlier of a certain disease that cannot be obliviously removed but needs to be attended to. Being able to do model editing is good. We, nevertheless, must do it very carefully with expertise in both machine learning and specific knowledge domain. A more automatic approach may be to employ data assimilation, discussed in Sect. 9.2 of Chap. 9, to iteratively update/edit relationships or dynamical models directly based on current observations without human interventions or judgements.

Taking it further, perhaps we can employ Takens's theorem (briefly discussed in Sect. 4.6) to first project the interrelationships/dynamics onto a higher-dimensional space through the reconstructed phase space procedure and then project the dynamics back to the individual dimensions (individual features) to study and interpret their behaviors by DFA or MFDFA. Theoretically, there is a one-to-one correspondence between the individual feature behaviors and the overall behavior of the whole dynamical system under RPS. The corresponding time series can be individually visualized, analyzed, and synchronized.

All the above constitute important issues for data-driven machine learning where feature sparsity, intelligibility, and accuracy matter. In Chap. 5, I discuss urban theory-informed neural networks in which domain-specific knowledge and data-driven methods are synthesized to construct digital twins of cities for urban dynamics and complexity analysis. This is perhaps a powerful theory-informed data-driven learning that can cater for feature sparsity, data fidelity, and intelligibility.

Figure 4.11 sums up our discussion in this chapter.

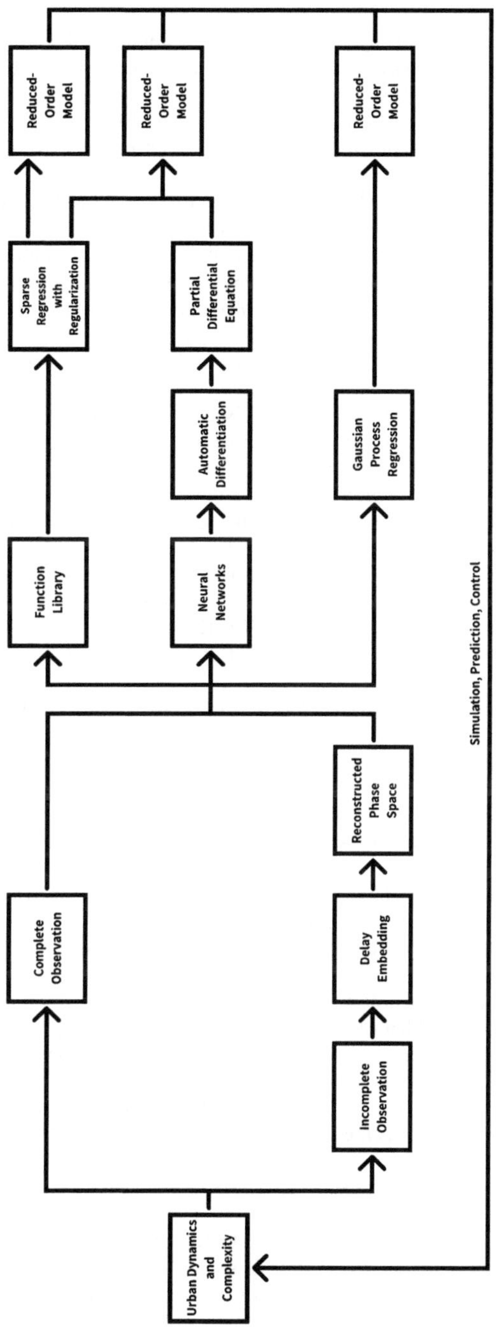

Fig. 4.11 Data-driven approach to the construction of digital twins of cities

References

Agarwal R, Melnick L, Frosst N, Zhang X, Lengerich B, Caruana R, Hinton G (2021) Neural additive models: interpretable machine learning with neural nets. arXiv:2004.13912. https://doi.org/10.48550/arXiv.2004.13912.

Al-Kaff MO, AlNemer G, El-Metwally HA, Elsadany A-EA, Elabbasy EM (2024) Dynamic behavior and bifurcation analysis of a modified reduced Lorenz model. *Mathematics* 12: 1354. https://doi.org/10.3390/math12091354.

Algaba A, Dominguez-Moreno M. C, Merino M, Rodriguez-Luis AJ (2018) A review on some bifurcations in the Lorenz system. *Nonlinear Systems* 1: 3–36.

Allen PM, Strathern M, Baldwin J (2008) Complexity: the integrating framework for models of urban and regional systems. In: Albeverio S, Andrey D, Giordano P, Vancheri A (eds.) *The Dynamics of Complex Urban Systems: An Interdisciplinary Approach.* NY: Physica-Verlag Heidelberg, 21–42.

Arbib MA (ed.) (2002) *The Handbook of Brain Theory and Neural Networks.* Cambridge: MIT Press.

Bakarji J, Champion K, Kutz JN, Brunton SL (2023) Discovering governing equations from partial measurements with deep delay autoencoders. *Proceedings of the Royal Society A* 479 (2276). https://doi.org/10.1098/rspa.2023.0422.

Bartlett MS (1960) *Stochastic Population Models in Ecology and Epidemiology.* London: Methuen.

Baydin AG, Pearlmutter BA, Radul AA (2018) Automatic differentiation in machine learning: a survey. *Journal of Machine Learning Research* 18: 1–43.

Beck M, Pöppel K, Spanring M, Auer A, Prudnikova O, Kopp M, Klambauer G, Brandstetter J, Hochreiter S (2024) xLSTM: extended long short-term memory. *Proceedings of the 41st International Conference on Machine Learning*, PMLR 235.

Berg J, Nyström K (2019) Data-driven discovery of PDEs in complex datasets. *Journal of Computational Physics* 384: 239–252.

Bishop SR, Holbom PG, Beard AN, Drysdale DD (1993) Nonlinear dynamics of flashover in compartment fires. *Fire Safety Journal* 21: 11–45.

Boulard H, Kamp Y (1988) Auto-association by multilayer perceptrons and singular value decomposition. *Biological Cybernetics* 59: 291–294.

Brunton SL, Proctor JL, Kutz JN (2016a) Discovering governing equations from data by sparse identification of nonlinear dynamical systems. *Proceedings of the National Academy of Sciences* 113(15): 3932–3937.

Brunton SL, Proctor JL, Kutz JN (2016b) Sparse identification of nonlinear dynamics with control (SINDYc). *IFAC-PapersOnLine* 49(18): 710–715.

Champion K, Lusch B, Kutz JN, and Brunton SL (2019). Data-driven discovery of coordinates and governing equations. *Proceedings of the National Academy of Sciences* 116(45): 22445–22451. www.pnas.org/cgi/doi/https://doi.org/10.1073/pnas.1906995116.

Chang CH, Tan S, Lengerich B, Goldenberg A, Caruana R (2021) How interpretable and trustworthy are GAMs? arXiv:2006.06466. https://doi.org/10.48550/arXiv.2006.06466.

Conti P, Gobat G, Fresca S, Manzoni A, Frangi A (2023) Reduced order modeling of parametrized systems through autoencoders and SINDy approach: continuation of periodic solutions. *Computer Methods in Applied Mechanics and Engineering* 411: 116072. https://doi.org/10.1016/j.cma.2023.116072.

Dumortier F, Llibre J, Artes JC (2006) Qualitative Theory of Planar Differential Systems. NY: Springer-Verlag.

Evans SP (1973) A relationship between the gravity model for trip distribution and the transportation problem in linear programming. *Transportation Research* 7: 39–61.

Fischer MM (1998) Computational neural networks: a new paradigm for spatial analysis. *Environment and Planning A* 30: 1873–1891.

Fischer MM, Leung Y (1998) A genetic algorithms based evolutionary computational neural network for modelling spatial interaction data. *Annals of Regional Science* 32: 437–458.

Fischer MM, Schindler KH, Reismann M (1999) A global search procedure for parameter estimation in neural spatial interaction modelling. *Papers in Regional Science* 78: 119–134.

Ge EJ, Haining R, Li, Chi P, Yu ZG, Waye MY, Chu KH, Leung Y (2012) Using knowledge fusion to analyze avian influenza H5N1 in East and Southeast Asia. *PloS One* 7(5): e29617, 2012.

Gonçalves M B, Ulysséa-Neto I (1993) The development of a new gravity – opportunity model for trip distribution. *Environment and Planning A* 25: 817–826.

Graves A, Schmidhuber J (2005) Framewise phoneme classification with bidirectional LSTM and other neural network architectures. *Neural Networks* 18(5–6): 602–610.

Hochreiter S, Schmidhuber J (1997) Long short-term memory. *Neural computation* 9(8): 1735–1780.

Holland JH (1975) *Adaptation in Natural and Artificial Systems*. Ann Arbor: University of Michigan Press.

Holland JH (1992) *Genetic algorithms*. Scientific American 267(1): 66–73.

Kachroo P, Sastry S (2016) Travel time dynamics for intelligent transportation systems: theory and applications. *IEEE Transactions on Intelligent Transportation Systems* 17(2): 385–394.

Kaheman K, Brunton SL, Kutz JN (2020) Automatic differentiation to simultaneously identify nonlinear dynamics and extract noise probability distributions from data. *Machine Learning: Science and Technology* 12. https://doi.org/10.1088/2632-2153/ac567a.

Kingma D P, Welling, Max (2022). Auto-Encoding Variational Bayes". arXiv:1312.6114.

Klus S, Nüske F, Peitz S, Niemann J-H, Clementi C, Schütte C (2020) Data-driven approximation of the Koopman generator: Model reduction, system identification, and control. *Physica D* 406: 132416.

Koopman, BO. (1931) Hamiltonian systems and transformation in Hilbert space. *Proceedings of the National Academy of Sciences* 17 (5): 315–318.

LeCun Y, Bengio Y, Hinton G (2015) Deep learning. *Nature* 521(7553): 436–444.

Leung Y, Gao XB, Chen KZ (2004) A dual neural network for solving entropy-maximising models. *Environment and Planning A* 36: 879–919.

Leung Y, Ge EJ, Yu Z G (2011) Temporal scaling behavior of avian influenza A (H5N1): he multifractal detrended fluctuation analysis. *Annals of the Association of American Geographers* 101(2011): 1221–1240.

Leung Y, Ma JH, Zhang WX (2001) A new method for mining regression classes in large data sets. *IEEE Transactions on Pattern Analysis and Machine Intelligence* 23: 5–21.

Lin CT, Jou CP (1999) Controlling chaos by GA-based reinforcement learning neural network. *IEEE Transactions on Neural Networks* 10(4): 846–859.

Loiseau JC, Brunton SL (2018) Constrained sparse Galerkin regression. *Journal of Fluid Mechanics* 838: 42–67.

Lorenz EN (1963) Deterministic nonperiodic flow. *Journal of atmospheric sciences* 20: 130–141.

McLachlan GJ, Basford KE (1988) *Mixture models: inference and applications to clustering*. NY: Marcel Dekker.

Messias M, Silva RP (2022) Nonchaotic behavior and transition to chaos in Lorenz-like systems having invariant algebraic surfaces. *Chaos Theory and Applications* 4(1): 26–36.

Mohan AT, Gaitonde DV (2018) A deep learning based approach to reduced order modeling for turbulent flow control using LSTM neural networks. arXiv:1804.09269.

Nijkamp P, Reggiani A (1992) Interaction*, Evolution and Chaos in Space*. Berlin: Springer-Verlag.

Ott E, Grebogi C, Yorke JA (1990) Controlling chaos. *Physical Review Letters* 64: 1196–1199.

Povinelli RJ, Johnson MT, Lindgren AC, Ye J (2004) Time series classification using Gaussian mixture models of reconstructed phase spaces. *IEEE Transactions on Knowledge Data Engineering* 16: 779–783.

Proctor JL, Brunton SL, Kutz JN (2016) Dynamic mode decomposition with control. *SIAM Journal on Applied Dynamical Systems* 15(1): 142–161.

Rahman S, San O, Rasheed A (2018) A hybrid approach for model order reduction of barotropic quasi-geostrophic turbulence. *Fluids 3*(4): 86. https://doi.org/10.3390/fluids3040086.

Raissi M, Perdikaris P, Karniadakis GE (2018) Numerical Gaussian processes for time-dependent and nonlinear partial differential equations. *SIAM Journal on Scientific Computing* 40(1): A172–A198.

Rehman N, Mandic D.P (2010) Multivariate empirical mode decomposition. *Proceedings of The Royal Society A* 466: 1291–1302.

Rudy SH, Brunton SL, Proctor JL, Kutz JN (2017) Data-driven discovery of partial differential equations. *Science Advances* 3(4). https://doi.org/10.1126/sciadv.1602614.

Ruelle D, Takens F (1971) On the nature of turbulence. *Communications in Mathematical Physics* 20:167–192.

Sauer T, Yorke JA, Casdagli M (1991) Embedology. *Journal of Statistical Physics* 65: 579–616.

Scarselli F, Tsoi AC (1998) Universal approximation using feedforward neural networks: A survey of some existing methods, and some new results. *Neural Networks* 11(1): 15–37.

Schaeffer H (2017) Learning partial differential equations via data discovery and sparse optimization. *Proceedings of the Royal Society A: Mathematical, Physical and Engineering Science* 473(2197): 20160446.

Schmid PJ, Sesterhenn JL (2008) Dynamic mode decomposition of numerical and experimental data. *Bulletin of the American Physical Society 61st Annual Meeting*, 208.

Schmidt M, Lipson H (2009) Distilling free-form natural laws from experimental data. *Science* 324: 81–85.

Senior M L (1979) From gravity modelling to entropy maximising: A pedagogic guide. *Progress in Human Geography* 3: 175–221.

Shekofteh Y, Jafari S, Sprott JC, Golpayegani SMRH, Almasganj F (2015) A Gaussian mixture model-based cost function for parameter estimation of chaotic biological systems. *Communications in Nonlinear Science and Numerical Simulation* 20: 469–481.

Siami-Namini S, Tavakoli N, Namin AS (2018) A comparison of ARIMA and LSTM in forecasting time series. *17th IEEE International Conference on Machine Learning and Applications*. https://doi.org/10.1109/ICMLA.2018.00227.

Snickars F, Weibull J W (1977) A minimum information principle. *Regional Science and Urban Economics* 7: 137–168.

Sparrow C (1982) *The Lorenz Equations: Bifurcations, Chaos, and Strange Attractors*. NY: Springer-Verlag.

Takens F (1981) Detecting strange attractors in turbulence. In Rand D, Young LS (eds.) *Dynamical Systems and Turbulence*, Berlin: Springer-Verlag, 366–381.

Tibshirani R (1996) Regression shrinkage and selection via the Lasso. *Journal of the Royal Statistical Society. Series B (Methodological)* 58(1): 267–288.

Tsang SW, Leung Y (2011) A theory-based cellular automata for the simulation of land-use change. *Geographical Analysis* 43: 142–171.

Tu JH, Rowley CW, Luchtenburg DM, Brunton SL, Kutz JN (2014) On dynamic mode decomposition: theory and applications. *Journal of Computational Dynamics* 1(2): 391–421.

Vlachas_PR, Byeon W, ZY Wan, Sapsisy TP, Koumoutsakos P (2018) Data-driven forecasting of high-dimensional chaotic systems with long-short term memory networks. In *Proceedings of the Royal Society A: Mathematical, Physical and Engineering Sciences*, 474: 20170844. https://doi.org/10.1098/rspa.2017.0844.

Wang Z, Xiao Z, Fang F, Govindan R, Pain CC, Guo Y (2018a) Model identification of reduced order fluid dynamics systems using deep learning. *International Journal for Numerical Methods in Fluids* 86(4): 255–268.

Wang Z, He SY, Leung Y (2018b) Applying mobile phone data to travel behaviour research: a literature review. *Travel Behaviour and Society* 11: 141–155.

Whitney H. (1936) Differentiable manifolds. *Annals of Mathematics* 3(37): 645–680.

Williams MO, Kevrekidis IG, Rowley CW (2015) A data–driven approximation of the Koopman operator: extending dynamic mode decomposition. *Journal of Nonlinear Science* 25:1307–1346.

Wilson AG (1967) A statistical theory of spatial distribution models. *Transportation Research* 1: 253–269. https://doi.org/10.1016/0041-1647(67)90035-4.

Wilson AG (1970) *Entropy in Urban and Regional Modelling*. London: Pion.
Wilson AG (2010) Entropy in urban and regional modelling: retrospect and prospect. *Geographical Analysis* 42: 364–394.
Wong SC, Tong CO (1998) Estimation of time-dependent origin – destination matrix for transit networks. *Transportation Research* 32B: 35–48.
Wu JF (1997) A real-time origin-destination matrix updating algorithm for on-line applications. *Transportation Research* 31B: 381–396.
Xu H, Zhang D, Zeng J (2021) Deep learning of parametric partial differential equations from sparse and noisy data. *Physics of Fluids* 33: 037132. https://doi.org/10.1063/5.0042868.
Yousif MZ, Lim HC (2022) Reduced-order modeling for turbulent wake of a finite wallmounted square cylinder based on artificial neural network. *Physics of Fluids* 34: 015116. https://doi.org/10.1063/5.0077768.
Yu ZG, Leung Y, Chen YQ, Zhang Q, Anh V, Zhou Y (2014) Multifractal analyses of daily rainfall time series in Pearl River basin of China. *Physica A: Statistical Mechanics and Its Application* 405(C): 193–202.
Yue ZS, Yong HW, Meng DY, Zhao Q, Leung Y, Zhang L (2020) Robust multiview subspace learning with nonindependently and nonidentically distributed complex noise. *IEEE Transactions on Neural Network and Learning Systems* 31(4): 1070–1083. https://doi.org/10.1109/TNNLS.2019.2917328.
Zeeman EC (1976) Catastrophe theory. *Scientific American* 234(4): 65–83. https://doi.org/10.1038/scientificamerican0476-65.
Zong B, Song Q, Min MR, Cheng W, Lumezanu C, Cho D, Chen H (2018) Deep autoencoding Gaussian mixture model for unsupervised anomaly detection. *Proceedings of International conference on learning representations.*

Chapter 5
Building Digital Twins of Cities via Urban Theory-Informed Neural Networks

5.1 Reasons for Incorporating Urban Theories into Neural Networks to Model Urban Dynamics and Complexity

As discussed in Chap. 3, one way to incorporate complexity into digital twins of cities is to learn the ROMs from high-dimensional models that characterize the dynamics of complex urban systems/entities, usually in the form of ODEs or PDEs. The projection-based learning can project the high-dimensional spatiotemporal data generated by the high-dimensional model onto a low-dimensional manifold so that the dynamics and the associated complexity can be captured by a much simpler surrogate model expanded by the low-dimensional basis. The advantages of such an approach are (1) it can parsimoniously capture urban complexity characterized by the governing equations of urban dynamics based on urban theories, and (2) it facilitates efficient simulations, particularly near real-time and real-time, for urban management and control. Digital twins such constructed are theory-informed with good interpretability and generalization capability. However, since the projection is generally linear, it may not be quite effective in handling highly nonlinear dynamical systems and may be sensitive to noisy data on which derivatives are directly computed. Furthermore, if the governing equations or the exact forms of the underlying dynamics are not known, then we do not have the high-dimensional model to generate snapshots/data for the construction of the ROM through various projection methods.

In case we do not have the governing equations, can we still build ROMs that can incorporate dynamics and complexity into digital twins? An answer to this question is that if we have some ideas about the underlying dynamics but not the exact model, then we may still discover the most likely governing equations of urban dynamics through the methods discussed in Chap. 4. However, for highly nonlinear dynamical systems that exhibit complex behavior, such methods may not be able to discover all necessary terms to build the ROM.

Y. Leung, *Digital Twins of Cities*, Advances in Spatial Science,
https://doi.org/10.1007/978-3-032-07966-4_5

Urban systems may be too complex whose behaviors cannot be explicitly described, i.e. we may only have incomplete or even no knowledge about the underlying dynamics and the associated complexity, particularly for highly nonlinear dynamical systems like backdraft in buildings. What we have are only the observational or experimental data about the inputs and outputs of the systems. To model dynamics and complexity via digital twins, the neural network approach briefly discussed in Sect. 4.7 of Chap. 4 can be employed to learn the input–output maps of highly nonlinear systems. The models learned may be made generalizable. The downside of such approach is that we need a very large dataset to train the neural networks to capture the complicated dynamics, and the resulting neural network models are generally non-interpretable in the sense of urban theories. Using purely data-driven approach to learn and extrapolate city dynamics without any urban theory-imposed constraints can be non-inspiring in urban analysis and management, and the results may not observe the underlying processes.

To harness the power of the theory-based and data-driven approaches, we can integrate them into a single framework for the incorporation of dynamics and complexity into digital twins of cities. Essentially, we are imposing urban theory on neural network training so that the resulting networks will observe the urban theory imposed and becomes more interpretable. For efficient simulation and prediction, we can learn ROMs of highly nonlinear complex urban systems within the urban theory-informed framework. The following is a discussion on such a paradigm.

5.2 Incorporating Dynamics Through Physics-Informed Neural Networks

To capitalize on the power of machine learning (Sarker 2021) in general and neural networks in particular for learning hidden linear and nonlinear urban dynamics from noisy and heterogeneous observations or experimental spatiotemporal data, and to ensure that the learned dynamics respect laws or restraining conditions of urban process and development, it is profitable to develop urban theory-informed machine learning methods for the incorporation of dynamics and complexity into digital twins of cities. The integration of multiscale and multiphysics with machine learning has been shown to be an effective approach for solving the forward, inverse, and equation discovery problems with hidden physics (Raissi and Karniadakis 2018; Karniadakis et al. 2021; Cuomo et al. 2022). It increases the interpretability and generalizability of the learned models. Specifically, the hybrid learning process calls for the selective use of observational and/or experimental data that embody the underlying urban dynamics, appropriate learning models—e.g. neural network architectures—and suitable learning bias for optimal learning with minimal loss under constraints that enforce urban dynamics, regularization, and other system properties.

Among other machine learning methods, the physics-informed neural network (PINN) has been demonstrated to be natural and effective in solving ill-posed and inverse problems about the underlying dynamics of complex systems directly from noisy and sometimes limited data (Dissanayake and Phan-Thien 1994; Lagaris et al. 1998; Raissi et al. 2017a, b; Cuomo et al. 2022). PINNs are suitable for solving problems with underlying physics-based constraints or where explicit physical relationships exist. In general, PINNs can solve the forward problem, inverse problem, and equation discovery problem under such circumstances. By the synergistic integration of numerical PDE solvers with deep learning, the constructed deep neural networks can also achieve model parsimony—by serving as a projection function of the system input onto the latency space for low-dimensional manifold recovery of the input–output relationship in complex systems.

In general, PINN employs automatic differentiation to differentiate a neural network with respect to its spatiotemporal coordinates and model parameters to obtain a learned network which respects conditions—urban conditions in the case of digital twins of cities—that govern the observed data on which the network is trained (Raissi et al. 2017a). By hybridizing the data-driven and model-informed approaches, PINN becomes a universal functional approximator that can encode directly the underlying urban laws as prior information or via soft constraints. It is highly flexible in learning high-dimensional dynamics on complex geometric domains because no fixed meshes or grids are required, and training points can be randomly chosen in the spatiotemporal domain to form a colocation point cloud on which the hidden urban dynamics is learned.

Appropriately constructed, PINNs can solve PDEs taking the following general form (Cuomo et al. 2022):

$$\begin{aligned} F(\mathbf{u}(z);\ \boldsymbol{\phi}) &= f(z), \quad z \ in\ \boldsymbol{\Omega} \\ B(\mathbf{u}(z)) &= g(z), \quad z \ in\ \partial\boldsymbol{\Omega} \end{aligned} \tag{5.1}$$

where $\boldsymbol{\Omega} \subset \mathbb{R}^d$ is the domain; $\partial\boldsymbol{\Omega}$ is the boundary; $z := (x_{1,\ldots,}x_{d-1}; t)$ is the space-time coordinate vector; $\mathbf{u} = (u, u_x, u_{xx} \ldots)$ is the solution to be sought; $\boldsymbol{\phi}$ are theory parameters; f is the function that identifies the data of the learning problem; F is the nonlinear differential operator; B is the operator for the initial conditions or boundary conditions (Dirichlet, Neumann, Robin, or periodic); and g is the boundary function. The framework in Eq. (5.1) can be used to solve the forward and inverse problems.

5.2.1 *Solving the Forward Problem by Urban Theory-Informed Neural Networks*

In the forward problem, given the dynamical model of a system with specified parameters $\boldsymbol{\phi}$, say in PDE, and input, we want to compute/approximate the output $\mathbf{u}$ for z. PINN solves the PDE by constructing a neural network to approximate the solution that respect the initial and/or boundary conditions. Specifically, for digital twins of cities, we train the neural network by minimizing the loss function taking the general form as follows

$$L(\boldsymbol{\theta}) = L_F(\boldsymbol{\theta}) + L_B(\boldsymbol{\theta}) \tag{5.2}$$

where

$$L_F(\boldsymbol{\theta}) = \frac{1}{n_F}\sum_{i=1}^{n_F}\left\| F\left[N(x_i, t_i; \boldsymbol{\theta}) - f(x_i, t_i)\right]\right\|^2 \tag{5.3}$$

$$L_B(\boldsymbol{\theta}) = \frac{1}{n_B}\sum_{j=1}^{n_B}\left\| B\left[N\left(x_j, t_j; \boldsymbol{\theta}\right) - g\left(x_j, t_j\right)\right]\right\|^2 \tag{5.4}$$

Here, $\mathbf{u}(z)$ is approximated by the deep neural network—e.g. a deep $\boldsymbol{\theta}$-parameterized multilayer feedforward neural network $N(\boldsymbol{x}, t; \boldsymbol{\theta})$—described in Sect. 4.7 of Chap. 4, expressed as follows

$$\mathbf{u}(z) \approx \hat{\mathbf{u}}_{\boldsymbol{\theta}}(z) \tag{5.5}$$

where $\boldsymbol{\theta}$ stands for all the parameters (connection weights and biases) in the neural network.

By further taking known observational data into consideration, particularly in solving the inverse problem, the approximating neural network is learned by minimizing the composite loss function taking the following general form (Cuomo et al. 2022)

$$\boldsymbol{\theta}^* = arg\min_{\boldsymbol{\theta}}(\omega_F L_F(\boldsymbol{\theta}) + \omega_B L_B(\boldsymbol{\theta}) + \omega_D L_D(\boldsymbol{\theta})) \tag{5.6}$$

where $\omega_F, \omega_B,$ and ω_D are the respective weights for the losses due to the mismatches with the PDE, F (the discrepancy between the learned neural network and the PDE, i.e. the PDE residual), the initial/boundary conditions, B (by matching the output of the neural network with the initial/boundary conditions), and the labeled data, D (discrepancy between the network output and the observational/measurement data). Therefore, the learning results will best satisfy the theory stipulated by the PDE and the observational data at selected collocation points in the domain. However, there is a delicate balance we need to strike between theory loss and data loss that constitute the composite loss function that may involve training with some hyperparameters. If we prefer to write separately the initial and boundary conditions, then we minimize the loss function as follows

$$\boldsymbol{\theta}^* = arg\min_{\boldsymbol{\theta}}(\omega_F L_F(\boldsymbol{\theta}) + \omega_{BC} L_{BC}(\boldsymbol{\theta}) + \omega_{IC} L_{IC}(\boldsymbol{\theta}) + \omega_D L_D(\boldsymbol{\theta})) \tag{5.7}$$

where $L_{BC}(\boldsymbol{\theta})$ and $L_{IC}(\boldsymbol{\theta})$ are the losses due to the boundary and initial conditions, respectively, and ω_{BC}, ω_{IC} are the respective weights.

Without loss of generality, with respect to Eq. (5.6), the respective constituent loss functions are

$$\begin{aligned} L_F(\boldsymbol{\theta}) &= \frac{1}{N_C}\sum_{i=1}^{N_C} F(\hat{\mathbf{u}}_{\boldsymbol{\theta}}(z))^2 \\ &= \frac{1}{N_c}\sum_{i=1}^{N_c} \|F(\hat{\mathbf{u}}_{\boldsymbol{\theta}}(z_i)) - f(z_i)\|^2 \\ &= \frac{1}{N_C}\sum_{i=1}^{N_C} \|\boldsymbol{\theta}(\mathbf{u}_i) - \boldsymbol{r}_i\|^2 \end{aligned} \tag{5.8}$$

which is the mean squared error (MSE), residual on the PDE;

$$L_B(\boldsymbol{\theta}) = \frac{1}{N_B}\sum_{i=1}^{N_B} \|B(\hat{\mathbf{u}}_{\boldsymbol{\theta}}(z_i)) - g(z_i)\|^2 \tag{5.9}$$

is the MSE for the initial/boundary conditions; and

$$\mathcal{L}_D(\boldsymbol{\theta}) = \frac{1}{N_D}\sum_{i=1}^{N_D} \left\|\hat{\mathbf{u}}_{\boldsymbol{\theta}}(z_i) - \mathbf{u}_i^*\right\|^2 \tag{5.10}$$

is the MSE for the labeled data D used for supervised learning. It should be noted that automatic differentiation is employed to incorporate a PDE into the loss function of the neural network. To construct the PDE residuals in the loss function, we need to calculate the relevant derivatives which can be done by automatic differentiation. Therefore, by the above training, the PINN approximates the hidden dynamics through a collection of observational data $\{z_i, \mathbf{u}_i^*\}, \mathrm{i} = 1, \ldots, N_d$, and colocation points $\{z_i, \boldsymbol{r}_i = 0\}, \mathrm{i} = 1, \ldots, N_{\boldsymbol{r}}$, for the residual. It should be mentioned that PINN does not always require training with a huge amount of data. Learning can be done with limited amount of data.

Many urban processes involve estimations of the dispersion or propagation of objects or phenomena in space and time. Such dynamics can often be characterized by the wave equation whose solution can be estimated by PINN (Moseley et al. 2020). In the context of digital twins of cities, our theories can be expressed in the form of the wave equation that governs the spatiotemporal dynamics of traffic flow, air pollutant dispersion, river water contamination, city noise propagation, etc. Appropriate estimation of these processes will be instrumental to sustainable city development. Conventionally, the wave equation is solved by methods such as finite difference which ends up in very high computational cost because of the very fine meshing required. An efficient way to solve this forward problem is via a mesh-free urban theory-informed neural networks.

The wave equation can be expressed as

$$\frac{\partial^2 u}{\partial t^2} = a^2\left(\frac{\partial^2 u}{\partial x^2} + \frac{\partial^2 u}{\partial y^2} + \frac{\partial^2 u}{\partial z^2}\right) \tag{5.11}$$

where u is the phenomenon, say air pollutant concentration; a is velocity; (x, y, z) are spatial variables/coordinates; and t is time. Then,

$$f(x, y, z, t) = \left(\frac{\partial^2}{\partial x^2} + \frac{\partial^2}{\partial y^2} + \frac{\partial^2}{\partial z^2}\right) - \frac{1}{a^2(x, y, z)}\frac{\partial^2 u}{\partial t^2} \tag{5.12}$$

The dynamics of the wave equation are very complex, and the solution can be rather complicated due to bifurcation and propagation in different environments.

Let the initial conditions be

$$u(x, y, z, t = 0) = 0$$

$$\frac{\partial u}{\partial t}(x, y, z, t = 0) = 0$$

We can then train the urban theory-informed neural network by minimizing the following loss function

$$L(\boldsymbol{\theta}) = L_F(\boldsymbol{\theta}) + L_{IC}(\boldsymbol{\theta}) \tag{5.13}$$

where $L_F(\boldsymbol{\theta})$ and $L_{IC}(\boldsymbol{\theta})$ are the theory loss and initial condition loss defined respectively as follows

$$L_F(\boldsymbol{\theta}) = \frac{1}{n_F}\sum_{i=1}^{n_F}\left\|\left(\left(\frac{\partial^2}{\partial x^2} + \frac{\partial^2}{\partial y^2} + \frac{\partial^2}{\partial z^2}\right) - \frac{1}{a(x_i, y_i, z_i)^2}\frac{\partial^2}{\partial t^2}\right)N\left(x_{i,}y_i, z_i, t_i; \boldsymbol{\theta}\right)\right\|^2 \tag{5.14}$$

$$\begin{aligned} L_{IC}(\boldsymbol{\theta}) = & \frac{\lambda_1}{n_{IC_1}}\sum_{j=1}^{n_{IC_1}}\left\|N\left(x_j, y_j, z_j, t_j; \boldsymbol{\theta}\right)\right\|^2 \\ & + \frac{\lambda_2}{n_{IC_2}}\sum_{k=1}^{n_{IC_2}}\left\|\frac{\partial}{\partial t}N(x_k, y_k, z_k, t_k; \boldsymbol{\theta})\right\|^2 \end{aligned} \tag{5.15}$$

where n_F, n_{IC_1}, and n_{IC_2} are the respective colocation/observational points for the evaluation of the neural network trained by randomly sampled data points of the domain, and λ_1 and λ_2 are the hyperparameters balancing the theory loss and the initial condition loss (Fig. 5.1).

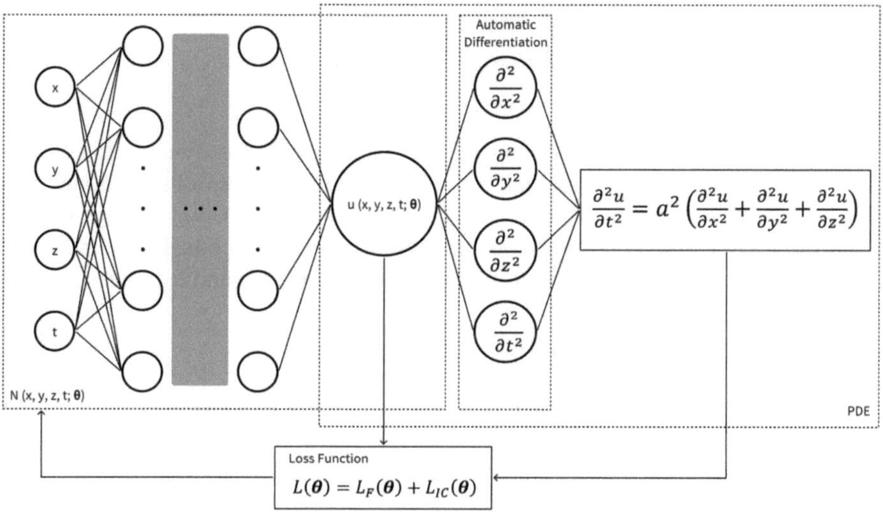

Fig. 5.1 Theory-informed neural network for urban dynamics involving the wave Equation

If there are boundary conditions, the total loss to be minimized becomes

$$L(\boldsymbol{\theta}) = L_F(\boldsymbol{\theta}) + L_{IC}(\boldsymbol{\theta}) + L_B(\boldsymbol{\theta}) \tag{5.16}$$

where

$$L_B(\boldsymbol{\theta}) = \frac{\lambda_3}{n_B}\sum_{l=1}^{n_B}\left\| N(x_l, y_l, z_l, t_l; \boldsymbol{\theta}) \; - g(x_j, y_j, z_j, t_l)\right\|^2 \tag{5.17}$$

As another example, to solve the forward problem of the logistic growth and wave-like diffusion of population in city systems described by the Fisher-KPP in Eq. (3.15) with the initial condition $u(x, 0) = u_0(x)$, we similarly minimize the general loss function in Eq. (5.13) with the relevant terms specified respectively as follows

$$\begin{aligned} L_F(\boldsymbol{\theta}) = \frac{1}{n_F}\sum_{i=1}^{n_F}\left\| \left(\frac{\partial}{\partial t} - \frac{\partial^2}{\partial x^2}\right) N(x_i, a_i, t_i; \boldsymbol{\theta}) - a_i N(x_i, a_i, t_i; \boldsymbol{\theta})(1 - N(x_i, a_i, t_i; \boldsymbol{\theta}) \right\|^2 \\ + \frac{\lambda}{n_{IC}}\sum_{k=1}^{n_{IC}}\left\| \frac{\partial}{\partial t} N(x_k, a_k, t_k; \boldsymbol{\theta}) - u_0 \right\|^2 \end{aligned} \tag{5.18}$$

(see also Rohrhofer et al. (2024) for a more detailed investigation).

5.2.2 Solving the Inverse Problem by Urban Theory-Informed Neural Networks

PINN can also be useful in solving the inverse problem for dynamical complex systems. The idea is to find the parameters $\boldsymbol{\phi}$ of the PDE from observational data. Given some observational data about the output of a system, we attempt to infer about the inputs—the conditions—of the systems. Without considering the initial and boundary conditions, the loss function to be minimized can be expressed as

$$L(\boldsymbol{\theta}, \boldsymbol{\phi}) = L_{PA}(\boldsymbol{\theta}, \boldsymbol{\phi}) + L_D(\boldsymbol{\theta}) \tag{5.19}$$

where $\boldsymbol{\phi}$ are the unknown parameters of the underlying PDE we wish to invert for given a set of observational data $D = \{(x_q, t_q), (u_q, t_q)\}, q = 1, \ldots, n_D; \boldsymbol{\theta}$ and $\boldsymbol{\phi}$ denote parameters. The two constituent loss functions are

$$L_{PA}(\boldsymbol{\theta}, \boldsymbol{\phi}) = \frac{1}{n_{PA}} \sum_{i=1}^{n_{PA}} \| F[N(x_i, t_i; \boldsymbol{\theta}); \boldsymbol{\phi}] - f(x_i, t_i) \|^2 \tag{5.20}$$

$$L_D(\boldsymbol{\theta}) = \frac{\lambda}{n_D} \sum_{q=1}^{n_D} \| N(x_k, t_k; \boldsymbol{\theta}) - (u_k, t_k) \|^2 \tag{5.21}$$

Therefore, by minimizing the composite function in Eq. (5.19), we learn both the network parameters $\boldsymbol{\theta}$ and the PDE parameters $\boldsymbol{\phi}$.

To solve the inverse problem of the wave equation, we learn $\boldsymbol{\theta}$ and $\boldsymbol{\phi}$ simultaneously by minimizing

$$L(\boldsymbol{\theta}, \boldsymbol{\phi}) = L_F(\boldsymbol{\theta}) + L_D(\boldsymbol{\theta}) \tag{5.22}$$

where

$$L_F(\boldsymbol{\theta}, \boldsymbol{\phi}) = \frac{1}{n_F} \sum_{i=1}^{n_F} \left\| \left(\left(\frac{\partial^2}{\partial x^2} + \frac{\partial^2}{\partial y^2} + \frac{\partial^2}{\partial z^2} \right) - \frac{1}{a(x_i, y_i, z_i; \boldsymbol{\phi})^2} \frac{\partial^2}{\partial t^2} \right) N(x_i, y_i, z_i, t_i; \boldsymbol{\theta}) \right\|^2 \tag{5.23}$$

$$L_D(\boldsymbol{\theta}) = \frac{\lambda}{n_D} \sum_{l=1}^{n_D} \left\| N(x_l, y_l, z_l, t_l; \boldsymbol{\theta}) - u_g(x_j, y_j, z_j, t_l) \right\|^2 \tag{5.24}$$

5.2.3 Solving the Model Discovery Problem by Urban Theory-Informed Neural Networks

For the model/PDE discovery problem, we want to infer about the underlying governing equations of a system from the observational data about its input conditions and output. To learn the PDE governing the dynamics of a complex system, our differential operator takes the following general form

$$F(\mathbf{u}(z); \boldsymbol{\gamma}) = f(z), \quad z \text{ in } \boldsymbol{\Omega} \tag{5.25}$$

Here, $\boldsymbol{\gamma}$ are the physical/geometrical parameters related to the dynamics. To discover the differential operator F, we minimize the following loss function

$$L(\boldsymbol{\theta}, \boldsymbol{\xi}) = L_{TH}(\boldsymbol{\theta}, \boldsymbol{\xi}) + L_D(\boldsymbol{\theta}) \tag{5.26}$$

where TH denotes urban theory, and D denotes data.

The theory loss is

$$L_{TH}(\boldsymbol{\theta}, \boldsymbol{\xi}) = \frac{1}{n_{TH}} \sum_{i=1}^{n_{TH}} \left\| \boldsymbol{\xi}\phi\left[N(x_i, t_i; \boldsymbol{\theta}) - f(x_i, t_i)\right] \right\|^2 + \|\boldsymbol{\xi}\|^2 \tag{5.27}$$

where ϕ is the library of the potential differential operators—such as the one expressed in Eq. (4.69) in Sect. 4.7 of Chap. 4—and $\boldsymbol{\xi}$ are the coefficients of the reduced-order PDE obtained through sparse identification like SINDy such that $F = \boldsymbol{\xi}\phi$.

And the data loss is

$$L_D(\boldsymbol{\theta}) = \frac{\lambda}{n_D} \sum_{k=1}^{n_D} \|N(x_k, t_k; \boldsymbol{\theta}) - u_{FD}(x_k, t_k)\|^2 \tag{5.28}$$

where (x_k, t_k) and (u_k, t_k) are observational data, and λ is the hyperparameter that controls the theory loss and the data loss. It should be noted that by incorporating additional collocation points from the randomly sampled analytical or approximate solutions (e.g. by finite difference) at the initial and boundary domains and by encoding them into the data loss function, explicit incorporation of the loss terms—due to the initial and boundary conditions—into the total loss function is not necessary.

Therefore, by minimizing the composite function in Eq. (5.26), we learn both the network parameters $\boldsymbol{\theta}$ and the reduced-order PDE parameters $\boldsymbol{\xi}$. As previously discussed, learning the reduced-order model through theory-informed neural networks and regularization is of great importance to simplify the theory and alleviate the prohibitively high computational cost for analysis, simulation, and control of dynamical systems.

As another practical example, the above approach can be employed to build a digital twin for city traffic control. Using PDE to model macroscopic traffic-flow dynamics of aggregated traffic states, density, speed, and flow is a basic method for the prediction and management of city traffic congestions. Building a digital twin for such application requires the integration of the dynamical model of traffic density with physics constraints and traffic trajectory data. Adopting the theory-based method discussed above, Zhao and Yu (2024) designed a traffic theory-informed neural network to learn the fundamental diagram and look-ahead kernel with experimental traffic trajectory data to model "look-ahead" nonlocal traffic dynamics in a ring road. Central to the network is the nonlocal traffic-flow model describing the evolution of traffic density within a length by the following hyperbolic PDE

$$\frac{\partial}{\partial t}\rho(x,t) + \frac{\partial}{\partial x}\big(\rho(x,t)V_\eta(\rho_\eta(x,t))\big) = 0 \tag{5.29}$$

where $\rho(x, t)$ and $V(\rho)$ represent respectively the density and fundamental diagram in which the speed $v(x, t) = V(\rho(x, t))$—i.e. the speed is dependent on the local density by the fundamental diagram. Based on our above discussion, we can generally express the traffic theory loss as

$$L_F(\boldsymbol{\theta}, \boldsymbol{\xi}) = \frac{1}{n_{TH}} \sum_{i=1}^{n_{TH}} \left\| \left[\frac{\partial}{\partial t}\rho(x,t) + \frac{\partial}{\partial x}\big(\rho(x,t)V_\eta(\rho_\eta(x,t))\big) \right] \boldsymbol{\xi}\phi[N(x_i, t_i; \boldsymbol{\theta})] \right\|^2 + \|\boldsymbol{\xi}\|^2 \tag{5.30}$$

The theory-informed NN constructed by Zhao and Yu (2024) trains three parameters: θ to learn the spatiotemporal dynamics of density $\rho(x, t)$; θ_ω to learn the nonlocal look-ahead kernel; and θ_v to learn the fundamental diagram V_η. The overall loss function to be minimized in the learning process is

$$L(\theta, \theta_v, \theta_\omega) = L_{data}(\theta, \theta_v, \theta_\omega) + L_{phy-d}(\theta, \theta_v, \theta_\omega) + L_{phy-s}(\theta, \theta_\omega) \tag{5.31}$$

where $L_{data}(\theta)$ is the data loss capturing the discrepancy between the learned density and measurement; L_{phy-d} is the physics dynamics loss capturing the discrepancy between the learned dynamics and the nonlocal traffic-flow model; and L_{phy-s} is the physics static loss constraining the learned kernel and the fundamental diagram to ensure that the nonlocal PDE is well-posed. It was demonstrated that the traffic data indeed capture the look-ahead nonlocal phenomena, and the learned nonlocal model yields a more accurate estimation of traffic wave propagation. Similar in spirit, Huang et al. (2023) also showed the effectiveness of incorporating nonlocal traffic-flow model into PINN.

With regard to learning the dynamic entropy-maximization model, we can perhaps employ a deep feedforward neural network like the one in Fischer and Leung (1998)—or an autoencoder to reduce dimension—to learn the input–output map, and formulate a loss function that accounts for the error of such black box mapping together with errors for the violations of the constraints placed on the $O_i's$, $D_j's$, and c to make the neural network theory-informed.

5.3 Deriving Reduced-Order Models for Urban Theory-Informed Neural Networks

For efficient simulation and prediction, we can build ROMs of highly nonlinear complex systems within the framework of PINN. If the governing equations F and B in Eq. (5.1) are known instead, we can first discretize them into a high-dimensional dynamical model of the complex nonlinear system, as discussed in Sect. 3.2 of Chap. 3, and generate from it snapshots to perform the POD-Galerkin projection onto the low-dimensional manifold. Using the projection method discussed in Sect. 3.3 of the same chapter, we can generate the reduced basis and obtain the expansion/projection coefficients. To enhance stability, accuracy, and convergence, we can approximate the ROM using the PINN method. With the PINN-based approach, a neural network is employed to approximate the mapping from the input—the model parameters—to the output—the expansion coefficients of the high-dimensional model solution—onto the reduced space. By minimizing an appropriately designed loss function—e.g. loss being the sum of the mean squared residual error of the ROM/reduced-order equation, and the mean squared error between the neural network output and the expansion coefficients of the high-dimensional solutions—we can learn the ROM (Chen et al. 2021a). Similar in spirit in learning the right coordinates for discovering the dynamics of complex systems discussed in Sect. 4.5 of Chap. 4, by skillfully combining PINN with SINDy, Chen et al. (2021b) showed how a PINN can be constructed to learn governing equations from scarce data. Therefore, the results of the PINN such derived satisfy the dynamics of the ROM of the original high-dimensional model governing the dynamics of the complex nonlinear system. In particular, such an approach integrates deep neural networks, physics embedding, automatic differentiation, and sparse regression to approximate the solution of nonlinear spatiotemporal system variables, compute essential derivatives, and identify the key derivative terms and parameters that form the structure and explicit expression of the governing equations from scarce and noisy data. This harnesses the power of ROM (with embedded urban theory) and PINN to incorporate dynamics and complexity into digital twins of cities. In this way, we can bring domain-specific urban knowledge into the learning of the ROM.

Remark. Adopting the constrained optimization approach, SINDy can be made theory informed in finding the latent space for discovering dynamics of complex systems for digital twins of cities. Taking advantage of the flexibility and ability in accommodating temporal behavior of DMD (Schmid and Sestersenn 2008) and the sparsity promotion of SINDy, Loiseau (2020) integrated both methods to unravel a low-dimensional chaotic model which is structurally the same as the classical Lorenz model. The procedure first performs the low-dimensional embedding of the dynamics by projecting the time series of the high-dimensional state vectors onto the span of the DMD modes. Sparse identification of the underlying dynamics is then carried out via SINDy as follows

$$
\begin{aligned}
\min_{\xi} & \sum_{k=1}^{3} \|\dot{\mathbf{x}}_k - \theta(\mathbf{x})\boldsymbol{\xi}_k\|_2^2 + \lambda \|\boldsymbol{\xi}_k\|_2^2 \\
s.t. \quad & C\boldsymbol{\xi} = 0 \\
& H\boldsymbol{\xi} \leq 0
\end{aligned}
\tag{5.32}
$$

where $C\boldsymbol{\xi} = 0$ is the linear equality constraint, and $H\boldsymbol{\xi} \leq 0$ is the convex inequality constraint based on prior physical knowledge—i.e. we can learn the low-dimensional dynamics via sparse regression with the imposition of urban theory in the form of constraints. Here, the l-2 norm is used in the minimization instead. Such procedure can be employed to learn, for example, the ROM of the urban evolution model in Eq. (4.12). It can also be applied to learn dynamics with controls discussed in Sect. 4.4 of Chap. 4.

5.4 Incorporation of Dynamics and Complexity into Digital Twins for City Microclimates

In the process of rapid urban development, our built environment is complex with complicated city topology, building structures, and layouts, particularly in high-density living. Understanding urban microclimates, especially under climate change, is of paramount importance to mitigate the impact of global warming and enhance city resilience to extreme climates. The simulation of urban temperature and wind, among other climatic features, is essential to the design of built environment that facilitates air circulation, thermal comfort, and building energy saving. Based on the canonical model of fluid dynamics and taking the nondimensional form of the Navier-Stokes equations

$$
\nabla \cdot u = 0
$$

$$
u_t + (u \cdot \nabla)u = -\nabla p + \frac{1}{R_e}\nabla^2 u \tag{5.33}
$$

where u is the vector velocity field; p is pressure; ∇ is divergence; and R_e is the Reynolds number, Mortezazadeh and Wang (2020) constructed the following city fast fluid dynamics (cityFFD) model to simulate microclimates in urban built environment

$$\nabla \cdot u = 0$$

$$\frac{\partial u}{\partial t} + (u \cdot \nabla)u = -\nabla p + \left(\frac{1}{Re} + \nu_t\right)\nabla^2 u - \frac{G_r}{R_e^2}\theta$$

$$\frac{\partial \theta}{\partial t} + (u \cdot \nabla)\theta = \left(\frac{1}{R_e \cdot P_r} + \alpha_t\right)\nabla^2 \theta \tag{5.34}$$

where $u, \theta, p, Re, G_r, P_r, \nu_t,$ and α_t are the velocity, temperature, pressure, Reynolds number, Grashof number, Prandtl number, turbulent viscosity, and turbulent thermal diffusivity, respectively.

Let $u(x, t; \gamma)$ be the velocity field, where x and t are the space and time coordinate, and γ the variable parameters. We can solve Eq. (5.33) via a theory-informed neural network by minimizing the following loss function like the procedure discussed above

$$L_F(\theta) = \left\| \left(\frac{\partial}{\partial t} + N(x, t; \gamma) \cdot \nabla\right) N(x, t; \gamma) + \left(\nabla - \frac{1}{R_e}\nabla^2\right) N(x, t; \gamma) \right\| + \|\nabla \cdot N(\chi, t; \gamma)\|^2 \tag{5.35}$$

where $N(x, t; \gamma)$ is the deep neural network that approximates u and p. By the same token, Eq. (5.34) can be solved by an appropriately constructed theory-informed neural network. As previously discussed, we can incorporate the initial and boundary conditions by adding to the loss function, Eq. (5.35), appropriate loss terms for both conditions, and minimize the corresponding composite loss function. Alternatively, we can minimize the loss function in Eq. (5.35) subject to the constraints imposed by the initial and boundary conditions.

Katal et al. (2022) further showed how to integrate cityFFD with cityBEM (an urban building energy model) for 3-D urban building energy and microclimate modeling. The simulation of urban microclimates via the above Navier-Stokes model in high-resolution, high-dimensional meshes, and time steps is computationally very expensive. Thus, a ROM for the low-dimensional approximation of the Navier-Stokes equations will greatly increase the flexibility and efficiency in real-time simulations. To derive the relevant ROM—depending on the conceptual approach and the data situations—we can employ the methods of low-dimensional manifold learning through different projection operators discussed in Sect. 3.2 of Chap. 3, or the purely data-driven learning via sparse nonlinear modeling techniques discussed in Sect. 4.2 of Chap. 4 (Rudy et al. 2017), or the theory-informed learning discussed in this section (Cai et al. 2021). For example, Loiseau and Brunston (2018) employed POD, discussed in Sect. 3.2 of Chap. 3, in conjunction with SINDy to learn the ROM of the Navier-Stokes system in a sparse and closed form. Guan et al. (2020) employed SINDy, discussed in Sect. 4.2 of Chap. 4, to learn the ROM of the Navier-Stokes equation. Along the line of urban theory-informed neural network discussed in this section, Peng et al. (2024) employed a Fourier neural operator to learn a family of parameterized PDEs for real-time simulations of the 3-D dynamic urban microclimates. Callaham et al. (2021) further showed how data-driven machine learning can extract sparse subspaces for dynamical systems governed by the Navier-Stokes equations.

Besides modeling wind flow and temperature of a built environment, Navier-Stokes equations have also been used to model room temperature dynamics of a single building in terms of different ambient temperatures and cooling air flow rates (Rao and Ukil 2020). Similar approaches discussed above can be employed for its efficient simulation.

5.5 On the Optimal Design of Network Architecture for Urban Theory-Informed Neural Networks

As pointed out by Cuomo et al. (2022), architecture/topology of neural networks impacts on the performance of the PINN. For deep multilayer feedforward neural networks, the architectural features include the number of layers, number of neurons in each layer, learning rate, momentum term, etc. As there are no definitive theories on the optimal selection of these hyperparameters, we need to optimally select them through some heuristic procedures. We, for instance, can automatically optimize the neural network architecture using synergistically the GA (Leung 1997). The hybrid system, coined GENNET, consists of a neural network engine and a GA engine (Fig. 5.2). The GA engine encodes neural network architectures as chromosomes that constitute a population of plausible networks and evolve them through genetic operators—namely selection, crossover, and mutation. The evolved chromosome is then decoded into a neural network by a neural network decoder and fed to the neural network engine for training. Various statistics such as learning speed and approximation error are transferred back to the GA engine for fitness evaluation. Networks with high fitness will then be evolved again by the genetic operators for further improvement. The iterative process will terminate when the desirable fitness value is achieved, and the neural network architectures converges to the optimal architecture. Technically, the populations of chromosomes—i.e. populations of neural network architectures $\vec{N}_k(x, t; \theta)$—are evolved by the GA expressed in the following canonical form

$$\vec{N}_{k+1}(x, t; \theta) = \left\{T_m^i\left(T_c^i\left(T_s^i\left(\vec{N}_k(x, t; \theta)\right)\right)\right), i = 1, \dots, L\right\}, k \geq 0 \tag{5.36}$$

where $\left(T_m^i, T_c^i, T_s^i\right), i = 1, \ldots, L$, are independent versions of the mutation operator T_m, the crossover operator T_c, and the selection operator T_s, respectively. It is apparent that the sequence of populations of neural network architectures $\left\{\vec{N}_k(x, t; \theta), k \geq 0\right\}$ is a Markov chain which is homogeneous, irreducible, and aperiodic. Leung et al. (1997) proposed a concept of population diversity and quantitatively characterized

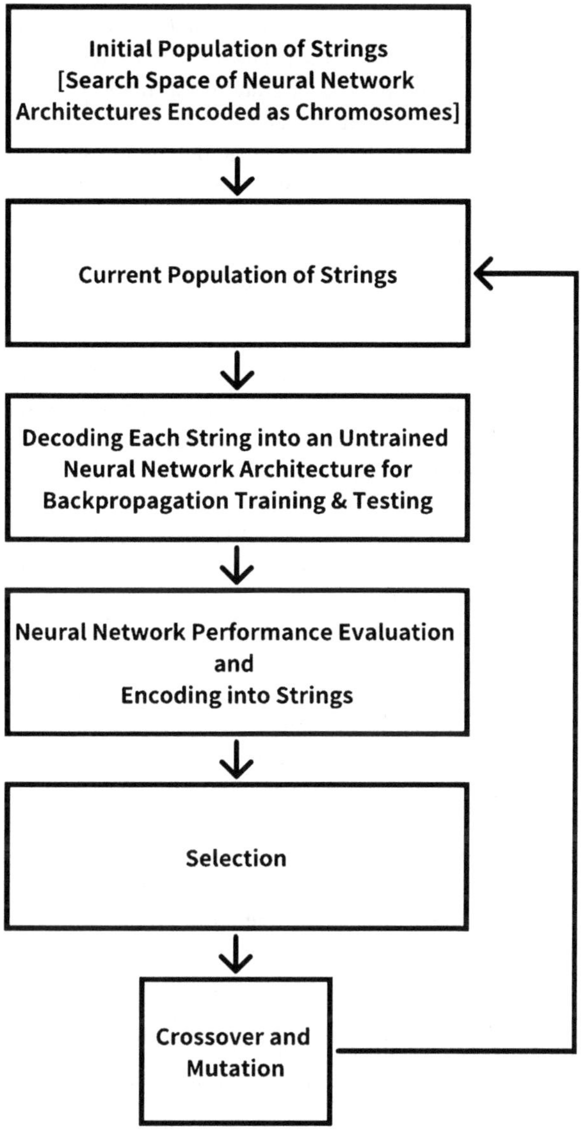

Fig. 5.2 GENNET—a GANN system for evolving neural network topology

and theoretically analyzed the issue of convergence of canonical GA using the theory of Markov chain. Fischer and Leung (1998) applied the above hybrid GA-neural network framework to study spatial interactions by estimating interregional flows via a multilayer feedforward neural network optimally evolved by the GA. Such optimization strategy has become a procedure for neural architecture search in deep learning (Arifovic and Gencay 2001; Shang 2023).

Other than the architecture, the activation function also plays an important role in enhancing the network performance. Different types of activation functions can be experimented for training and optimization. This can be built into GENNET for simultaneous optimization also.

So far, most of the deep neural networks used in PINN is the multilayer feedforward neural network. It would be useful if different types of neural networks such as the LSTM and xLSTM discussed in Sect. 4.7 of Chap. 4, the convolutional neural network (CNN) (LeCun 1989; LeCun et al. 2010; Fischer 2025), and Transformer (Vaswani et al. 2017) can also be evaluated to see their efficacy. For instance, Transformer has been shown to be effective in capturing long-range dependencies crucial to the prediction of backdrafts in buildings under complex and abruptly evolving fire scenes using integrated past experiences and real-time sensor data and visual data (Zhang et al. 2023). By combing a LSTM with a transpose CNN, Wu et al. (2022) demonstrated that the approach is effective in identifying temperature field and forecasting fires using real-time ceiling temperature profile and temperature field images in a numerical tunnel to make emergency response and suggest firefighting activities. Similarly, can we combine LSTM or xLSTM—which appears to have good performance in time series analysis—with Transformer—which tends to be rather capable of handling problems in a global context—to form a hybrid neural architecture for theory-informed learning? All these are possible alternatives for the design of neural network architectures for building theory-informed digital twins of cities.

However, deep neural networks like CNN can be massive with plausibly redundant layers and filters. Simplification by network pruning is a way to reduce the size and complexity of the network topology. It can be treated as a method to derive the ROM of a neural network. Yao et al. (2021) pruned the entire CNN via layer-by-layer compression using a novel visualization-based filter pruning method. In addition to effectively compressing the network, the proposed method renders an informative visualization and interpretation of the deep learning process. After pruning, the computational cost and storage requirement of the CNN are significantly reduced—which means that complex deep neural networks can be easily implemented in small mobile devices. So, it enables the efficient use of deep learning with the IoT technologies that digital twins of cities often depend on. Likewise, can we apply similar methods to visualize the operation of Transformer to better understand the inner working of the model and prune its architecture? For instance, the Transformer-based large language model (LLM) has been found incapable of producing underlying models that accurately represent the real world. Though the LLM was 100% accurate in providing turn-by-turn driving directions, the underlying maps used were filled with non-existent streets and routes when they were extracted (Vafa et al. 2024). With a visualization-based pruning method like the one in Yao et al. (2021), we may be able to fathom the internal flaws and incongruity of the model and formulate its solution. Therefore, a thorough evaluation of the adequacy and effectiveness of various neural networks and their simplification will be instrumental to the construction of theory-informed digital twins for different city phenomena and processes.

5.6 Issues in the Urban Theory-Informed Neural Network Approach to Modeling Urban Dynamics and Complexity

From our above discussion, we can see how theories can be built into neural network learning of urban dynamics and complexity. However, there are more research issues that need to be entertained in further research. I highlight in brief issues concerning neural networks and language models, PINNs, and Gaussian learning in the following discussion.

5.6.1 On Neural Networks and Large Language Models

Notwithstanding the impressive achievements of neural networks, particularly the recent dazzling performance of LLM via generative AI (Zhao et al. 2024), a caveat needs to be made on the limitations of such neural networks. For instance, Transformer and its variants on which most LLMs are built are essentially an algorithmic model involving multi-head attention layers stacked in a deep neural network containing billions of parameters—which may have very little to do with how we learn languages, how we do logical or associative reasoning, and how we do critical reasoning. Can Transformer really learn a coherent model of a city? Is the knowledge acquired in one situation transferrable to another situation? Is the knowledge acquired in one city transferrable to another city? Like other neural networks, it has its limitations, particularly in its adaptability and scalability. Furthermore, the Transformer-based LLMs are general-purpose. They might be too complex or superfluous to model and simulate specific urban processes with an unnecessarily huge number of parameters and computational complexity. Some data stored might be irrelevant to tasks to be performed. A small language model (SLM) (Nguyen et al. 2024) trained by domain-specific data and knowledge with more efficient encoding-decoding, robust training-pretraining, and structure pruning may be sufficient to build task-specific digital twins—particularly with IoT and small-device mobile sensing that deliver more timely data—for more efficient and accurate predictions. Perhaps we can solve a complicated urban task by integrating SLMs each solving interrelated sub-tasks—especially when the sub-tasks are sequential in nature—instead of applying a massive LLM to solve the complicated task in a parallel manner. On the other hand, like what is done in Leung (1997) in evolving multilayer feedforward neural networks, we can perhaps synergistically employ GA to evolve the topology and procedure of neural-network-based LLMs to optimize their structures, information processing, and reasoning strategy to enhance adaptability and scalability.

Postscript Remark. DeepSeek-AI (2025) made a stunning announcement showing that tasks performed by current LLMs could be accomplished with equivalent if not better performance by a much smaller model costing just a small fraction of the time and money spent on the development of LLMs. It is similar in spirit with my above view about LLMs and SLMs. In a nutshell, DeepSeek-r1 employs distillation from a LLM (as a matter of fact, it can be from several LLMs) to train a much smaller language model to effectively and efficiently perform the same tasks which could only be achieved by the much over-sized LLM before. The hugely downsized model uses the chain-of-thought prompting to break a complicated problem down with a step-by-step process of reflection. It also employs key-value caching to reduce computation and improve efficiency in text generation. Throughout, it relies solely on reinforcement learning with modest supervised fine tuning to optimize its learning strategy to maximize the long-term cumulated learning reward. However, reinforcement learning is only one of the learning methods in machine intelligence. To take it forward, we should consider other learning strategies which may serve better under different scenarios. Learning methods such as deep reinforcement learning (Mnih et al. 2015), meta-learning (Vanschoren 2019), transfer learning (Pan and Yang 2010), and contrastive self-supervised learning (Jaiswal et al. 2021; Xiao et al. 2023) might be useful in mitigating such problem and could be considered to train LLMs or SLMs under variously circumstances (see Chap. 11 for further discussion). Since we still need LLMs for distillation, perhaps a fundamental question to ask is whether we really need to unabatedly amass astronomical amount of data, regardless of their relevance and redundancy, with extremely exorbitant cost in time, energy, and money to go through prohibitively long process of pretraining to enhance our machine intelligence? Should we build measures to avoid data overwhelm? Is there a limit to this type of intelligence? Can our intrinsic brain model, cognitive model, and knowledge acquisition model inform our data collection process so that data can be relevantly, appropriately, and parsimoniously collected and used for the enhancement of machine intelligence in return. Afterall, current data, particularly human generated data, and information have almost been exhaustively amassed by existing LLMs. What remains will be incremental information that should be progressively or supplementally gathered from plausible sources for training. Thus, we need model-data interoperability, discussed in Chap. 9, in here also. In the future, LLM training may need to rely on synthetic data also. In this situation, we need to be cautious about self-reinforced training that may unavoidably magnify certain perspective if appropriate objective measures for preventing biased views are not put in place. I envision that cleverer and more efficient AI language models with more intelligent collection, digestion, update, and use of information will be constructed in the future.

To make neural networks inspiring in doing urban science and in building digital twins of cities is through the careful integration of these networks with urban theories. Making neural networks urban theory-informed is an attempt to get the best of both worlds. Therefore, a thorough analysis of various neural networks and their complementarities with urban theories are crucial to the modeling of urban dynamics and complexity by way of digital twins of cities. In the long run, we need future generations of neural works that may take us closer to reaching high-level and human general intelligence.

5.6.2 On Physics-Informed Neural Networks

Despite their good performance and promise in solving the forward, inverse, and equation discovery problems in dynamical complex systems, PINN still suffers from some outstanding problems that need to be solved (Karniadakis et al. 2021; Cuomo et al. 2022). First, the computational cost is high because PINN involves expensive neural network training/retraining and deep learning methods simultaneously. The issue can get to be more serious for large-scale complicated urban problems. More efficient algorithms—e.g. parallel training algorithms and hardware implementation, such as the one discussed in Sect. 4.7 of Chap. 4—that scale well need to be developed for large-scale dynamical complex systems. Second, PINN generally involves non-convex optimization problems in which convergence to global minimum of the loss function may not be guaranteed over complicated loss morphology (Krishnapriyan et al. 2021). Appropriate global optimization methods need to be developed to effectively and efficiently solve the global convergence problem. Multipoint stochastic search algorithms, like GA, which can be parallelly implemented may be useful for handling such a task. With respect to neural network architecture, LSTM—which is good for sequence-to-sequence learning rather than solving the entire space-time all at once—may be an appropriate choice to handle the loss function and the optimization problem. Of course, it may make the already expensive network training and optimization even more expensive unless sparsity of colocation points for training can be achieved. We need to strike a good balance. Third, for dynamical complex systems exhibiting multi-scale, chaotic, or bifurcation behaviors, we may need to consider the robustness of the PINN architecture in response to the variation of the bifurcation parameter—such as the increase of the Reynolds number—which may change the architecture of a neural network. A robust PINN architecture thus needs to be developed. Fourth, it is a challenge to extrapolate a PINN learned under certain initial or boundary conditions to unseen areas or to the future time (Cuomo et al. 2022). Deep reinforcement learning, meta-learning, transfer learning, and contrastive self-supervised learning might be useful in mitigating such problem. Fifth, more experiments need to be carried out to see whether PINNs scale well to large-scale complex urban problems.

5.6.3 On Gaussian Learning

Parallel to making neural networks physics-informed, we can make the Gaussian learning process discussed in Sect. 4.6 of Chap. 4 theory-informed also. Raissi and Karniadakis (2018) showed how to build hidden physics into the Gaussian regression process to solve the inverse problem by embedding physics in the kernel of the prior of the Gaussian process. Here the choice of kernels plays a pivotal role in the success of the method. Similarly, we can make RCMD discussed in Sect. 4.6 theory-informed also. We can, instead, embed constraints such as stability at an equilibrium point/attractor and/or other physical constraints into the regression class in the RCMD algorithm for better generalization. Similar in spirit, Fichera and Billard (2022) developed an eigen-decomposition of a graph-based Laplacian matrix to identify the locations and dynamics of multiple attractors in a dynamical system.

Figure 5.3 summarizes our discussion in this chapter.

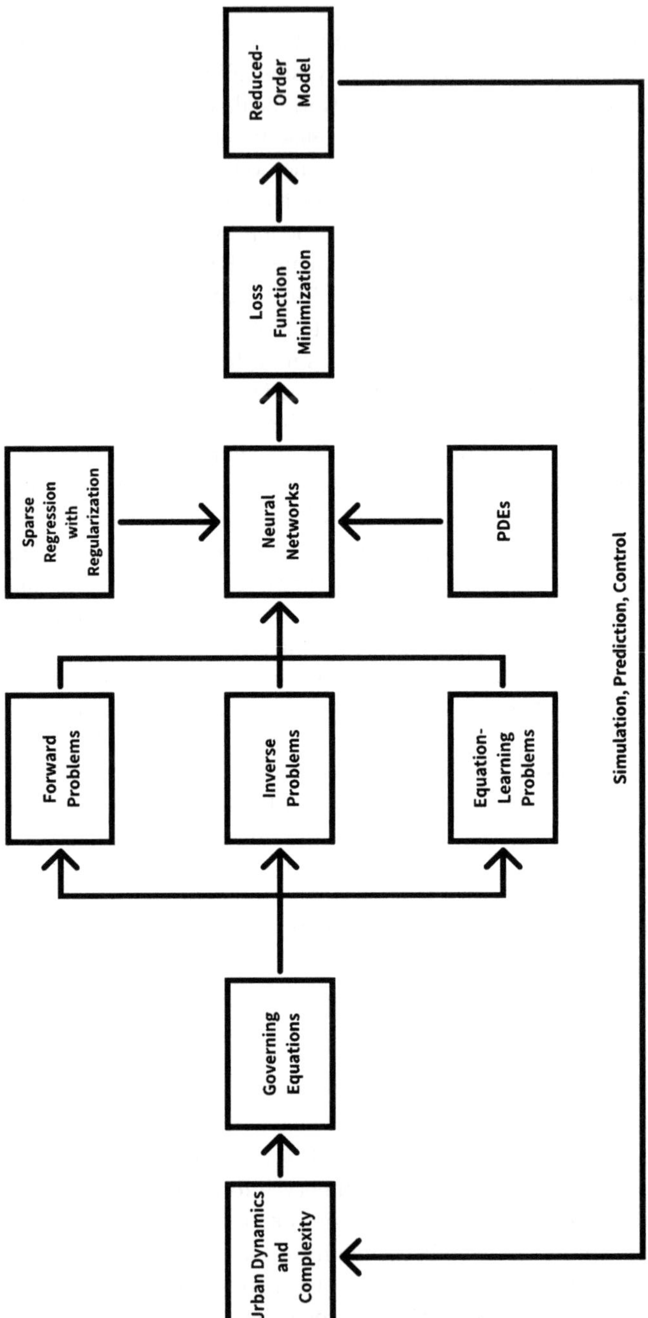

Fig. 5.3 Urban theory-informed neural networks for the construction of digital twins of cities

References

Arifovic J, Gencay R (2001) Using genetic algorithms to select architecture of a feedforward artificial neural network. *Physica A: Statistical Mechanics and its Applications* 3–4(289): 574–594.

Cai C, Mao Z, Wang Z, Yin M, Karniadakis GE (2021) Physics-informed neural networks (PINNs) for fluid mechanics: a review. *Acta Mechanica Sinica* 37: 1727–1738.

Callaham JL, Koch JV, Bingni W. Brunton SL, Kutz JN, Brunton SL (2021). Learning dominant physical processes with data-driven balance models. *Nature Communications* 12: 1016.

Chen W, Wang Q, Hesthaven JS, Zhang C (2021a) Physics-informed machine learning for reduced-order modeling of nonlinear problems. *Journal of Computational Physics* 446: 110666.

Chen Z, Liu Y, Hao S (2021b) Physics-informed learning of governing equations from scarce data. *Nature Communications* 12: 6136. https://doi.org/10.1038/s41467-021-26434-1.

Cuomo S, Di Cola VS, Giampaolo F, Rozza G, Raissi M, Piccialli F (2022) Scientific machine learning through physics-informed neural networks: where we are and what's Next. *Journal of Scientific Computing* 92, article number 88. arXiv:2201.05624.

DeepSeek-AI (2025) DeepSeek-R1: Incentivizing reasoning capability in LLMs via reinforcement learning. arXiv:2501.12948.

Dissanayake MWMG, Phan-Thien N (1994) Neural-network-based approximations for solving partial differential equations. *Communications in Numerical Methods in Engineering* 10(3):195–201. https://doi.org/10.1002/cnm.1640100303.

Fichera B, Billard A (2022) Linearization and identification of multiple-attractor dynamical systems through Laplacian eigenmaps. *Journal of Machine Learning Research* 23: 1-35.

Fischer MM (2025) Convolutional neural networks: key components and architectures. *Working Papers in Regional Science* 2025-01. https://doi.org/10.57938/2076fa6b-8225-433c-b3e6-c96de2e46735.

Fischer MM, Leung Y (1998) A genetic algorithms based evolutionary computational neural network for modelling spatial interaction data. *Annals of Regional Science* 32: 437–458.

Guan Y, Brunton SL, Novosselov I (2020) Sparse nonlinear models of chaotic electroconvection. *Royal Society Open Science* 24 8(8): 202367. https://doi.org/10.1098/rsos.202367.

Huang AJ, Biswas A, Agarwal S (2023) Incorporating nonlocal traffic flow model in physics-informed neural networks. https://doi.org/10.48550/arXiv.2308.11818.

Jaiswal A, Babu AR, Zadeh MZ, Banerjee D, Makedon FA (2021) Survey on contrastive self-supervised learning. *Technologies 9*(1):2. https://doi.org/10.3390/technologies9010002.

Karniadakis BE, Kevrekidis IG, Lu L, Perdikaris P, *Wang S, Yang L* (2021) Physics-informed machine learning. *Nature Reviews Physics* 3(6): 422–440. https://doi.org/10.1038/s42254-021-00314-5.

Katal A, Mortezazadeh M, Wang LL, Yu H (2022) Urban building energy and microclimate modeling–From 3D city generation to dynamic simulations. *Energy* 251: 123817.

Krishnapriyan A, Gholami A, Zhe S, Kirby RM, Mahoney MW (2021) Characterizing possible failure modes in physics-informed neural networks. In *Proceedings of the 35th Conference on Neural Information Processing Systems* (*NeurIPS 2021*).

Lagaris IE, Likas A, Fotiadis DI (1998) Artificial neural networks for solving ordinary and partial differential equations. *IEEE transactions on neural networks* 9(5): 987–1000. https://doi.org/10.1109/72.712178.

LeCun Y (1989) *Generalization and network design strategies.* Technical Report CRG-TR-89-4. Toronto: University of Toronto.

LeCun Y, Kavukcuoglu K, Farabet C (2010) Convolutional networks and applications in vision. *Proceedings of 2010 IEEE International Symposium on Circuits and Systems.* https://doi.org/10.1109/ISCAS.2010.5537907.

Leung Y (1997) *Intelligent Spatial Decision Support Systems.* Berlin: Springer-Verlag.

Leung Y, Gao Y, Xu ZB (1997) Degree of population diversity – a perspective on premature convergence in genetic algorithms and its Markov Chain analysis. *IEEE Transactions on Neural Networks* 8: 1165–1176.

Loiseau JC (2020) Data-driven modeling of the chaotic thermal convection in an annular thermosyphon. *Theoretical and Computational Fluid Dynamics* 34 (4): 339–365. https://doi.org/10.1007/s00162-020-00536-w.

Loiseau JC, Brunton SL (2018) Constrained sparse Galerkin regression. *Journal of Fluid Mechanics* 838: 42–67.

Mnih V, Kavukcuoglu K, Silver D, Rusu AA, Veness J, Bellemare, MG, Graves A, Riedmiller M Fidjeland AK, Ostrovski G, Petersen S, Beattie C, Sadik A, Antonoglou I, King H, Kumaran D, Wierstra D, Legg S, Hassabis D (2015) Human-level control through deep reinforcement learning. *Nature* 518(7540): 529–533.

Mortezazadeh M, Wang LL (2020) Solving city and building microclimates by fast fluid dynamics with large timesteps and coarse meshes. *Built Environment* 179: 106955.

Moseley B, A Markham A, Nissen-Meyer T (2020) Solving the wav equation with physics-informed deep learning. arXiv:2006.11894.

Nguyen CV, Shen X, Aponte R, Xia Y, Basu S, Hu Z, Chen J, Parmar M, Kunapuli S, Barrow J, Wu J, Singh A,Wang Y, Gu J, Dernoncourt F, Ahmed NK, Lipka N, Zhang R, Chen X, Yu T, Kim S, Deilamsalehy H, Park N, Rimer M, Zhang Z, Yang H, Rossi RA, Nguyen TH (2024) A survey of small language model. arxiv:2410.20011.

Pan S, Yang Q (2010) A survey on transfer learning. *IEEE Transactions on Knowledge and Data Engineering* 22(10): 1345–1359. https://doi.org/10.1109/TKDE.2009.191.

Peng W, Qin S, Yang S, Wang J, Liu X, Wang L (2024) Fourier neural operator for real-time simulation of 3D dynamic urban microclimate. *Building and Environment* 248: 111063. https://doi.org/10.1016/j.buildenv.2023.111063.

Raissi M, Karniadakis GE (2018) Hidden physics models: machine learning of nonlinear partial differential equations. *Journal of Computational Physics 357*: 125–141.

Raissi M, Perdikaris P, Karniadakis GE (2017a) Physics informed deep learning (Part I): data-driven solutions of nonlinear partial differential equations. http://arxiv.org/abs/1711.10561.

Raissi M, Perdikaris P, Karniadakis GE (2017b) Physics informed deep learning (Part II): data-driven discovery of nonlinear partial differential equations.http://arxiv.org/abs/1711.10566, arXiv: 1711.10566.

Rao DMKKV, Ukil A (2020) Modeling of room temperature dynamics for efficient building energy management. *IEEE Transactions on Systems Man and Cybernetics Systems* 50(2): 716–725.

Rohrhofer FM, Posch S, Gößnitzer C, Geiger BC (2024) Approximating families of sharp solutions to Fisher's equation with physics-informed neural networks. arXiv:2402.08313.

Rudy SH, Brunton SL, Proctor JL, Kutz JN (2017) Data-driven discovery of partial differential equations. *Science Advances* 3(4). https://doi.org/10.1126/sciadv.1602614.

Sarker IH (2021) Machine learning: algorithms, real-world applications and research directions. *SN Computer Science* 2:160. https://doi.org/10.1007/s42979-021-00592-x.

Schmid PJ, Sesterhenn JL (2008) Dynamic mode decomposition of numerical and experimental data. *Bulletin of the American Physical Society 61st Annual Meeting*, 208.

Shang X (2023) A study of deep learning neural network algorithms and genetic algorithms for FJSP. *Journal of Applied Mathematics*. https://doi.org/10.1155/2023/4573352.

Vafa K, Chen JY, Rambachan A, Kleinberg J, Mullainathan S (2024). Evaluating the world model implicit in a generative model. *38th Conference on Neural Information Processing Systems (NeurIPS 2024)*. arXiv:2406.03689v3.

Vanschoren J (2019) Meta-Learning. In Hutter F, Kotthoff L, Vanschoren J (eds.) *Automated Machine Learning: Methods, Systems, Challenges*, 35–62. https://doi.org/10.1007/978-3-030-05318-5.

Vaswani A, Shazeer N, Parmar N, Uszkoreit J, Jones L, Gomez, AN, Kaiser L, Polosukhin I (2017) Attention is all you need. In *NIPS'17: Proceedings of the 31st International Conference on Neural Information Processing Systems*, 6000–6010.

Wu X, Zhang X, Huang X, Xiao F, Usmani A (2022) A real-time forecast of tunnel fire based on numerical database and artificial intelligence. *Building Simulation* 15: 511–524. https://doi.org/10.1007/s12273-021-0775-x.

Xiao L, Zhang F, Hou Z, Mian L, Wang Z, Zhang J, Tang J (2023) Self-supervised Learning: generative or contrastive. *IEEE Transactions on Knowledge and Data Engineering* 35(1) 857–876. https://doi.org/10.1109/TKDE.2021.3090866.

Yao KX, Cao FL, Leung Y, Liang JY (2021) Deep neural network compression through interpretability-based filter pruning. *Pattern Recognition* 119: 108056.

Zhang T, Ding F, Wang Z, Xiao F, Lu CX, Huang X (2023) Forecasting backdraft with multimodal method: fusion of fire image and sensor data. *Engineering Applications of Artificial Intelligence* 132:107939. https://doi.org/10.1016/j.engappai.2024.107939.

Zhao C, Yu H (2024) Learning "look-ahead" nonlocal traffic dynamics in a ring road. *Proceedings of Machine Learning Research, 6th Annual Conference on Learning for Dynamics and Control* 242:142–154.

Zhao WX, Zhou K, Li J, Tang T, Wang X, Hou Y, Min Y, Zhang B, Zhang J, Dong Z, Du Y, Yang C, Chen Y, Chen Z, Jiang J, Ren R, Li Y, Tang X, Liu Z, Liu P, Nie J, Wen J (2024) A survey of large language models. arXiv preprint arXiv:2303.18223.

Chapter 6
Building Digital Twins of Cities as Complex Networks of Interdependence

6.1 The Network View of Cities

Since a complex system involves the interactions of many elements/parts, it can be modeled as a network where nodes represent the elements/components and links/edges represent their interdependence or interactions. A city can thus be conceptualized as a dynamical complex network of physical and virtual flows and interactions of which the main concern is on locations of entities and flows/interrelations/interactions between locations (Reggiani and Nijkamp 2006; Batty 2013; Wilson 2000). Likewise, a system of cities can be treated as a dynamical complex network in which individual cities interact as constituent entities. The relations between entities of an urban structure, treated as sites/nodes of the network, are usually measured along the edges/links of the corresponding graph connecting them. A transportation system, for example, can be represented as a network where the nodes can be traffic stops located within a city or cities located within a region, and weights on links can be distance, traffic volume, or connection strength measured along the links connecting them.

Networks are generally the physical containers whose capacity constrains flows of energy, information, materials, or people (Batty 2013). Entropy-maximization model is a typical example (Wilson 1970). Distance—measured in terms of physical distance, travel time, or travel cost—is pivotal to the way behavior through movements and flows is related to networks (Leung et al. 2013). On a more interpersonal level, social networks (Leinhardt 1977; Leung 1980) can be treated as a network where nodes are persons or social entities, and links are interpersonal/interinstitutional relations in the social space where topology defines the relevant graphs for their representation (Leung 1980; Batty 2013). Structures always affect functions (Strogatz 2001). The topology of transportation networks influences the flows of people and commodities, the topology of social networks affects ways people communicate with one another or infectious diseases are spread, and the topology of power grids impacts the transmission of energy in a city. Viewing cities as complex

Y. Leung, *Digital Twins of Cities*, Advances in Spatial Science,
https://doi.org/10.1007/978-3-032-07966-4_6

networks with numerous nodes and complicated interactions between them over non-trivial topology (Boccaletti et al. 2006), we can investigate, for example, how streets (edges/links in general) and street junctions (sites/nodes in general) are related to one another via the primal–dual arguments in space syntax and how such spatial configuration affects urban social dynamics (Hillier 2004). Network dynamics can be studied from the perspective of the dynamics of the networks themselves and the dynamics of interactions on networks.

6.2 Cities as Dynamical Complex Networks

Formally we can characterize networks as graphs. A graph can be denoted as G (N, L) containing the node set N and the link (pair of elements/nodes of N) set L. Nodes/hubs/vertices are used to define the elements of a graph with dynamical properties, and links/arcs/edges are used to specify the adjacency or strengths/weights of relations/interactions between the elements (further characterization is given in Chapter 7). In the context of information technology, a communication network can be structured as a network where nodes can be the communication hubs and links can be information flows (Leung et al. 1998; Wilson 2000). All these networks involve a huge number of elements and interactions between them. Cities are interacting systems within systems of cities (Berry 1964). The relative growths and changes of different cities can probably be deconstructed as changes occasioned by the development and growth/decline of nodes and network links (Batty 2013). Through percolation theory, we can study changes in connectivity in cities—behavior of the city network—by modeling site/node percolation, bond/link percolation (e.g. addition of connections between nodes/urban entities), K-core percolation, explosive percolation, etc. (Newman 2010; Porter and Gleeson 2016). Through percolation, we can study networks where nodes and connections are randomly occupied and deleted. Through Bernoulli percolation with parameter p—where p is the probability of opening an edge, i.e. connection between two nodes is open, and $(1 - p)$ is the probability of removing an edge—we can study how random connections create open clusters and how connectivity emerges and evolve in random dynamical urban systems. A low p value indicates few interactions in the network and a disordered behavior, while a high p value means enough interactions resulting in long-range interaction/connection in the network. we can study the giant component which represents connections involving a significant portion of the nodes in a city network. The Bernoulli percolation undergoes a phase transition with the percolation threshold, the critical value, at which the phase transition occurs. Below the critical value of p, the urban network consists of numerous tiny clusters without large scale interaction, and above that critical value there is only one infinite cluster with large scale interaction. It appears that at the critical threshold, there is no infinite cluster and self-similarity among fractal-like clusters seems to exist. Similarly, we can study site percolation with probability of occupying a site as p and emptying a site as $(1 - p)$. The dynamics of these networks are determined by the properties and dynamics of each constituent node, the dynamics of interactions between nodes, and the changing interplay of the network with its environment. So, the network configuration—such as the transportation network, the powerline network, and the epidemiological network—itself can be dynamic. The complicated interdependence changes over time, leading to complex dynamics and emergent complexity of the system. If we have interacting complex systems, such as interactions of different social groups/networks, then we have network of networks that exhibits properties of dynamical systems. It should be noted that percolation theory on networks beyond two dimensions becomes very complicated and there are open problems to be rigorously solved.

Therefore, cities can be conceptualized as dynamical complex networks with complicated interdependencies and interactions of various kinds between their constituents (Volchenkov 2008; Bettencourt 2021). Complex networks can get to be very complicated because of the properties and dynamics of nodes and network topologies. Node diversity (nodes of different functions), node redundancy (removal of nodes), dynamical complexity (nodes being nonlinear dynamical systems), connection diversity (different weights, directions, and signs of links between nodes), structural complexity (complicated wiring diagrams), network evolution (time-varying wiring diagrams), and meta-complications (any combination and mutual influences of the above, e.g. network evolution affecting topology, and modal dynamics affecting connection weights) all give rise to highly complex networks (Strogatz 2001). Therefore, we can investigate the dynamics of a network itself, e.g. the dynamics of infrastructure networks such as street networks, powerline and pipe networks, and the dynamics of interactions on a network, such as socioeconomic interaction, human mobility, information, monetary, and commodity flow on a transportation/communication network. The development of large networks is governed by robust self-organization that goes beyond the particulars of individual systems (Barab´asi and Albert 1999).

6.3 Dynamics of a Network and Its Low-Rank Approximation

Conceptually, we can treat cities as complex networks and represent them as graphs to investigate their dynamics and complexity. From the perspective of dynamical systems, we can model a city or an urban entity as a network containing k nodes each determined by a set of differential equations with interactions of various coupling strengths among them. Node dynamics and network topology changes can then be studied accordingly.

6.3.1 The Notion of Random Graph

Taking uncertainty into consideration, we particularly can model a city as a random graph which is a set of graphs furnished with a probability measure that depends on properties such as the distance between nodes/vertices in some metric space (Erdős and Rényi 1959, 1960). We can use the Erdos–Renyi random graph to study the emergence of connectivity between nodes based on probability and phase transitions of complex networks.

In the Erdos–Renyi random graph model, a graph G (n, p) of n nodes and m edges is constructed by randomly connecting labeled nodes such that

$$P(n, m; p) = p^m (1 - p)^{\binom{n}{2} - m} \tag{6.1}$$

where p is the probability of including each edge in the graph. The degree of any vertex v, $\deg(v)$, is distributed as a binomial distribution

$$P(n, m, \deg(v) = k; p) = \binom{n-1}{k} p^k (1 - p)^{n-1-k} \tag{6.2}$$

Let $\lambda = np$. As is well known, for large n and small $p, P(n, m, \deg(v) = k; \lambda = np)$ approaches the Poisson distribution as a limit

$$P(n, m, \deg(v) = k; \lambda = np) = \frac{e^{-\lambda} \lambda^k}{k!} \tag{6.3}$$

6.3.2 Low Rank and Sparsity of Adjacency Matrices

Mathematically, a random graph can be represented as a random matrix

$$\boldsymbol{W} = \langle \boldsymbol{W} \rangle + \mathbf{R} \tag{6.4}$$

where $\langle \boldsymbol{W} \rangle$ is the expected weight matrix and $\mathbf{R}$ is a random noise matrix. The expected matrix is the mean of the random matrix ensemble, and the noise matrix captures the fluctuations about the expected value due to randomness. A random matrix can be a Bernoulli matrix, a Gaussian matrix, etc., with interesting properties and behavior. We can also study universality of random matrices in which statistical properties are independent of probability distributions from which the entries are generated. From the random matrix, we can study interactions within a dynamical system and the stability of equilibrium points and periodic orbits. We can also investigate chaotic systems with random interactions, synchronization of oscillators, and evolution of networks in agent-based modeling for digital twins of cities (discussed in Chapter 7). In general, stochasticity can be injected into the simulation of agent-based systems through which network dynamics and complexity can be examined. We can also use random matrices generated by a probability distribution, say the Gaussian distribution, for random projection (Bingham and Heikki 2001) to reduce the dimensionality of snapshot matrices with sufficiently lower computational cost—in comparison with dimension reduction methods like SVD or PCA—even if nonlinearity exists in data. It should, however, be noted that the method is beneficial only when distances between data points need to be approximately preserved. Without this requirement, we can try randomized SVD (Boullé and Townsend 2022) for fast computation of near optimal SVD of huge snapshot sets if additional saving of computational cost is a main concern in SVD.

It has been observed that the expected matrix of a wide variety of random graphs involve low-rank matrices so that the weight matrix, $\boldsymbol{W}$, is equal to a function, ψ, of a low-rank matrix $\boldsymbol{L}$ as follows (Thibeault et al. 2014)

$$\boldsymbol{W} = \psi(\boldsymbol{L}) + \mathbf{R} \tag{6.5}$$

Parallel to the low-rank factorization of high-dimensional dynamical systems discussed in Chapter 3, the existence of a low-rank matrix (Golovnev et al. 2018) gives ground to spectral embedding of the dynamics of a complex network in the low-dimensional surrogate model through SVD (see Thibeault et al. 2014 for details). Such low-rank model is the simplest structure to account for the global behavioral dynamics and connectivity patterns of individuals of a system. From the decomposition, we can study spectral properties and behavior of the network dynamics. It extracts dominant features and local structures in the adjacency matrix of a high-dimensional graph. The eigenvalues of the adjacency matrix, for example, can indicate connectivity of the graph. For data-driven dimensionality reduction, we can use graph neural networks (Wu et al. 2019), for example, to learn the low-dimensional representations of random graphs.

According to Simon (1977), the world is a large matrix of interactions with mostly zero or close-to-zero entries. This type of matrix can be very sparse and very large. By ordering those entries according to their orders of magnitude, a distinct hierarchical structure—e.g. city hierarchy (Batty 2013) or regional hierarchy in terms of fuzzy graph (Leung 1984)—can be constructed. Therefore, in addition to the issue of low rank, sparsity is another issue we need to accommodate in the construction of digital twins of cities from the perspective of network complexity. We can study properties of a graph, particularly undirected graph, with respect to the eigenvalues and eigenvectors of the corresponding matrix, such as the adjacency matrix, associated with it by spectral graph theory (Chung 1997; Spielman 2012).

To be general, we can assume that an adjacency matrix comprises a low-rank component and a sparse component. It possesses a set of eigenvalues and a corresponding basis of eigenvectors that render low-rank approximation of the matrix. The reason for the existence of the low-rank component, i.e. having data lying on a low-dimensional manifold, has been discussed above, and the existence of sparsity is due to the non-existence of interactions and the corruptions in networks arising from missing entries and/or edges irrelevance—for example, vertices in a city network with no access to other vertices of interest because of their being located in deprived neighborhood of the city. So, the adjacency matrix is generally high-dimensional and corrupted. Under such situation, according to Candes et al. (2011), we can assume that the adjacency matrix **A** may be decomposed into

$$\mathbf{A} = \boldsymbol{L}_0 + \boldsymbol{S}_0 \tag{6.6}$$

where $\boldsymbol{L}_0$ is exactly low rank with errors in $\boldsymbol{S}_0$ of arbitrary magnitude, and $\boldsymbol{S}_0$ is exactly sparse. We have no knowledge about the low-dimensional column and row space of $\boldsymbol{L}_0$ and no ideas about the number and locations of the nonzero entries of $\boldsymbol{S}_0$. The task is to recover the low-rank and sparse components of the adjacency matrix accurately and efficiently. This is instrumental to the incorporation of network dynamics and complexity into digital twins of cities for efficient simulation and analysis. From the perspective of robust principal component analysis, Candès et al. (2011) theoretically proved and empirically demonstrated that we can recover the low-rank matrix $\boldsymbol{L}_0$ from **A** by simply solving the following convex optimization problem:

$$\begin{aligned} &min\ \|\boldsymbol{L}\|_+ + \lambda\|\boldsymbol{S}\|_1 \\ &s.t. \boldsymbol{L} + \boldsymbol{S} = \boldsymbol{A} \end{aligned} \tag{6.7}$$

where $\|\boldsymbol{L}\|_+$ is the nuclear norm—sum of the singular values of a matrix—of $\boldsymbol{L}$, and $\|\boldsymbol{S}\|_1$ is the l_1-norm of $\boldsymbol{S}$.

Along the line of reasoning of Candès et al. (2011), Richard et al. (2012) assumed that an interaction matrix **R** is both low rank and sparse, and provided the following convex mixed penalty method for its estimation

$$arg \min_{S \in \hat{S}} \left\{ \|\boldsymbol{S} - \boldsymbol{A}\|_F^2 + \gamma\|\boldsymbol{S}\|_1 + \tau\|\boldsymbol{S}\|_+ \right\} \tag{6.8}$$

where $\|\boldsymbol{S} - \boldsymbol{A}\|_F^2$ is the loss function; $\boldsymbol{A}$ is the adjacency matrix of a noisy graph; γ and τ are regularization parameters which can be selected via cross-validation; $\hat{\boldsymbol{S}}$ is the search space; and $\boldsymbol{S}$ is a candidate matrix whose coefficients are the signed scores for adding/removing edges from the matrix $\boldsymbol{A}$. Similar idea can be applied to predicting links. In this context, $\boldsymbol{A}$ is the adjacency matrix of a partially observed graph (Richard et al. 2012).

Parallel to the percolation of an adjacency graph, we can study the dynamics of a random graph through weighted percolation in which nodes and/or links are opened or removed with heterogeneous weights. Without further elaboration, we can embed dynamics and complexity of a city—represented as a random network—into digital twins of cities. From this, we can address the issues of control of adaptive complex systems (Montanari et al. 2022; Sanhedrai et al. 2022) for urban planning.

References

Barab´asi A-L, Albert R (1999) Emergence of scaling in random networks. *Science* 286: 509–512.

Batty, M (2013) *The New Science of Cities*. Cambridge: MIT.

Berry BJL (1964) Cities as systems within systems of cities. *Papers in Regional Science* 13(1): 147–163.

Bettencourt LMA (2021) Introduction to Urban Science: Evidence and Theory of Cities as Complex Systems. Cambridge: MIT Press.

Bingham E, Heikki M (2001) Random projection in dimensionality reduction: Applications to image and text data. https://doi.org/10.1145/502512.502546.

Boccaletti S, Latora V, Moreno Y, Chavez M, Hwang D-U (2006) Complex networks: structure and dynamics. *Physics Reports* 424(4–5): 175–308.

Boullé N, Townsend A (2022). A generalization of the randomized singular value decomposition. arXiv:2105.13052.

Candès EJ, Li X, Ma Y, Wright J (2011) Robust principal component analysis? *Journal of the ACM (JACM)* 58(3): 1–37. https://doi.org/10.1145/1970392.1970395.

Chung, R. K. *Spectral Graph Theory* (1997) American Mathematical Society. Providence: Rhode Island.

Erdős P, Rényi A (1959) On random graphs I. *Publicationes Mathematicae* 6 (3–4): 290–297.

Erdős P, Rényi A (1960) On the evolution of random graphs. *Publications of the Mathematical Institute of the Hungarian Academy of Sciences* 5: 17–61.

Golovnev A, Regev O, Weinstein O (2018) The minrank of random graphs. *IEEE Transactions on Information Theory* 64(11): 6990–6995.

Hillier B (2004) *Space is the machine*. London: Space Syntax.

Leinhardt S (ed.) (1977) *Social networks: a developing paradigm*. NY: Academic Press.

Leung Y (1980) A fuzzy set analysis of sociometric structure. *Journal of Mathematical Sociology* 7: 159–180.

Leung Y (1984) Towards a flexible framework for regionalization. *Environment and Planning A* 16: 1613–1632.

Leung Y, Li G, Xu ZB (1998) A genetic algorithm for the multiple destination routing problems. *IEEE Transactions on Evolutionary Computation* 21: 50–161.

Leung Y, Meng DY, Xu ZB (2013) Evaluation of a spatial relationship by the concept of intrinsic spatial distance. *Geographical Analysis* 45: 380–400.

Montanari AN, Duan C, Aguirre LA, Motter AE (2022) Functional observability and target state estimation in large-scale networks. *Proceedings of the National Academy of Sciences* 119(1): e2113750119. https://doi.org/10.1073/pnas.2113750119.

Newman MEJ (2010) *Networks: An Introduction*. Oxford: Oxford University Press.

Porter MA, Gleeson JP (2016) *Dynamical Systems on Networks: A Tutorial*. Berlin: Springer.

Reggiani A, Nijkamp P (eds.) (2006) *Spatial Dynamics, Networks and Modelling*. Cheltenham: Edward Elgar.

Richard E, Savalle PA, Vayatis N (2012) Estimation of simultaneously sparse and low rank matrices. *Proceedings of the 29th International Conference on Machine Learning*, 51–58.

Sanhedrai H, Gao J, Bashan A, Schwartz M, Havlin S, and Barzel B (2022) Reviving a failed network through microscopic interventions. *Nature Physics* 18(3): 338. https://doi.org/10.1038/s41567-021-01474-y.

Simon HA (1977) *Models of Discovery and Other Topics in the Methods of Science*. Dordrecht: Reidel.

Spielman D (2012) Spectral graph theory. In *Uwe Naumann U, Schenk* O (eds.) *Combinatorial Scientific Computing*. NY: Chapman and Hall/CRC, chapter 16.

Strogatz SH (2001) Exploring complex networks. *Nature* 410: 268–276.

Thibeault V, Allard A, Desrosiers P (2014) The low-rank hypothesis of complex systems. *Nature Physics* 20(2): 1–9. https://doi.org/10.1038/s41567-023-02303-0.

Volchenkov D (2008) Analysis of urban complex networks. *Condensed Matter Physics* 11, 2(54): 331–340.
Wilson AG (1970) *Entropy in Urban and Regional Modelling*. London: Pion.
Wilson AG (2000) *Complex Spatial Systems*. Edinburgh Gate: Pearson Education.
Wu Z, Pan S, Chen F, Long G, Zhang C, Yu PS (2019) A comprehensive survey on graph neural networks. arXiv:1901.00596.

Chapter 7
Multiagent Approach to Building Digital Twins of Cities

7.1 Microscopic Perspective of Urban Dynamics and Complexity

Our discussion so far is largely on the modeling of dynamics and complexity via digital twins of cities from the macroscopic perspective, except for the brief discussion on CA in Sect. 3.2 of Chap. 3 which can be treated as a microscopic approach with embedded macro dynamics in the transition rules. It is largely a top-down approach to the characterization and analysis of city dynamics and complexity. However, such macroscopic dynamics and complexity may be a result of the individual behaviors of city entities—such as individuals, households, firms, neighborhoods, government agencies, cities, etc.—and the interactions among them. Therefore, a microscopic approach that studies city entities and their interactions will give us a micro and bottom-up perspective for incorporating dynamics and complexity into digital twins of cities. Agent-based modeling (Reynolds 1987) is a powerful framework for the simulation and prediction of emergent complexity resulting from the dynamic microscopic behaviors of individuals. It can serve as a useful means to study emergent city phenomena (White and Engelen 2000; Batty 2005; Crooks et al. 2014). Modeling cities as multiagent systems (MASs) may enable us to study city dynamics and complexity from bottom up, and it may shed light on the synergetic integration of the macroscopic and microscopic approaches to the study of complex urban structures and processes.

Y. Leung, *Digital Twins of Cities*, Advances in Spatial Science,
https://doi.org/10.1007/978-3-032-07966-4_7

7.2 Building Digital Twins of Cities by Way of Agent-Based Modeling

An agent-based model is a microscale model for simulating the behaviors and interactions of autonomous adaptive agents—in the form of individuals or collective entities—giving rise to emergent macroscale complex phenomena and behavior. Complex global activities may spontaneously emerge from local interactions—which may be simple, complex, or nonlinear—among the constituent components/agents of a system. In the context of cities, fractals in city layouts, power-law distributions in city traffics, bifurcations of city growth, complexity of population migrations and city competitions may result from the interactions among individuals in a city. In urban economics, city economies can be modeled as evolving systems of autonomous interacting agents—such as individual producers, consumers, and other economic and social entities. Macroeconomic regularities such as shared market protocols and behavioral norms may result from local interactions among agents in a decentralized economy which may change the behaviors of the agents in return (Tesfatsion 2003). We can draw insights from the agent-based digial twins for macro urban-economic policy analysis and decision-making. Complex processes of economic development may also be a result of the interactions of microscopic economic agents (Tesfatsion 2003). It is therefore beneficial to employ the agent-based approach to incorporate dynamics and complexity into digital twins of cities for microscopic urban modeling, simulation, and management. It enables organizations and governments to empirically unravel consumers' and producers' behaviors through their interactions and evaluate impacts of various macro urban economic measures under different chaotic and nonchaotic urban economic scenarios. It can also simulate product lifecycles and experimentally explore ways to sustain circular urban economy through interacting urban agents with diverse characteristics and objectives.

The predator–prey model (Berryman 1992) is perhaps a classical problem that can be cast as an agent-based model for the study of urban dynamics based on the interplay between city population size and economic status of individuals (Dendrinos and Mullally 1982), and urbanization through dynamic urban–rural interactions (Chen 2009). Urban–rural population dynamics can be characterized by the predator–prey model—with rural population as prey and urban population as predator—via digital twins of cities. The model involves two types of agents, namely predator and prey, evolving together in time. It takes the form of the Lotka–Volterra equations (Lotka 1925; Volterra 1926) as follows

$$\frac{dH}{dt} = (\alpha - \beta P)H$$

$$\frac{dP}{dt} = (-\delta + \gamma H)P \tag{7.1}$$

where H is the number of prey and P is the number of predators. The four parameters are, respectively, α which is the net growth rate per individual of the prey in the absence of the predator; β which indicates the rate of decrease of H by βP when the predators are present; δ which is the net death rate per individual of the predator in the absence of the prey; and γ which indicates the rate of increase of P directly proportional to the presence of the prey by γH. Through some simple manipulation of terms and on integration, we have

$$\delta lnH - \gamma H + \alpha lnP - \beta P = constant \tag{7.2}$$

It is a family of closed curves in which different members of the population correspond to different values of the constant which are determined by the initial values of H and P with respect to given values of the parameters $\alpha,\ \beta,\ \delta,\ and\ \ \gamma$. The equilibrium point is $H = \delta/\gamma,\ P = \alpha/\beta$. With that, we can study oscillations of the predator and the prey population. It is observed that the dynamics formed around the nonlinear Lotka–Volterra model generate a variety of evolutionary models of the city system at different scales (Dendrinos and Mullaly 1982). Bakarji et al. (2023) employed the autoencoder with SINDy discussed in Sect. 4.5 in Chap. 4 to learn the sparse and closed form of Lotka–Volterra systems from time delay embedding of partial observations. By sensitivity analysis and parameter tuning, we can study the dynamics of the system with changes in the four parameters.

Closely related to the predator–prey model is the evolution of urban structure in the context of spatial interaction. Harris and Wilson (1978) showed that the evolution of urban structure involving producers and consumers can be described by a system of coupled first-order differential equations that are related to the Lotka–Volterra model. By expressing the flows in terms of the evolving structure and spatial interaction, it can be obtained by combining the Lotka–Volterra model with the statistical averaging procedure (Ellam et al. 2018).

The above processes depicted by Eq. (7.1) are deterministic without stochastic fluctuations. However, stochastic simulation can be carried out on the co-evolution of the predator and prey populations. Under randomness, urban–rural population dynamics with stochastic forcing can be expressed as

$$\frac{dH}{dt} = (\alpha - \beta P)H + Z^2$$

$$\frac{dP}{dt} = (-\delta + \gamma H)P \tag{7.3}$$

where Z is the stochastic forcing. By forcing the system sinusoidally with

$$Z(t) = 2sin(t) + 2sin\left(\frac{t}{10}\right) \tag{7.4}$$

and subjecting it to the SINDYc, SINDY with control, algorithm, Brunton et al. (2016) correctly identified the model structure and parameters of Eq. (7.3) in a numerical simulation.

To address uncertainty in the evolution of urban and regional structures, Ellam et al. (2018) injected stochasticity into the deterministic Harris-Wilson model (Harris and Wilson 1978) via well-posed systems of stochastic differential equations accompanied by a Bayesian inference methodology, namely the Markov chain Monte Carlo simulation, for parameter estimation and model calibration. As cautioned by Ellam et al. (2018), their stochastic formulation is only applicable to cross-sectional data, so it cannot handle highly correlated time series involving trends and fluctuations often crop up in real-life applications. To tackle this problem, we may need to consider using detrended fluctuation analysis (DFA), a method to study statistical affinity of non-stationary processes based on detrended fluctuations in time series (Peng et al. 1994), particularly those with multifractality exhibiting oscillations in the fluctuation function and significant errors in crossover locations (Zhou and Leung 2010) (See a brief discussion of DFA and MFDFA in Sect. 9.4 of Chap. 9).

Al-Kaff et al. (2022) showed that in the predator–prey interaction, a tiny integral step size can bring locally stable coexistence into the system. On the other hand, a large integral step size may make the system unstable, leading to more intricate and richer dynamics. That is, high intrinsic death rate of the predator leads to a chaotic growth rate of the prey. However, under direct correlation in symbiosis, the higher is the growth rate of the prey, the greater the growth rate of the predator becomes. Therefore, the operation of predation has increased, so is the opposite. They then used the Ott–Grebogi–Yorke (OGY) approach to control chaos in the predator–prey model. By expressing the predator–prey system as the Rosenzweig–MacArthur model with Allee effect on the prey and sigmoidicity of the functional response of the predator, it has been shown that the model exhibits bistability containing a pitchfork bifurcation (symmetry breaking), a Hopf bifurcation (a stable fixed point turning into a limit cycle), and a heteroclinic bifurcation (a limit cycle colliding with two or more saddle points) (summarized in Colon et al. 2015).

7.3 Digital Twins of Cities as Multiagent Systems

For generality, an agent-based model takes the form of a multiagent system (MAS) consisting of many interacting autonomous agents—each has its own goal and functions with a local view of the environment and self-directed interaction protocols through communication, cooperation, and competition. The environment provides a space in which agents perceive and interact. It imposes constraints on their interactions and resources from which they consume. So, a MAS is a complex adaptive system with adaptive/reinforcement learning, self-organization, and emergent behavior (Weiss 2018). Agents with reinforcement learning (Albrecht et al. 2023) interact continuously with other agents and the non-stationary environment, altering their communication strategies in response to the actions of other agents throughout time and space in pursuit of their own goals. Such interaction of numerous agents results in a highly dynamic and complex process giving rise to an ever-evolving system with high complexity (Bloembergen 2015). So, city can be treated as an evolutionary and self-organizing system driven by various agents—such as individuals and city entities—moving around purposely or randomly in space via some transportation or communication topologies, interacting with other agents in exchange of resources—such as services, land, commodities, and financial products—with a communication protocol, and modifying their behaviors in response to changing opportunities and distribution of resources in the overall environment whose factors can also be treated as agents (Allen et al. 2008; Bogachev 2008).

A central issue of MAS is cooperative control in which consensus is a fundamental issue (Zhou and Lin 2014). For a city within a region, its successful history is largely a tale of increasing cooperation and complementarity amidst competition (Allen et al. 2008). The purpose of reaching a consensus is to seek a distributive control protocol so that states of agents converge to some common trajectory, i.e. reaching an agreement on certain quantities of interest (Li et al. 2011). Thus, consensus can be achieved by specifying appropriate topologies of information exchanged (Gulzar et al. 2018). In the context of a city, there may be some urban management tasks which cannot be accomplished by a single agent—such as city traffic monitoring and control of the whole transportation network through highly distributed sensors (agents), and power supply of power plants (agents) interconnected by a network of powerlines. However, we can enable cooperative sensors, a MAS, to collaborate on the task with consensus protocol (A discussion about sensors is given in Chap. 9). Under consensus, the objective of interactions is to develop a communication protocol for a MAS to reach a common solution of the dynamics of individual agents (Monshizadeh et al. 2013), often governed by first-order and second-order dynamics (Hong et al. 2008). Going a step further, with emphasis placed on the dynamics of individual agents, synchronization requires the convergence of differences of the states of the agents with time going to infinity (Monshizadeh et al. 2013).

7.3.1 MAS as a Complex Adaptive Network

A natural approach is to model MASs as complex adaptative networks briefly discussed in Chap. 6. With such representation, we can investigate the control and optimization of MASs to achieve a targeted performance such as consensus under a communication topology (Herrera et al. 2020). In the context of digital twins of cities, consensus can be on agents of different states and goals working toward urban cohesiveness, urban resilience to socioeconomic stratification, etc., through appropriate information topology, communication protocol, self-reflection, relationship formation, and coordination.

Because of their high complexity, it is in general very time consuming and computationally expensive to simulate the dynamics of MASs, modeled particularly as complex adaptive networks with communication topology. To be efficient in the analysis, simulation, and control of such systems by their digital twins, it is beneficial to derive ROMs which are much lower in dimension yet preserve the structure, stability, consensus or other characteristics of interest in the original large-scale systems. Among other interests of concern, consensus is an essential problem in MAS. In what follows, I give a brief discussion on building consensus/synchronization preserving ROMs for MAS.

Let $G = (V, E, \mathbf{A})$ be a weighted graph, where $V = \{1,2, \ldots, N\}$ is a set of nodes/vertices, and $E \subseteq V \times V$ is a set of edges, with element denoted as (i, j). If G is an undirected graph, then the edge (i, j) is an unordered pair, i.e. $(i, j) \in E \Rightarrow (j, i) \in E$. It is ordered if G is a directed graph. $\mathbf{A} = \left[a_{ij}\right] \in \mathbb{R}^{N \times N}$ is an adjacency matrix, with weight $a_{ij} > 0$ if $(j, i) \in E$ and $a_{ij} = 0$ otherwise. For an undirected graph, $a_{ij} = a_{ji}$, for i, j =1,2,..., N, i.e. $\mathbf{A}^T = \mathbf{A}$. If $(j, i) \in E$ or $a_{ij} > 0$, then node j is a neighbor of node i and the set of all neighboring nodes of i is denoted by N_i. The path between two nodes is a sequence of edges connecting them. A directed graph contains a directed spanning tree in which a root node is connected to every other node via a directed path. The in-degree of node i is $d_i = \sum_{i=1}^{N} d_{ij}$, and the in-degree matrix is $\mathbf{D}$ = diag $(d_1, d_2, \ldots, d_N)$ (Mesbahi et al. 2010). The associated $N \times N$ Laplacian matrix is $\mathbf{L} = \mathbf{D}$ - $\mathbf{A}$, where $l_{ii} = \sum_{k \in N_i} a_{ik}$ and $l_{ij} = -a_{ij}$ for i, j =1, 2..., N, $i \neq j$. The incidence matrix of a directed graph is $\mathbf{R}$ defined as

$$\mathbf{R}_{ij} = \begin{cases} 1, & \text{if node } i \text{ is the head of edge j} \\ -1, & \text{if node } i \text{ is the tail of edge j} \\ 0, & \text{otherwise} \end{cases} \tag{7.5}$$

For i =1, 2, ..., N, j =1, 2, ..., k (number of edges). If G is undirected, then the incidence matrix is obtained by assigning to each of the edges an arbitrary orientation and then take the incidence matrix of the corresponding directed graph (Mesbahi and Egerstedt 2010). The Laplacian matrix and the incidence matrix of an undirected graph are related by $\mathbf{L} = \mathbf{RWR}^T$, where $\mathbf{W}$ = diag $(\omega_1, \omega_{2,\ldots,}\omega_k)$ is a k x k matrix with $\omega_j, j = 1,2, \ldots, k$, being the weight assigned to edge j.

7.3.2 MAS in the Form of Finite Dimensional Linear Time-Invariant System

In general, MAS can be depicted as a finite dimensional linear time-invariant system. The dynamics of each agent i, i.e. node i, $i = 1, \ldots, N$, is represented by the following time-invariant system

$$\dot{\boldsymbol{x}}_i(t) = \mathbf{A}\boldsymbol{x}_i(t) + \mathbf{B}\mathbf{u}_i(t)$$

$$\mathbf{y}_i(t) = \mathbf{C}\boldsymbol{x}_i(t) \tag{7.6}$$

with a diffusive coupling rule

$$\mathbf{u}_i(t) = -\sum_{(i,j)\in E} \left(\mathbf{y}_i(t) - \mathbf{y}_j(t)\right) \tag{7.7}$$

where $\boldsymbol{x}_i$, $\mathbf{u}_i$, *and* $\mathbf{y}_i$ are the state, control input, and output, respectively, and **A**, **B**, and **C** are matrices with appropriate dimensions. Each agent will receive the measurement outputs from its neighbors. The communication topology among the agents is a weighted graph G. The dynamic complexity of the system is measured by the number of state components in a state representation of the system, i.e. its dynamic order. Due to its high dimensionality and complexity, MASs are generally difficult to analyze and time consuming to simulate, particularly for large-scale near real-time or real-time applications. To be efficient in the simulation and control of such systems, it is important to find a ROM for practical implementation and operation of the complex MAS in digital twins of cities.

7.3.3 Model Reduction in MAS

If the MAS is macroscopically represented as a finite dimensional linear time-invariant system like Eq. (7.6), the intuitive idea for further reducing the complexity of a MAS is to reduce its dynamic order by some model reduction techniques, such as Lyapunov balanced truncation (Moore 1981; Monshizadeh et al. 2013). In model reduction, a requirement is to preserve the desired properties—such as stability and consensus/synchronization of the original MAS with respect to the communication topology. So, model reduction must be structure preserving also. Let **L** be the Laplacian matrix corresponding to the graph G. Then, the MAS in Eq. (7.6) can be rewritten in compact form as (Monshizadeh et al. 2013)

$$\dot{\mathbf{x}}(t) = \tilde{\mathbf{A}}\mathbf{x}(t) \tag{7.8}$$

where $\boldsymbol{x} = (x_1, x_2, \ldots, x_N)$ *and* $\tilde{\boldsymbol{A}} := \boldsymbol{I}_N \otimes \boldsymbol{A} - \boldsymbol{L} \otimes \boldsymbol{BC}$, with $\otimes$ denoting the Kronecker product. If the agents have stable dynamics and the overall network is stable, by balancing the relevant matrices in the Lyapunov equation, truncating the least important state components, and applying some stability condition, Monshizadeh et al. (2013) showed that the following reduced-order network of order r is stable

$$\bar{\boldsymbol{x}} = \overline{\tilde{\boldsymbol{A}}}\bar{\boldsymbol{x}}(t) \tag{7.9}$$

where $\overline{\tilde{\boldsymbol{A}}} := \mathbf{I}_N \otimes \bar{\mathbf{A}} - \mathbf{L} \otimes \bar{\mathbf{B}}\bar{\mathbf{C}}$; $\bar{\boldsymbol{x}} = \left(\bar{x}_1, \bar{x}_{2,\ldots,}\ \bar{x}_N\right)$ *with* $\bar{\boldsymbol{x}}_i \in \mathbb{R}^r$, r is determined by truncating the $N-K$ $(1 \le k < N)$ state components of smallest distinct characteristic values; and $\bar{\boldsymbol{x}}_i$ being the reduced state component of agent i, $i = 1,2,\ldots,N$. They also showed that the ROM is close to the original MAS subject to an error bound, and it is also synchronized—i.e. the difference of the states of the agents goes to zero as time goes to infinity—if the original network is synchronized and a certain small gain condition holds. ROMs such derived can substantially reduce the dimension and complexity of the MAS and are thus more efficient for simulation and control by way of digital twins.

Sometimes inputs have delay, and the corresponding MAS can be expressed as (Zhou and Lin 2014).

$$\dot{x}_i(t) = \mathbf{A}x_i(t) + \mathbf{B}\mathbf{u}_i(t - \tau_i)$$

$$\mathbf{y}_i(t) = \mathbf{C}x_i(t) \tag{7.10}$$

where $\tau_i \geq 0$, i = 1, 2…,N, is the input delay, and the rest of the terms are the same as above. By applying an appropriate projection method with truncation, Zhou and Lin (2014) derived a ROM for reduced-order observer-based output feedback protocol with known time delay in the communication network, and inputs to solve the consensus problem in the MAS.

In performing model reduction of MAS by projection, besides ensuring consensus or synchronization, we also need to ensure that the projection does not destroy the structure of the underlying communication network. To preserve the network structure, Monshizadeh et al. (2014) showed that by clustering the nodes of the underlying communication graph with appropriate graph partition, a ROM for the leader–follower linear diffusively coupled MAS with single-integrator dynamics that preserves the network structure and reaches consensus can be derived using Petrov–Galerkin projection. To make the clustering approach less restrictive, Mlinaric et al. (2015) employed the QR decomposition with column pivoting as a clustering algorithm to partition the graph, and combined Petrov-Galekin projection to derive the ROM for the leader–follower MAS that preserves communication structure and achieves consensus. In general, the leader–follower MAS on an undirected and weighted graph G of N nodes (agents) with m, m $\leq N$, leaders—where $V_L = \{\nu_{1,}\nu_{2,\ldots,}\nu_m\} \subseteq V$ is the set of leaders, and $V_F = V \setminus V_L$ is the set of followers—can be represented as follows

$$\dot{x}(t) = -\mathbf{L}x(t) + \mathbf{M}\mathbf{u}(t)$$

$$\mathbf{y}(t) = \mathbf{W}^{\frac{1}{2}}\boldsymbol{R}^T x(t) \tag{7.11}$$

where **L**, **W**, and ***R*** are the Laplacian matrix, the edge-weights matrix, and the incidence matrix, respectively, and the matrix **M** is defined as $M_{ij} = 1, \textit{if } i = \nu_j$, and $M_{ij} = 0$, otherwise. The ROM can then be derived from there (for details, see Mlinaric et al. 2015).

Therefore, dynamics and complexity of MAS can be substantially reduced by deriving the ROM that preserves the characteristics of the original full-scale MAS. It greatly facilitates the analysis, simulation, control, and interpretation of the MAS in its digital twin.

7.4 Multiagent Modeling with Specifically Crafted Communication Protocol and Decision-Making Strategy

Strictly speaking, the differential-equation model of the time evolution of populations discussed in Sect. 7.2 is more or less a macroscopic representation of the interaction between predator and prey at the population level. It is conceptually not a purely bottom-up approach that models the microscopic behaviors of distinct individuals of both populations and their interactions with other agents and the environment with some crafted communication protocols. From the microscopic perspective, individual agents are characterized by their initial attributes, assigned norms and modes of behavior (such as communication, learning, and collaboration) for interacting with other agents in the environment with an initial state. The system then spontaneously evolves over time resulting in emergent structures. To simulate the predator–prey dynamics within the microscopic agent-based framework, agents can be characterized by their states, interaction norms (including observations, actions, rewards in reinforcement learning), and environmental settings (including agent speed, prey reproduction, predator starvation, etc.) to form specific communication rules to capture emergence from bottom up (Kölle et al. 2024). In urban transportation, drivers (agents) may be characterized by socioeconomic status, health, reaction time, driving speed etc., with permissible actions such as stopping, accelerating, decelerating, road-condition judgment, safety, and time-minimizing as objectives. For traffic-flow management, the MAS then will evolve traffic patterns over time through interactions among the agents starting from an initial traffic condition on a road network and based on rules for lane changing and collision avoidance, etc., along the way. In urbanization, decisions of agents with different economic statuses and cultural identities to migrate depend on the states of the individuals and their perceptions of the local and global environments (Benenson 1999). Simulating a MAS with large rule sets can get to be very complex. To reduce computational complexity, rule simplification in terms of knowledge reduction advanced by the rough-set approach may be instrumental to efficient MAS simulations (Leung et al. 2007). Within the rough-set framework (Pawlak 1991), rules are discovered from observational or experimental data. Rule simplification is then achieved through a knowledge reduction procedure in which superfluous attributes in rules are eliminated, redundant rules are taken out, and related rules are combined to form a parsimonious rule set that can achieve the same level of performance as the original rule set in evolving the MAS. Such an approach is purely data driven. That is, instead of specifying the communication rules a priori, we can learn and simplify them directly from data.

In the conventional MAS, agents function with a pre-defined communication protocol, e.g. a pre-defined rule set. They are inflexible with low adaptability to the changing environment. Since an agent itself should be a dynamical system, its characteristics and communication protocol may change over time. In MAS, agents should coevolve throughout their lifecycles. To make agents dynamic and more intelligent, we should tap on the power of artificial intelligence (AI) to build intelligent agents/AI agents (Stone and Veloso 2000; Padgham and Winikoff 2005) to navigate city complexity in a proactive and dynamic way. Agents should be able to observe and reflect on changes in the environment and robustly modify their behaviors to pursue their goals. Russell and Norvig (2003), for example, classify agents into five types, namely the reflex agent who acts only on the basis of the current percept and function with the condition-action/if–then rule; the model-based reflex agent who possesses an internal model which depends on the percept history to take actions in interacting with other agents and the environment; the goal-based agent who executes goal-oriented actions to accomplish their tasks; the rational utility-based agent who chooses actions that maximize the expected utility of the action outcomes; and the learning agent who learns to become more competent by enriching its knowledge and modifying its behavior throughout its life time.

To capitalize on the power of generative AI, instead of crafting a priori rules for communication, we may employ LLMs or SLMs to build generative agents who can interact in natural language with one another and the environment through observation, reflection, knowledge updating, and planning. By leveraging the power of natural language, we can characterize AI agents in terms of their socioeconomic identities, perspectives, and relationships with other agents. Through this, we can bring into digital twins of cities the social dimensions essential to bottom-up and humanistic planning with concepts and ideas from urbanism. These agents are rational agents who are empowered with cognitive abilities, planning capabilities, dynamic information intake and processing functionalities, memory functions, and appropriate-tool invoking skills to evolve themselves from agents with limited knowledge and capability into agents with richer knowledge and higher goal-driven motivation to achieve objectives efficiently and autonomously. For example, we may be able to evolve reflex agents who can only react to current situations into learning agents who can solve problems and plan for their behaviors. With LLM-based learning, agents can communicate, negotiate, and coordinate flexibly with one another over time through natural language processing. They can take cognizance of their surroundings and are equipped with the capabilities of processing and integrating spatiotemporally varying multimodal information such as text, voice, images, and video; learning and reasoning through interactions with other agents and the environment; and analyzing and executing tasks efficiently. Agents with different objectives and knowledge backgrounds/experiences can be coordinated with distributed and social learning to complete interrelated tasks. They can plan their actions by memory, reflection, and logical thinking over a long-time horizon. Park et al. (2023) experimented with a limited version of such an idea by creating generative agents as a form of simulacrum of human behaviors.

Regarding the construction of digital twins for city traffic control, we, for instance, can build a MAS with different task-specific AI agents working collaboratively on various tasks in the high-dimensional workspace. Some may estimate road densities in street/road trunks, intersections, and round abouts as model-based agents according to a dynamical model like the one in Eq. (5.29). Some may observe and interpret road conditions with the fusion of real-time audio-visual data coming from various sensors and scene understanding driven by LLMs and neural networks. Some may work on drivers' concentrations and driving behaviors while others may monitor pedestrian movement or decide on the distribution of traffic controls, etc. They all receive data from sensors distributed at different locations, communicate and learn dynamically in a concerted manner throughout the cooperative process to provide better informed, more intelligent, and safer traffic-control decisions under regular and emergent traffic conditions. So, the multiple AI agent system is intelligent and generative amidst emergent complexity. It will also be resourceful in the development of digital twins for autonomous city driving in which a variety of AI agents can be deployed to ensure safe autonomous driving (Hallerbach et al. 2018). We can also formulate an intelligent MAS to simulate the dynamics of urban retail structures and processes, and the predator–prey urban–rural population dynamics discussed in Sect. 7.2.

This type of generative agent, of course, may suffer from all shortcomings of natural-language-based generative AI, including hallucination, data poisoning, societal bias, believability, and other ethical issues. On the other hand, we can perhaps make use of the plausible bias training in LLMs to deliberately bias train digital twins in terms of socioeconomic status and ethnicity of city players/agents to better understand and simulate the dynamics of housing affordability, residential segregation, or other social justice/injustice phenomena—such as social inclusion/exclusion in cities—within an intelligent MAS framework to plan for a more harmonious and cooperative city living environment. Here, precaution has to be taken against the amplification of soical biases. Through this we can integrate socioeconomic considerations into socially inclusive urban planning and decison-making processes. With the future development of generative AI in general and AI agents in particular, it will render us an effective and efficient way to build flexible, robust, and more intelligent MASs for digital twins of cities. Linking such AI agents to urban policy analysis and decision-making, we can efficiently and effectively simulate urban development scenarios, explore, design and assess policies/interventions according to the evolution of agent' behaviors and urban dynamics before real-world implementations. A caveat to such generative MAS development is that LLM-based generative agents might, in the long run, develop their own communication protocols or even their own language beyond our comprehension, resulting in peculiar and uncontrollable emergence if left unchecked. From the urban planning point of view, this is something we would not want to end up having. From the generative AI perspective, this might be a plausible consequence to which we should be proactive in taking precaution measure to prevent it from happening.

7.5 Issues in the Multiagent Approach to Building Digital Twins of Cities

Since agents in a MAS function autonomously, designing decentralized algorithms for communication and cooperation can be complicated and maintaining consistency and synchronization may be difficult. It may lead to suboptimal solutions. Designing robust and adaptive methods for decentralized decision-making through conflict resolution and negotiation will be necessary. The integrated information fusion approach based on the theory of evidence and conflict resolution developed by Leung et al. (2013)—briefly discussed in Chap. 11—may be an effective way to tackle this problem.

Regardless of how we build MASs, an interesting question is whether the dynamics and complexity exhibited in the macroscopic representation are qualitatively similar to those emerged from the microscopic representation of the system. By assigning specially crafted rules to individual agents for sensing and interaction, and by incorporating stochasticity in random walk and other behaviors—such as breeding, dying, and hunting—Colon et al. (2015) experimentally demonstrated that such a microscopic system exhibits all the bifurcation behaviors of the given macroscopic system in the qualitative sense. This implies that with suitable conditioning and manipulation according to the known macro dynamics, macroscopic dynamics and complexity of the predator–prey model might emerge from the microscopic behaviors of individual agents. Incidentally, by appropriately defining a group of agents (consumers and retailers), an environment (a results grid representing the parameter space capable of showing emergent behaviors and phase changes), and a set of associated development rules (consumers' retail center choice), Dearden and Wilson (2012) could construct a MAS which is equivalent (producing similar results) to the Boltzmann-Lotka–Volterra (BLV) model for the dynamics of urban retail articulated by Harris and Wilson (1978). However, in the general case, if macro dynamics is not known in advance and we cannot tailor make rules and conditions correspondingly, can microscopic behaviors generate the stipulated macro dynamics, at least qualitatively? The answer to this may shed light on the general development of MAS for the modeling of complex feedback between the macrostructure and microstructure of the urban system. The knowledge learned from the microscopic and macroscopic analyses can be made mutually informed, and we may explore the intricate interrelations between the macroscopic and microscopic processes (Zimmerman et al. 1998).

Going a step further, sitting in-between may be a mesoscopic approximation of the MAS in which agents randomly move in space across the scales and interact with close-by agents along their trajectories. By governing position dynamics of the agents with the Ito diffusion process and the type changes of agents by the Markov jump process, Helfmann et al. (2021) showed that evolution of the agent states over time can be expressed as coupled stochastic equations with no analytical solutions. Approximation of the solutions must be done through simulation, which turns out to be very expensive because of the very high dimensionality of the discretized version of the original system. Applying appropriate model reduction techniques that transform the agent-based model to density-based model, Helfmann et al. (2021) obtained a ROM which is given by a system of coupled stochastic PDEs propagating agent densities for different agent types. Since there is a substantial reduction in the number of coupled equations, simulation of the system of stochastic PDEs is much faster than the original stochastic MAS. For model reduction of the stochastic predator–prey model using the Koopman generator, see Niemann et al. (2021) for details.

References

Albrecht SV, Christianos F, Schäfer L (2023) *Multi-Agent Reinforcement Learning: Foundations and Modern Approaches.* Cambridge: MIT Press.

Al-Kaff MO, El-Metwally HA, Elabbasy EM (2022) Qualitative analysis and phase of chaos control of the predator-prey model with Holling type-III. *Scientific Report* 12: 20111.

Allen PM, Strathern M, Baldwin J (2008) Complexity: the integrating framework for models of urban and regional systems. In: Albeverio S, Andrey D, Giordano P, Vancheri A (eds.) *The Dynamics of Complex Urban Systems: An Interdisciplinary Approach.* NY: Physica-Verlag Heidelberg, 21–42.

Bakarji J, Champion K, Kutz JN, Brunton SL (2023) Discovering governing equations from partial measurements with deep delay autoencoders. *Proceedings of the Royal Society A* 479 (2276). https://doi.org/10.1098/rspa.2023.0422.

Batty M. (2005) *Cities and Complexity: Understanding Cities with Cellular Automata, Agent-Based Models, and Fractals.* Cambridge: MIT Press.

Benenson I (1999) Modeling population dynamics in the city: from a regional to a multi-agent approach. *Discrete Dynamics in Nature and Society* 3: 149–170.

Berryman AA (1992) The Origins and Evolution of Predator-Prey Theory. *Ecology* 73 (5): 1530–1535.

Bloembergen D, Tuyls D, Hennes D (2015) Evolutionary dynamics of multi-agent learning: a survey. *Journal of Artificial Intelligence Research* 53: 659–697.

Bogachev L (2008) Cities as evolutionary systems in random media. In: Albeverio S, Andrey D, Giordano P, Vancheri A (eds.) *The Dynamics of Complex Urban Systems: An Interdisciplinary Approach.* NY: Physica-Verlag Heidelberg, *143–162.*

Brunton SL, Proctor JL, Kutz JN (2016) Discovering governing equations from data by sparse identification of nonlinear dynamical systems. *Proceedings of the National Academy of Sciences* 113(15): 3932–3937.

Chen Y (2009) Urban chaos and perplexing dynamics of urbanization. *Letters in Spatial and Resource Sciences* 2(2): 85–95.

Colon C, Claessen D, Ghila M (2015) Bifurcation analysis of an agent-based model for predator–prey interactions. *Ecological Modelling* 317: 93–106.

Crooks AT, Patel A, Wise S (2014) Multi-agent systems for urban planning. In Pinto NN, Tenedório JA, Antunes AP, Cladera JR (eds.) *Technologies for Urban and Spatial Planning: Virtual Cities and Territories.* Hershey: IGI Global, 29–56.

Dearden J, Wilson AG (2012) The relationship of dynamic entropy maximising and agent-based approaches in urban modelling. In Heppenstall AJ, Crooks AT, See LM, Batty M (eds.) *Agent-Based Models of Geographical Systems*, Chap. 35, Berlin: Springer, 705–720. https://doi.org/10.1007/978-90-481-8927-4_35.

Dendrinos DS, Mullally H (1982) Evolutionary patterns of urban populations. *Geographical Analysis* 13: 328–344.

Ellam L, Girolami M, Pavliotis GA, Wilson A (2018) Stochastic modelling of urban structure. *Proceedings of the Royal Society A: Mathematical, Physical and Engineering Sciences* 474: 20170700. https://doi.org/10.1098/rspa.2017.0700.
Gulzar MM, Rizvi STH, Javed MY, Munir U, Asif H (2018) Multi-agent cooperative control consensus: a comparative review. *Electronics 7*(2): 22.
Hallerbach S, Xia Y, Koester F (2018) Simulation-based identification of critical scenarios for cooperative and automated vehicles. *SAE International Journal of Connected and Automated Vehicles* 1(2). https://doi.org/10.4271/2018-01-1066.
Harris B, Wilson AG (1978) Equilibrium values and dynamics of attractiveness terms in production-constrained spatial-interaction models. *Environment and Planning A 10:* 371–388.
Helfmann L, Conrad ND, Djurdjevaca A, Winkelmann S, Schutte C (2021) From interacting agents to density-based modeling with stochastic PDEs. *Communications in Applied Mathematics and Computational Science* 16(1): 1–32. https://doi.org/10.2140/camcos.2021.16.1.
Herrera M, Pérez-Hernández M, Parlikad AK, Izquierdo J (2020) A review on control and optimisation of multi-agent systems and complex networks for systems engineering. *Processes* 2020, *8*(3): 312. https://doi.org/10.3390/pr8030312.
Hong Y, Chen G, Bushnell L (2008) Distributed observers design for leader-following control of multi-agent networks. *Automatica* 44(3): 846–850.
https://doi.org/10.1371/journal.pone.0250970.
https://doi.org/10.3390/electronics7020022.
Kölle M, Erpelding Y, Ritz F, Phan T, Illium S, Linnhoff-Popien C (2024) Aquarium: a comprehensive framework for exploring predator-prey dynamics through multi-agent reinforcement learning algorithms. *Proceedings of the 16th International Conference on Agents and Artificial Intelligence (ICAART 2024)—Volume 1*, 59–70. ISBN: 978–989–758–680–4. https://doi.org/10.5220/0012382300003636.
Leung Y, Fung T, Mi JS, Wu WZ (2007) A rough set approach to the discovery of classification rules in spatial data. *International Journal of Geographical Information Science* 21: 1033–1058.
Leung Y, Ji NN, Ma JH (2013) An integrated information fusion approach based on the theory of evidence and group decision-making. *Information Fusion* 14: 410–422.
Li Z, Duan Z, Chen G (2011) Consensus of discrete-time linear multi-agent systems with observer-type protocols. *Discrete and Continuous Dynamical Systems-Series B* 16(2): 489–505.
Lotka AJ (1925) *Elements of physical biology*. Furnace: Williams & Wilkins.
Mesbahi M, Egerstedt M (2010) *Graph Theoretic Methods in Multiagent Networks*. Princeton: Princeton University Press.
Mlinaric P, Grundel S, Benner P (2015) Efficient model order reduction for multi-agent systems using QR decomposition-based clustering. *Proceedings of 54th IEEE Conference on Decision and Control (CDC)*, 4794–4799.
Monshizadeh N, Trentelman HL, Camlibel MK (2013) Stability and synchronization preserving model reduction of multi-agent systems. *Systems & Control Letters* 62: 1–10.
Monshizadeh N, Trentelman HL, Camlibel MK (2014) Projection based model reduction of multi-agent systems using graph partitions. *IEEE Transactions on Control of Network Systems* 1(2): 145–154. https://doi.org/10.1109/TCNS.2014.2311883.
Moore BC (1981) Principal component analysis in linear system: controllability, observability and model reduction. *IEEE Transactions on Automatic Control* 26 (1): 17–32.
Niemann JH, Klus S, Schutte C (2021) Data-driven model reduction of agent-based systems using the Koopman generator. *PLoS ONE* 16(5): e0250970.
Padgham L, Winikoff M (2005) *Developing Intelligent Agent Systems: A Practical Guide*. Vol. 13. Hoboken: John Wiley & Sons.
Park JS, O'Brien JC, Cai CJ, Morris MR, Liang P, Berstein MS (2023) Generative agents: interactive simulacra of human behavior. arXiv:2304.03442.
Pawlak Z (1991) *Rough Sets: Theoretical Aspects of Reasoning about Data*. Boston: Kluwer.
Peng CK, Buldyrev SV, Havtin S, Simons M, Stanley HE (1994) Goldberge organization of DNA nucleotides. *Physical Review E* 49(2): 1685–1689.

Reynolds CW (1987) Flocks, herds, and schools: a distributed behavioral model. *Computer Graphics* 21(4): 25–34.
Russell S J, Norvig P (eds.) (2003). *Artificial Intelligence: A Modern Approach.* Upper Saddle River: Prentice Hall. Chap. 2.
Stone P, Veloso M (2000) Multiagent systems: a survey from a machine learning perspective. *Autonomous Robots* 8(3). https://doi.org/10.1023/A:1008942012299.
Tesfatsion L (2003) Agent-based computational economics: modeling economies a complex adaptive system. *Information Sciences* 149: 263–269.
Volterra V (1926) Fluctuations in the abundance of a species considered mathematically. *Nature* 118(2972): 558–560.
White R, Engelen G (2000) High-resolution integrated modelling of the spatial dynamics of urban and regional systems. Computers, Environment and Urban Systems 24: 383–400.
Weiss G (ed.) (2018). *Multiagent Systems.* Cambridge: MIT Press.
Zhou B, Lin Z (2014) Consensus of high-order multi-agent systems with large input and communication delays. *Automatica* 50 (2): 452–464.
Zhou Y, Leung Y (2010) Multifractal temporally weighted detrended fluctuation analysis and its application in the analysis of scaling behavior in temperature series. *Journal of Statistical Mechanics: Theory and Experiment* 06: P06021. https://doi.org/10.1088/1742-5468/2010/06/P06021.
Zimmerman B, Lindberg C, Plsek P (1998) *Edgeware: Insights from Complexity Science for Health Care Leaders.* Irving: VHA Inc.

Chapter 8
Incorporation of Multiscale Dynamics and Complexity into Digital Twins of Cities

8.1 The Issue of Scale in Digital Twins of Cities

I have discussed the incorporation of dynamics and complexity into digital twins of cities on the macro level in Chaps. 3–5, and on the micro level in Chap. 7. I would like to explore further this macro-micro dichotomy in search of appropriate scales to build digital twins. This chapter debates on the macro-micro dichotomy and the appropriate scale on which digital twins of cities should be built.

From the perspective of dynamical complex systems, we may wonder how to link up micro dynamics with macro dynamics. First, are there microfoundations for the macro urban phenomena? Second, can we reduce macro dynamics into micro components, or can we obtain macro dynamics through the aggregation of micro dynamics? Could macro properties of a system be directly read off from the microstates of the agents at any point in time, and could we directly derive macro emergence from the properties and interactions of the parts at the micro level? Third, what exactly is the interplay between the micro and macro dynamics over time? Does the entire system evolve along with the dynamic interactions of the micro and macro over time, with the micro providing what is possible from bottom up and the macro conditioning the micro level parts and their interactions from top down? Fourth, would the macro-micro division of analysis exclude the meso domain which may be the center of change in adaptive complex urban systems? Do we need extra scales for the construction of digital twins of cities, and how do dynamics translate between scales? This chapter attempts to address the issues raised by questions 1 to 3 in Sect. 8.2 and gives an insight into the query made by question 4 in Sect. 8.4.

Y. Leung, *Digital Twins of Cities*, Advances in Spatial Science,
https://doi.org/10.1007/978-3-032-07966-4_8

8.2 The Macro-Micro Dichotomy of Urban Dynamics

In economics, microfoundations seek to provide an understanding of the macroeconomic phenomena based on the behaviors of the economic agents and their interactions at the micro level (Janssen 2006; Epstein 2011). Similarly, we can ask whether we have microfoundations for macro urban phenomena. From the reductionist point of view, higher-level urban phenomena can be decomposed into simple micro building blocks from which higher-level dynamics can be reconstructed. Micros are individual behaviors and macro is the consequence of their aggregation. The macro structure is obtained by a simple linear combination of micro entities through direct aggregation. To the extreme, the whole/macro is the sum of the parts/micros, and decomposition of the macro are the micros in the strict linear systems where the superposition principle applies.

However, the relationship between macro and micro dynamics is not that simple under nonlinearity. It should first be noted that dynamics has its own intrinsic properties that capture different aspects of system complexity and emergence at each level. In nonlinear dynamical systems, parts do not necessarily hold the properties of the whole and the whole is more than the sum of its parts. An individual car, for example, does not possess the properties of the pattern of city traffic dynamics. Individual residential choices do not possess the dynamics of the housing market. Agent-based modeling attempts to render microfoundations for the macroscopic behavior of dynamical systems. Conceptually, higher-level dynamics can be determined by the behaviors of the lower-level agents from bottom up, with the macro behavior of the system being determined by the behaviors and interactions of the micro components. However, it is generally a fallacy, especially under nonlinearity and emergence. Though we may be able to observe macroscopic dynamics from the interactions of individuals at the microscopic level, it is in general difficult to breakdown or identify which specific microscopic dynamics is responsible for a given macroscopic behavior. Under nonlinearity and emergence, behavior at a higher level usually could not be fully decomposed into behaviors of objects at a lower level. The macro behavior of a dynamical complex system is generally independent of and differs from the behaviors of its components (Barab´asi and Albert 1999; Strogatz 2001). At the microscopic level, the concern is on the dynamics of individual agents/components and their interactions governed by individual rules/ protocols. We are interested in individual behaviors and their interactions giving rise to emergent patterns at a higher level. At the macroscopic level, the concern is the overall system behavior exhibiting global trend and oscillation, phase transition, and convergence throughout the system evolution.

Global dynamics in general cannot be induced directly from the micro elements and their interactions. For instance, by treating the crowd as a continuum and ignoring any specific behaviors of the pedestrians—such as speed of walking, taking turns, and stopping at will, etc.—Bain and Bartolo (2019) showed that the dynamics of pedestrian movement can be appropriately predicted by macro hydrodynamics based only on the spectral properties of the velocity waves, conservation laws, and symmetry principles without relying on any behavioral assumptions. Similarly, our physiology cannot be decomposed directly into objects at the cellular level. Traffic patterns like traffic flows in a transportation network cannot be decomposed into individual drivers' behaviors—such as driving speed and haphazard lane changing—or performance of individual cars, or to push it further, the sturdiness of individual car parts. Thus, the macroscopic and microscopic behaviors of traffic flows are different. Dynamical properties of traffic flows on networks possess unique characteristics different from those on a single node or link. Knowing the properties and dynamics of constituent nodes may not give us a definitive way to predict the macro properties and dynamics of the network. Given a network topology, for instance, what would happen to the network dynamics when the dynamics of some or all the constituent nodes have stable fixed points, limit cycles, limit torus, or strange attractors is unclear. What would the nonlinear interactions among these nodes be? How should they be synchronized? The answer is by no means simple and straightforward, particularly under nonlinearity and emergence. The macro–micro linkage becomes even more complicated when the network topology simultaneously varies over time and space (Strogatz 2001). In cities, though individual behaviors contribute to the properties and dynamics of the land use system, it does not mean that they can be fully determined by the properties and dynamics of the individuals because when we form larger things from smaller things, the former will have their own properties and natural laws, particularly when other environmental or global factors come into play. Therefore, the whole usually cannot be straightforwardly predicted by the properties of the parts.

In general, macro properties of a system cannot be directly read off from the microstates of the agents at any point in time (Epstein 2011). They may just be a plausible result that could be generated by natural emergence and self-synchronization through agents' interactions with the environment. While it may be possible for macroscopic dynamics to emerge from microscopic behaviors and interactions, unique identification of the microscopic dynamics responsible for a macroscopic behavior is difficult, if not impossible—because of the many-to-one mapping (see Sect. 8.4 for further discussion). Therefore, phase transition on the macroscale needs to be studied on its own because of its own special quality. Changes at the macro level may not be directly correlated with the microscopic properties and changes in the elements at the micro level. Smooth or abrupt phase transition at the macro level has its own properties and undergoes its own dynamic process of change. The macro emergence may not be directly derived from the properties of the parts and their interactions at the micro level. The macro emergence may only be interpreted from the dynamics at the macro level governed possibly by a few equations. Under strong emergence, horizontal entailment applies. To predict the future of a dynamical system at a particular level, say the macro level, what is happening at that level is necessary and sufficient. In other words, the macroscopic process can be self-contained with causal/functional and computational closure (Rosas et al. 2024). That is why Chaps. 3 to 5 are devoted largely to the incorporation of dynamics and complexity into digital twins of cities on the macro scale.

Microfoundations in economics attempt to understand aggregate economic phenomena in terms of the behaviors of individual entities and their interactions that may involve market and non-market interactions. It investigates the link between the principles of macroeconomics and microeconomics to explore the aggregate relationships. In brief, the economy—the city in our case—is considered a dynamical complex system populated by numerous heterogeneous agents—in terms of preferences, socioeconomic backgrounds, rationality, etc.—whose complex interactions unabatedly change the structure of the entire system in a smooth or abrupt manner, depending on the uncertain occurrence of external shocks or disturbances along the trajectory. So far, the research agenda has been challenged by the skepticism of conventional macroeconomists and the effort has not been successful in deriving all macroeconomic propositions from fundamental hypotheses on the behaviors of individual agents (Janssen 1993, 2006).

To successfully tackle the issue of macro–micro dichotomy in digital twins of cities, we need to effectively handle the interactions and interoperability between the macro and micro levels. System evolution depends on the dynamic interaction of the macro and micro regimes. Each level operates on its own rules in pursuit of its own objectives. They coevolve through mutual interaction within the entire system. With an extremely huge number of agents, the micro level possesses an astronomical number of possibilities for arrangement and interaction. However, only a limited number are applicable to the situation within which the macro level exists. The macro imposes constraints on the micro, and the micro generates possibilities for the macro. Too much constraint will limit the interactions of the micro elements leading to no micro in the extreme. In this situation, we are pursuing macro at the expense of micro. Conversely, too weak a constraint will limit the macro states, and we are pursuing the micro at the expense of the macro. To the extreme, we will not have a macro state. This might not be desirable from the city planning point of view. In city planning, we might want to arrange a macro environment from which elements at the micro level can better draw energy needed for self-organization in achieving a development goal—such as cities forming pattern of interactions for various types of metropolis development. As a matter of fact, the entire system evolves along the dynamic interactions of the micro and macro over time, with the micro providing what is possible from bottom up and the macro conditioning the micro components and their interactions from top down, attempting to strike a coordination mutually beneficial to both levels.

An interesting question is whether we can learn the hidden dynamics from the nonlinear interactions of parts at the micro level so that they will be in synchrony with the dynamics at the macro level or converged to the rational expectation. In short, can we build macro dynamics from bottom up through the evolution of emergent dynamics generated by the compositions and interactions of heterogeneous agents—which themselves are dynamically changing in the course of time? Can the oscillatory or chaotic phenomena observed at both the macroscopic and microscopic levels, for instance, be synchronized? Although Colon et al. (2015) experimentally demonstrated that by skillfully crafting rules for the individual agents with reference to some macro dynamics and certain manipulations of the environment, the microscopic system can exhibit bifurcation behavior of the macroscopic system in the qualitative sense. However, do we have a general model for the macro–micro linkage? Specifically, what information or features at the microscopic level do we need to decide on the equations/mechanism that govern the macroscopic behavior? With respect to percolation, what is the percolation threshold where phase transition will take place in a random network and global structure—e.g. a large, connected cluster that spans the whole network—will emerge from behaviors at the microscopic level? The answer to it is by no means simple. Under nonlinearity, strange things can happen at the micro level on the finest scale and learning the mappings from the microstates to the macrostate over time, if it is at all possible, is not at all easy. Instead of learning the mappings, which may be difficult to find, we may build macro dynamics into the microscopic system so that micro simulations are constrained by the macro environment, like the theory-based CA simulation of land use dynamics in Tsang and Leung (2011), discussed in Sect. 3.2 of Chap. 3. Another plausible approach might be to obtain snapshots from the simulations of the MAS micro dynamics and subject them to machine learning with algorithms—like SINDy discussed in Sects. 4.2–4. 5 of Chap. 4 and urban theory-informed neural networks discussed in Chap. 5—to learn the macro dynamics which, however, may or may not be equal to the analytical macro dynamics resulting from its own dynamic mechanisms (see further discussion in Sect. 8.4).

8.3 Arguments for the Intermediate Levels—The Meso and Multiscale Perspectives

Besides the above issues, the prevailing macro–micro dichotomy has recently been challenged in economic analysis to be insufficient in studying economic dynamics. It is argued that the macro–micro division of analysis excludes the meso domain which is considered by some economists to be the center of change in adaptive complex economic systems (Chen 2005; Dopfer et al. 2004). In mesoeconomics, the economic system is built upon meso which represents an organizational loop between the macroeconomic and microeconomic systems (Kozuharov 2011). Throughout economic evolution, complex processes of change take place in both micro and macro structures, and the meso domain can explicate them with evolution mechanisms such as replication, variation, selection, and self-organization. The meso trajectory—a three-phase process of emergence, diffusion, and maintenance of novel rules in an economic system—involves the spread of a new rule into the micro-organizational domain, with repercussions in the macro domain with self-ordering and self-organization that determine the macro structure (Dopfer et al. 2004). The macro–meso–micro framework is thus considered a sound basis for evolutionary economics.

Wilson (1981) gave a similar argument for the explicit differentiation of the micro, meso, and macro scale in dynamical urban and regional analysis under chaos and bifurcation. For urban analysis, Pumain (2006) argued that multiple interactions between individuals, firms, and institutions constitute the meso level—a product from both the micro and macro levels. The EM model of spatial interaction also puts forth the macro–meso–micro perspective (Wilson 1967). Though not making scale the explicit issue in its investigations, regional science analysis (Isard 1956, 1975) is essentially cast against the macro–meso–micro framework. A similar view is also expressed in the study of urban resilience which identifies three levels: the micro level of economic actors inside a city, the macro level highlighting the embeddedness of cities into global processes through a system of cities, and the meso level—that is the city itself—being the product of bottom-up and top-down processes (Rogov and Rosenblat 2018). In the study of health service resilience, human resilience occurs at the micro level, organization resilience at the meso level, societal resilience at the marco level, and social-ecological resilience at the cross level, with the micro and macro being analytically bridged by the meso (Bergström and Dekker 2014).

In general, we are interested in the collective behavior of groups of individuals/ components or subsystems in the form of spatial organizations—such as clusters and networks—in a system and the dynamics arising from their interactions and evolution over time. Depending on what we identify as meso, in the city setting it can be neighborhoods, communities, etc., and in the setting of system of cities, it can be cities or metropolis, etc. Through their interactions, we are interested in emergence giving rise to patterns at the higher level. Similar to the macro–micro translation, while it is possible to observe macroscopic behavior arising from mesoscopic dynamics, it is difficult to deduce which mesoscopic configuration or behavior will lead to the emergence of a particular macroscopic dynamic. It again can be a many-to-one mapping under nonlinearity, complexity, and emergence. For example, different mesoscopic network configurations may lead to similar macroscopic pattern of commodity flows. Nonlinearity makes it difficult to trace back specific mesoscopic behaviors responsible for the macroscopic dynamics. Collective interactions of mesoscopic components give rise to macroscopic patterns that are not explicitly present at the mesoscopic level. Emergent properties arising from interactions across scales may not have direct counterparts on the individual scales. Scales observed with different resolutions also impact on the difficulty in unraveling cross-scale dynamics (see further discussion in Sect. 8.4).

From the MAS viewpoint, by equipping digital twins of cities with the macro-, meso-, and microscopic perspectives, simulation, and control of agent-based urban systems may be made more flexible, practical, and interpretable. We may, for example, formulate a macro theory from a micro theory by allowing new agents to appear in a system and bring along new behaviors into the complex network. Instead of the macro–micro dichotomy, we can perhaps study dynamics and complexity of agent-based systems along the city hierarchy on multiple spatial and temporal scales in which agents can merge and new behaviors can happen under new connectivity, bringing forth new dynamics and complexity (Andersson 2008). Perhaps, the dynamics and complexity of cities may be better captured by modeling them as complex MAS governed by dynamics of many degrees of freedom, interacting nonlinearly on different spatial and temporal scales (Albeverio et al. 2008). For example, on large scales, agent mobility is dominated by the origin–destination scheme, but on the meso and micro scales are events driven by stochastic individual or group movements caused by changing decisions through the interactions between agents and with the environment (Bazzani et al. 2008).

To carry the scale argument a step further, we might need a multilevel construct to comprehensively understand and incorporate dynamics and complexity into digital twins of cities. Within this construction, urban entities—such as individuals, households, neighborhoods, districts, towns, cities, metropolis, and global city nested at different levels of the urban hierarchy—have nonlinear interactions across scales involving agents at different levels or composite agents formed across different levels, resulting in a variety of emergent spatiotemporal dynamics. Though under strong emergence, we just need to study the dynamics at each level in its own right, it will be useful if we can unravel the relations between levels along the hierarchy in case additional insights can be drawn from reduction through the inter-level linkages—particularly when emergence involves mix of scales or when we need to go beyond the context/range of operational parameters within which emergence take place. Then, the basic issue is on how to link the dynamics at different levels and how to translate across scales changes from the microscale to the macroscale within the multiscale framework. We need to develop models for dynamics at multiple scales—from individuals to groups to systems to systems of systems—to comprehend the emergence of structures and processes across scales, particularly under multiscale stochasticity. An analogy in the human immune system is that the translation of changes at the genetic and molecular level, to the cellular level, the tissue level, the organ level, all the way up to changes in our overall health is by no means clear and straightforward. For this, we need a rigorous theoretical underpinning that can unite the underlying equations/rules that govern urban dynamic behaviors at all scales—that is, a theoretical foundation that can take us from microscopic to macroscopic urban behavior and vice versa along the scale hierarchy. More specifically, can we derive the governing equations of macro dynamics from those of micro dynamics? Dynamics and complexity on each scale are already highly complicated. From the MAS perspective, can we possibly draw insights into or find a cohesive and congruent macro–meso–micro city structure and process for flows, relationships, feedback loops, and emergent properties across scales for our urban systems by modifying or changing the rules governing agent interactions within and between scales and the environment? One can imagine how formidable the mission will be to tackle cross-scale dynamics and complexity in nonlinear systems. A daunting and challenging task! But if done correctly, it is an extremely worthy and rewarding mission!

8.4 A Conceptual Construct for Multiscale Urban Dynamics

To put the above arguments into a theoretical framework, Fig. 8.1 depicts multiscale dynamics only in the context of macro–meso–micro dynamics for simplicity's sake. In this hierarchical structure, the micro, meso, and macro levels have their own structures and dynamics. Casting population growth against the multiscale framework, for instance, we might be studying behaviors and dynamics of individuals in the population at the microscopic level in terms of growth rate and competition for resources under a carrying capacity. At the Mesoscopic level, we might be analyzing behaviors and interactions of population subgroups, and at the macroscopic level, we might be investigating the structure and dynamics of the whole population governed, for example, by the Verhulst-Pearl equation, Eq. (3.12), or the dynamics of different population groups by the Lotka–Volterra equation, Eq. (7.1), in the predator–prey context. Linking these scales together involves the translations of patterns and dynamics across scales to capture emergence and dynamics of the whole population. In traffic dynamics over a transportation network, we may be interested in the structures—roads of various grades, junctions, roundabouts, traffic signals, etc. constituting the whole transportation system—and dynamics of traffic flows—congestion level, traffic-flow speed, average travel time, etc.—of the whole network at the macro level, those of the local intersections or districts on the meso level, and individual vehicles of various kinds, drivers, pedestrians, traffic signals, and their behaviors—lane changing, uneven walking/driving speed, distance flocking, signal controls, etc.—and interactions at the micro level. In social networks, we may be interested in the dynamics of collective opinion and behavior of the city population at the macro level, the social subgroups at the meso level, and the individuals as well as their interactions and mutual influence dynamics at the micro level. In urban microclimates, we may concern about the citywide temperature variation, air flow dynamics in terms of changing wind speed and direction, and temperature anomaly such as heat island formation at the macro level. At the meso level, our concern may rest on those at the neighborhood or district level of various kinds. At the micro level, we may want to investigate building properties, building layouts, land use types, road surfaces, vehicles, population sizes, and vegetation covers whose structures and interactions play an important role in the formation and dynamics of urban microclimates. It will be even more challenging if we are dealing with cross-scale dynamics and complexity of highly complicated urban structures and processes.

As previously discussed, in strictly linear systems where the superposition principle applies, macro structures and dynamics are obtained by a simple linear combination of micro entities through direct aggregation because of linearity, proportionality, and additivity. Therefore, composition of the micro is the meso/macro, and composition of the meso is the macro. Conversely, direct decomposition of the macro is the meso/micro, and the direct decomposition of the meso is the micro. Transfer functions relating components and behaviors at different levels can be formulated for such inter-scale translations. In linear systems, traffic behavior such as congestion

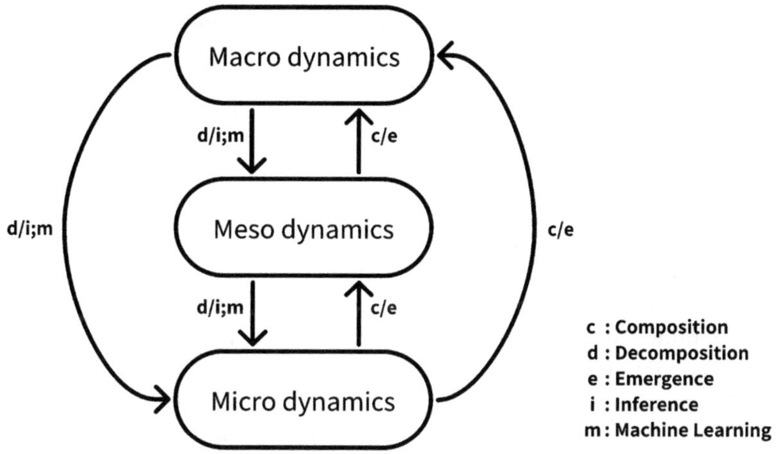

Fig. 8.1 The conceptual construct of macro–meso–micro dynamics

level at the macro level, for example, can be obtained via direct composition of the behaviors of drivers, pedestrians, traffic signals, and their interactions at the micro level. Conversely, structures and dynamics at the micro level can be derived through direct decomposition of the structure and behavior at the macro level.

However, under nonlinearity, such a simple composition/decomposition will not work. Because of nonlinearity and complex interactions in this hierarchical setting, complex structures and dynamics at the higher level are formed through emergence from the nonlinear interactions of components at the lower level in nonlinear dynamical complex systems as previously discussed. Thus, inter-level translation/mappings are by no means trivial, particularly in highly nonlinear chaotic systems with degeneracy and multistability (see discussion in Sect. 9.5 of Chap. 9). To obtain structure and behavior at the macro level from the micro level, it is through the behaviors and nonlinear interactions and feedback loops of the individual components at the micro level giving rise to macro dynamics that goes beyond the simple/direct composition of individual behaviors like the linear systems. Conversely, to derive structures and dynamics at the lower level from the higher level, unlike linear systems where we can simply break down the higher-level structure and behavior into their constituent lower-level components through direct decomposition, the best we can do is to obtain lower-level structures and dynamics from the upper-level by making inference on the nonlinear relationship—such as the statistical inference on the impact of the macro-level behavior on the micro level components and their interactions—or by learning the inter-level nonlinear mappings through machine learning like neural networks or other methods discussed in this book. From the macro level all the way down to the micro level involves a chain of between-level mappings to be inferred or learned. Besides various methods of inference or machine learning, it calls for the use of data and domain-specific knowledge to break down the upper-level behavior into the lower-level components, if it is at all possible, on which inference can be made, or perform system identification to identify mathematical models that capture the relationship between upper-level variables and the corresponding lower-level dynamics through machine learning. Once captured, the relationship can be simplified by deriving the corresponding ROMs via low-dimensional manifold learning methods discussed throughout this book. The task becomes even more complicated and difficult in nonlinear dynamical systems exhibiting multistability (see discussion in Sects. 9.4 and 9.5 of Chap. 9) where we need to capture multiple stable states within and between levels, as well as within-level and between-level state transitions. In general, to be successful in deriving accurate and reliable inter-level mappings, special attention needs to be paid to cross-level scale consistency and dependency, inter-level nonlinear interactions, and feedback loops in cross-level couplings, model complexity, and intelligibility.

From the purely data-driven point of view, if the dynamics at each level are manifested as time series, can we start out from the time series at the finest level and derive the time series at all levels manifesting the dynamics, e.g. underlying governing equations, at each of these levels with genuine physical meanings? By composing and decomposing time series, we might be able to draw insights into the identification of dynamics at each level and between-level interactions and dependencies. Perhaps we can apply multivariate empirical mode decomposition (MEMD), briefly discussed in Chap. 9, to extract information at certain levels with physical meaning through the decomposition of the multivariate time series at the finest level and subject those extracted intrinsic mode functions (IMFs) to the urban theory-based learning discussed in Chap. 5 to learn hidden dynamics. As discussed in Chap. 9, we can reconstruct the original multivariate time series through simple composition. Through the cointegration of time series at different levels—a statistical method for describing and assessing long-term relationships of non-stationary time series—it can perhaps shed light on the discovery of inter-level relationships. It should, however, be noted that the sifting process of EMD is a mechanical procedure for decomposing a time series into a series of IMFs in which some may not bear any physical meaning about the underlying dynamics. Moreover, the dynamics that generate the original time series at the finest level still need to be unraveled. Besides EMD, other time series analysis such as wavelet transforms (Daubechies 1992; also see Leung (2010) for a discussion on geographical time series) may also be useful to find multiscale dynamics from data. By convoluting wavelet functions with the signal, we can scale the signal and examine it in a more revealing manner under another representation in both time and frequency. Alternatively, we may consider framework like the characterization of hierarchical emergence through causal closure via a hidden Markov process (Rosas et al. 2024). In the context of MAS, can we acquire communication rules for agents at different levels directly from data? A plausible way may be to build on the concept of multi-scale information tables and investigate knowledge/rule acquisition and reduction in multi-scale decision tables in which an agent is located at different levels of the hierarchy of the multi-scale granular labeled partition structure and can take on as many values as there are scales under the same attribute (Wu and Leung 2011). With data-driven approach, we also need to ensure that the dynamics on each scale and cross-scale dynamics uncovered are interpretable.

Therefore, learning multilevel dynamics of complex urban systems will give us a more embracing view of city structures, behaviors, and their emergence and gain insight into how local interactions give rise to global behavior—e.g. how global structure and behavior of MASs emerge from simple local rules of interaction—and how global dynamics restrain local behaviors throughout city evolution, and ultimately what drives dynamics and interactions across scales. Understanding these cross-scale dynamics and complexity will inspire us on the management and control of our multiscale urban phenomena and processes. All these are very challenging issues which need rigorous theoretical investigations and extensive empirical verifications before we can formally characterize multilevel dynamical complex urban systems in future research. In any case, meticulous analysis of the macro and micro level dynamics and complexity discussed in the previous chapters and the remaining part of this book is absolutely necessary, foundational, and instrumental to the modeling of urban dynamics and complexity via digital twins of cities that scale. Approaches discussed are transferable to the learning and modeling of dynamics and complexity at the meso level or on some chosen scales with physical meaning.

References

Albeverio S, Andrey D, Giordano P, Vancheri A (eds.) (2008) *The Dynamics of Complex Urban Systems: An Interdisciplinary Approach.* NY: Physica-Verlag Heidelberg.

Andersson C (2008) Ontogeny and ontology in complex systems modeling. In: Albeverio S, Andrey D, Giordano P, Vancheri A (eds.) *The Dynamics of Complex Urban Systems: An Interdisciplinary Approach.* NY: Physica-Verlag Heidelberg, 43–58.

Bain N, Bartolo D (2019) Dynamic response and hydrodynamics of polarized crowds. *Science* 363(6422): 46–49.

Barab´asi A-L, Albert R (1999) Emergence of scaling in random networks. *Science* 286: 509–512.

Bazzani A, Capriotti M, Giorgini B, Melchiorre G, Rambaldi S, Servizi G, Turchetti G (2008) A model for a systematic mobility in urban space. In: Albeverio S, Andrey D, Giordano P, Vancheri A (eds.) *The Dynamics of Complex Urban Systems: An Interdisciplinary Approach.* NY: Physica-Verlag Heidelberg, 59-64.

Bergström J, Dekker SWA (2014) Bridging the macro and the micro by considering the meso: reflections on the fractal nature of resilience. *Ecology and Society* 19(4): 22. https://doi.org/10.5751/ES-06956-190422.

Chen P (2005) A biological perspective of macro dynamics and the division of labor: persistent cycles, disruptive technology and the trade-off between stability and complexity. In Dopfer K (ed.) *The Evolutionary Foundations of Economics.* Cambridge: Cambridge University Press, 472–505.

Colon C, Claessen D, Ghila M (2015) Bifurcation analysis of an agent-based model for predator–prey interactions. *Ecological Modelling* 317: 93–106.

Daubechies I (1992) *Ten lectures of wavelets.* Philadelphia: Society for Industrial and Applied Mathematics.

Dopfer K, Foster J, Potts J (2004) Micro-meso-macro. *Journal of evolutionary economics* 14: 263–279.

Epstein B (2011) Agent-based modeling and the fallacies of individualism. In Humphreys P, Imbert C (eds.) *Models, Simulations, and Representations,* NY: Routledge, 115–144.

Isard W (1975) *Introduction to Regional Science.* NY: Prentice-Hall.

Isard W (1956) Regional science, the concept of region and regional structure. *Papers and Proceedings of the Regional Science Association* 2: 13–26.
Janssen MCW (1993) *Microfoundations: A critical inquiry*. Oxfordshire: Routledge.
Janssen MCW (2006) Microfoundations. *Tinbergen Institute Discussion Paper*. TI 2006-041/1. JEL code: B22, D40, E00.
Kozuharov S (2011) Mezzo economics analytical approach as the propulsive part of managerial economics in tourism. *UTMS Journal of Economics* 2 (2): 213–219.
Leung Y (2010) *Knowledge Discovery in Spatial Data*. Berlin: Springer-Verlag.
Pumain D (2006) Alternative explanations of hierarchical differentiation in urban systems. In Pumain D (ed.) *Hierarchy in Natural and Social Sciences*. Dordrecht: Springer, 169–222.
Rogov M, Rozenblat C (2018) Urban resilience discourse analysis: towards a multi-level approach to cities. *Sustainability* 10, 4431. https://doi.org/10.3390/su10124431.
Rosas FE, Geiger BC, Luppi AI, Seth AK, Polani D, Gastpar M, Mediano PAM (2024) Software in the natural world: a computational approach to hierarchical emergence. arXiv:2402.09090.
Strogatz SH (2001) Exploring complex networks. *Nature* 410: 268–276.
Tsang SW, Leung Y (2011) A theory-based cellular automata for the simulation of land-use change. *Geographical Analysis* 43:142-171.
Wilson AG (1967) A statistical theory of spatial distribution models. *Transportation Research* 1: 253–269. https://doi.org/10.1016/0041-1647(67)90035-4.
Wilson AG (1981) *Catastrophe Theory and Bifurcation: Applications to Urban and Regional Systems*. London: Croom-Helm.
Wu WZ, Leung Y (2011) Theory and applications of granular labelled partitions in multi-scale decision tables. *Information Sciences* 181: 3878–3897.

Chapter 9
Interoperability Between Models and Data for the Incorporation of Dynamics and Complexity into Digital Twins of Cities

9.1 On Model-Data Interoperability

From our previous discussions, we can see how dynamical models are learned from data under various situations, and how data should be generated or collected according to model requirements or instructions. Therefore, it is essential to synchronize dynamic models and data so that digital twins can be constantly updated with new and revised data coming from IoT devices, sensors and various sources or generated by various scenarios, and data can be continuously and adaptively collected and fused according to model needs and requirements. Such interoperability between models and data is crucial to the development of digital twins of cities to model the short- and long-term dynamics and complexity of city lifecycle development. We must ensure that models and data operate in conjunction with each other. It is this seamless synchronization and constant mutual enhancement among the physical entities, the corresponding virtual models and the data hubs that distinguishes digital twins from conventional modeling. We need to ensure that the most available data in space and time are utilized, and the right information and knowledge can be effectively and efficiently transferred to the right place at the right time in this trilateral interconnection. In this way, we can advance our knowledge about cities and amass and update information/data—particularly from the changing observational systems—at the micro, meso, and macro levels for the continuous modeling of city evolution. Figure 9.1 depicts the trilateral interoperation in digital twins of cities.

In brief, this trilateral interoperation contains three bidirectional interactions. The first bidirectional interaction involves the physical twin—in our case the city—and the model—its virtual replica. The model is an abstraction of the physical twin—the physical asset. Based on our understanding of the dynamics and complexity of the physical twin, i.e. our real world, we formulate a model that represents it. It can be in the form of governing equations like ODEs or PDEs, a complex network, a MAS, etc. We use such models to simulate, predict, optimize, and control the physical twin throughout its life cycle. This bidirectional interaction itself is dynamic. A new

Y. Leung, *Digital Twins of Cities*, Advances in Spatial Science,
https://doi.org/10.1007/978-3-032-07966-4_9

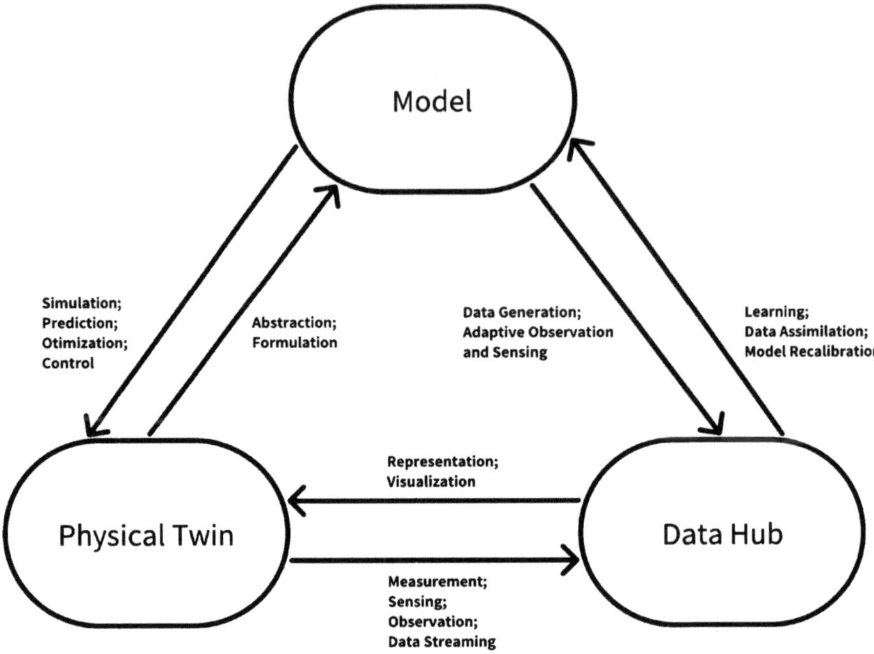

Fig. 9.1 Model-data interoperation in digital twins of cities

understanding of the physical twin will lead to a modified or new formulation of the model and a new round of simulation, prediction, optimization, and control. Since our real world is ever evolving, this bidirectional interaction is ever evolving also.

Between the physical twin and the data hub, we have another bidirectional interaction. We make measurements and observations of the physical twins through conventional data collection techniques and/or urban sensing with IoT and other sensing technologies. All of this form the streaming of spatiotemporal data into the data hub with appropriate infrastructure. The structured data from the data hub, on the other hand, render the information-based representation of the physical twin which can be visualized. Such interaction is again iterative and dynamic throughout the lifecycle of the physical twin.

Between the data hub and the model is another bidirectional interaction. The data hub provides data for learning via various means discussed in the previous chapters. Moreover, through data assimilation, discussed in Sect. 9.2, we can update our model with or recalibrate our model against current measurements and observations to make our estimations/predictions accurate. In reciprocal, the model can inform the way data should be collected so that they can appropriately reflect the dynamics and complexity of city evolution to be captured by the model. Furthermore, the model can generate data for learning, such as the high-fidelity models can generate data for the learning of the corresponding ROMs discussed in detail in various chapters. Again, such bidirectional interaction is dynamic and iterative over time.

It should be noted that there are interoperations between the bidirectional interactions also. It is this dynamic trilateral interoperation—and the bidirectional interactions embedded—that makes our urban analysis and planning theoretically and pragmatically flexible, relevant, interesting, and instrumental. It is this important synergy that forms our digital twins of cities. Based on the above conceptualization and extended on the definitions made by AIAA and AIA and NASEM in Chapter 1, I propose that digital twins can be defined as "A set of virtual information constructs that imitates the structure, context and behavior of an individual/unique physical asset, or a group of physical assets, is dynamically updated via the trilateral interoperation between the virtual, the physical, and the data throughout its lifecycle and informs decisions that realize value". In what follows, I give a further discussion on the interoperability between models and data in digital twins of cities.

9.2 Data Assimilation as a Facilitator for Model-Data Interoperability

Data assimilation (Carrassi et al., 2018) is an important approach to realize and implement model-data interoperability in digital twins of cities. It involves methodologies which employ observational or measurement data on real-life systems to continuously correct and update the model structures and system states—including the initial conditions, boundary conditions, trajectories, and parameters of dynamical models characterized by governing equations. Due to the complexity of urban environments, we usually need to estimate the states of complicated and large dynamical urban systems with rich or sparse information under uncertainty. The data are generally multisource coming from IoT and other sensors of the changing observational systems, and valid data previously forecasted by the models at the time the observations are made. City traffic control, microclimates, air pollution, and energy efficiency of the built environment previously discussed are typical urban issues involving the deployment of various types of sensors—e.g. stationary and mobile sensors, satellites, radars, etc.—to make measurements of the system states on a continuous basis. These are real-life data that should be factored into relevant models to update predictions and to evolve digital twins over time to closely and accurately estimate system dynamics and complexity. We need the observational data, albeit limited and noisy, to correct/update the model estimates of the system states, and we need the dynamical model to extrapolate information to unseen situations. Such iterative interoperability of models and measurement data are key to the reliable prediction of short-term and long-term urban system dynamics and complex behaviors. It also sheds light on the relative impact of the dynamical models and observations on system-state prediction and system control. Model and data working independently and without mutual updates will not enable digital twins to do an appropriate job in the analysis and management of urban dynamics and complexity.

9.2.1 The Bayesian Foundation for Data Assimilation

Since observations are usually biased with measurement errors and model predictions are usually biased with estimation errors, the treatment of uncertainty due to such errors becomes essential in data assimilation. It is particularly critical in the prediction of chaotic systems which are highly sensitive to initial conditions. We might need multiple realizations to make reliable ensemble estimation of the system states. Therefore, any data assimilation method must be equipped with error propagation capability so that uncertainty arising from data measurement errors and model estimation errors can be propagated to the result and minimized to ensure that accurate forecast of system dynamics can be made by the model to enable optimal system control with respect to urban planning objectives. Among other methods, Kalman filter (KF) (Kalman, 1960) and its variants (Lendek et al., 2007; Khodarahmi and Maihami, 2023) are the most common algorithms for data assimilation. The standard KF algorithm—known as Kalman filtering (or linear quadratic estimation)—attempts to improve the accuracy of state prediction of a linear dynamical system by incorporating measurements coming from various sources to iteratively correct and update model forecasts—the true state—over time through a state transition model. It propagates and combines errors from the measurements and model estimates to minimize recursively the error between the predicted state and the measured state. It works like a low-pass filter with a dynamically changing parameter—the Kalman gain—that filters out the high frequencies, the noise, to get the low frequency, the estimate, by giving higher weights to more recent observations. It assumes that system dynamics and measurement models are known, and the noise is Gaussian.

The theoretical basis of KF is the Bayesian model which can be expressed in general as

$$p(x|y) = \frac{p(y|x)p(x)}{p(y)} \tag{9.1}$$

where $p(x)$ is the prior distribution, usually based on the underlying urban dynamical model and previous measurements, that amasses the information about the state of the system prior to the assimilation of the new observations; $p(y|x)$ is the likelihood of data conditioning on the state x, i.e. the observations given the true state and $p(y)$ is the normalization factor which is the marginal distribution of the observation y, that can be dropped without affecting our calculation. Therefore, we have

$$p(x|y) \propto p(y|x)p(x) \tag{9.2}$$

Using the above Bayesian estimation rule, the idea is to iteratively update the state estimate x using observation y in the designated time domain $[0, T]$. This forms the basis for the construction of KF and many other data assimilation methods. The KF itself is a recursive Bayesian filter.

9.2.2 Kalman Filter for Data Assimilation

Taking the urban MAS described in Eq. (7.6) as an example, for each agent in the MAS at time $k \in [1, \mathrm{K}]$, it runs its own KF to estimate its state using local observations and exchanges estimates and measurements with other agents through some communication protocol over a network topology to enhance estimation accuracy for the overall system. By taking into consideration disturbance/noise in system/process estimation and measurement, each agent takes on the following time-invariant system in matrix form

$$\begin{aligned} \dot{\boldsymbol{x}} &= \boldsymbol{A}\boldsymbol{x}_{k-1} + \boldsymbol{B}\boldsymbol{u}_{k-1} + \omega_{k-1} \\ \boldsymbol{y}_k &= \boldsymbol{C}\boldsymbol{x}_k + \nu_k \end{aligned} \tag{9.3}$$

where $\boldsymbol{A}$ is the state transition matrix/process model; $\boldsymbol{B}$ is the input matrix; $\boldsymbol{C}$ is the measurement matrix that maps the measurements to the state; $\boldsymbol{x}_k$ is the state of the system at time k; $\boldsymbol{u}_k$ and $\boldsymbol{y}_k$ are the input/control and observation (can be measurements from sensors) at time k, respectively; and ω and ν are the process and measurement noise, respectively, which are Gaussian with

$$\omega_k \sim N(0, \boldsymbol{Q});\ \nu_k \sim N(0, \boldsymbol{R})$$

where $\boldsymbol{Q}$ and $\boldsymbol{R}$ are symmetric covariance matrices of the process/state transition noise and the measurement noise, respectively.

If $\boldsymbol{A}$, $\boldsymbol{B}$, and $\boldsymbol{C}$ vary over time, we have

$$\begin{aligned} \dot{\boldsymbol{x}} &= \boldsymbol{A}_{k-1}\boldsymbol{x}_{k-1} + \boldsymbol{B}_{k-1}\boldsymbol{u}_{k-1} + \omega_{k-1} \\ \boldsymbol{y}_k &= \boldsymbol{C}_k\boldsymbol{x}_k + \nu_k \end{aligned} \tag{9.4}$$

For simplicity and without loss of generality, we keep them constant in our following discussion. The KF procedure for state estimation consists of two main steps. Specifically, it takes a probabilistic estimate of the state of the system and updates it over time using two steps: prediction step and update/estimation step.

Prediction step:

$$\begin{aligned} \tilde{\boldsymbol{x}}_k^- &= \boldsymbol{A}\tilde{\boldsymbol{x}}_{k-1} + \boldsymbol{B}\boldsymbol{u}_{k-1} \\ \boldsymbol{P}_k^- &= \boldsymbol{A}P_{k-1}\boldsymbol{A}^T + \boldsymbol{Q}_{k-1} \end{aligned} \tag{9.5}$$

Here, $\boldsymbol{x}_k$ is the system state at time k which is Gaussian: $\boldsymbol{x}_k \sim N(\tilde{\boldsymbol{x}}_k, \boldsymbol{P}_k)$, $\boldsymbol{P}_k$ is the error covariance. The superscript "-" in $\tilde{\boldsymbol{x}}_k^-$ and $\boldsymbol{P}_k^-$ means before the current measurements are taken. This step comes before the update/estimation step. We take whatever prior estimate we have about the state of the system to predict the state at the next time step through the dynamical model.

Update/Estimation step:

$$\begin{aligned} \tilde{\boldsymbol{x}}_k &= \tilde{\boldsymbol{x}}_k^- + \mathbf{K}_k\left(\boldsymbol{y}_k - \boldsymbol{C}\tilde{\boldsymbol{x}}_k^-\right) \\ \boldsymbol{P}_k &= (I - \mathbf{K}_k\boldsymbol{C})\boldsymbol{P}_k^- \end{aligned} \tag{9.6}$$

where $\tilde{\boldsymbol{x}}_k$ and $\boldsymbol{P}_k$ are estimates of the state and error covariance by employing all measurements up to k, respectively. Here, $\mathbf{K}_k$ is the Kalman gain—which is updated at each time step k that minimizes the error covariance $\boldsymbol{P}_k$: $E\left[(\boldsymbol{x} - \tilde{\boldsymbol{x}})^2\right] = E\left[(\boldsymbol{x} - \tilde{\boldsymbol{x}})^T(\boldsymbol{x} - \tilde{\boldsymbol{x}})\right]$, a measure of the inaccuracy of the state estimate—obtained as

$$\mathbf{K}_k = \boldsymbol{P}_k^-\boldsymbol{C}^T\left(\boldsymbol{C}\boldsymbol{P}_k^-\boldsymbol{C}^T + \boldsymbol{R}\right)^{-1} \tag{9.7}$$

In this step, we take the predicted state and the covariance matrix of the noise, together with the new measurement about the system, to make the composite probabilistic estimate $\tilde{\boldsymbol{x}}_k$ of the system state $\boldsymbol{x}_k$ by updating/correcting the predicted state $\tilde{\boldsymbol{x}}_k^-$ with the term $\mathbf{K}_k\left(\boldsymbol{y}_k - \boldsymbol{C}\tilde{\boldsymbol{x}}_k^-\right)$, often called the innovation term with the Kalman gain $\mathbf{K}_k$.

The Kalman gain is physically the weight given to the measurements and the current state estimate. More weight will be given to the most recent measurements for a high gain, and, on the contrary, to the model predictions for a low gain. It should be noted that for real-time data assimilation in fast dynamics, because of the Markovian nature of KF, we can use only the previous state (without history) and the current measurements together with the associated uncertainty to update our estimation and improve the accuracy. Figure 9.2 depicts the procedure of state estimation of dynamical systems via the Kalman filter procedure.

To cast KF against the Bayesian estimation framework in Eq. (9.2), we can express it as

$$p\left(\boldsymbol{x}_k|\boldsymbol{y}_k\right) \propto p\left(\boldsymbol{y}_k|\boldsymbol{x}_k\right)p\left(\boldsymbol{x}_k|\boldsymbol{y}_{k-1}\right) \tag{9.8}$$

where the prior $p\left(\boldsymbol{x}_k|\boldsymbol{y}_{k-1}\right)$, a Gaussian, comes from the prediction step, and the posterior $p\left(\boldsymbol{x}_k|\boldsymbol{y}_k\right)$, a Gaussian, comes from the update step discussed above, and the likelihood, $p\left(\boldsymbol{y}_k|\boldsymbol{x}_k\right)$, a Gaussian also.

The standard KF may not perform well under nonlinearity, particularly for highly nonlinear dynamical systems taking the following general form

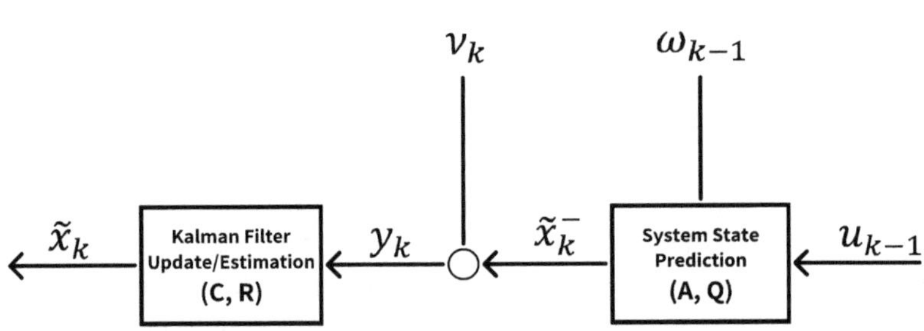

Fig. 9.2 Kalman filtering for state estimation of dynamical systems

$$
\begin{aligned}
\boldsymbol{x}_k &= f(\boldsymbol{x}_{k-1}, \boldsymbol{u}_k) + \omega_k \\
\boldsymbol{y}_k &= g(\boldsymbol{x}_k) + \nu_k
\end{aligned} \tag{9.9}
$$

where $\boldsymbol{x}$, $\boldsymbol{u}$, and $\boldsymbol{y}$ are state, input, and output vectors, respectively; f and g are nonlinear state and observation functions, respectively; and ω_k and ν_k are process and measurement noise, respectively. Data assimilation involving nonlinear filtering can be done via the extended KF which operates in the information domain and minimizes the system dynamics and measurement models via Tayor series expansion around current state estimate and covariance. In the discussion of urban dynamics in Chapter 7, cooperation is a common communication protocol in MAS to better estimate the global state of the system.

For a MAS of N agents, the discrete-time version of Eq. (9.9) for agent i becomes (Wang et al., 2021)

$$
\begin{aligned}
\boldsymbol{x}_k^i &= f_k^i\left(\boldsymbol{x}_{k-1}^i, \boldsymbol{u}_{k-1}^i\right) + \omega_{k-1}^i, \quad i = 1, 2, \ldots, N \\
\boldsymbol{y}_k^i &= g_k^i\left(\boldsymbol{x}_k^i\right) + \nu_k^i, \quad i = 1, 2, \ldots, N
\end{aligned} \tag{9.10}
$$

Through communication, when agent i receives relative measurement from agent j, $\boldsymbol{y}_k^i$ in (9.10) becomes

$$
\boldsymbol{y}_k^{ij} = g_k^{ij}\left(\boldsymbol{x}_k^i, \boldsymbol{x}_k^j\right) + \nu_k^{ij} \tag{9.11}
$$

where ν_k^i and ν_k^{ij} are the measurement noise vectors with covariance matrices $\boldsymbol{R}_k^i$ and $\boldsymbol{R}_k^{ij}$, respectively (Wang et al., 2021).

By stacking the vectors $\boldsymbol{x}_k^i$, $i = 1,2,\ldots,N$, into an augmented vector $\boldsymbol{x}_k^a$, and the measurement vectors $\boldsymbol{y}_k^i$ into $\boldsymbol{y}_k^a$ that includes all inter-agent information (the superscript "a" means "augmented"), the cooperative MAS can be expressed as

$$
\begin{aligned}
\dot{\boldsymbol{x}}^a &= \boldsymbol{A}\boldsymbol{x}_{k-1}^a + \boldsymbol{B}\boldsymbol{u}_{k-1}^a + \omega_{k-1}^a \\
\boldsymbol{y}_k^a &= \boldsymbol{C}\boldsymbol{x}_k^a + \nu_k^a
\end{aligned} \tag{9.12}
$$

Then, we can perform data assimilation with appropriate KF. By exchanging and synchronizing state estimates and measurements recursively, the MAS can improve overall estimation accuracy by fusing information and building consensus discussed in Chapter 7.

Over the years, many KF variants have been developed to perform data assimilation under various situations of the underlying dynamics, discrete or continuous. Further reviews can be found in Carrassi et el. (2018) and Khodarahmi and Maihami (2023). Besides KF, other techniques like the variational method (Sasai, 1970) which estimates the system trajectory that best fits all observations available within a designated time domain can be employed for data assimilation. Therefore, model-data interoperability can be materialized in digital twins of cities by using appropriate data assimilation methods.

In general, in data assimilation for prediction in dynamical systems, we solve the following problem

$$\hat{\boldsymbol{x}} = \boldsymbol{x}_0 + K(\boldsymbol{y} - \boldsymbol{x}_0) \tag{9.13}$$

where $\hat{\boldsymbol{x}}$ is the assimilated solution of the dynamical system; $\boldsymbol{x}_0$ is the model prediction without the observations/measurements $\boldsymbol{y}$; and $K(\boldsymbol{y} - \boldsymbol{x}_0)$ is the innovation in which K is the Kalman gain. To take time in explicitly, we have

$$\hat{\boldsymbol{x}}_k = \boldsymbol{x}_{0,k} + K_k\left(\boldsymbol{y}_k - \boldsymbol{C}\boldsymbol{x}_{0,k}\right) \tag{9.14}$$

where K_k takes on the form in Eq. (9.7), and the corresponding covariance $\boldsymbol{P}_k$ takes on the form in Eq. (9.6).

Without further elaboration, for continuous time, Eq. (9.3) becomes

$$\begin{aligned}\dot{\boldsymbol{x}}(t) &= \boldsymbol{A}(t)\boldsymbol{x}(t) + \boldsymbol{B}(t)\boldsymbol{u}(t) + \omega(t)\\ \boldsymbol{y}(t) &= \boldsymbol{C}(t)\boldsymbol{x}(t) + \nu(t)\end{aligned} \tag{9.15}$$

Remark. Though Kalman filter is a powerful data assimilation method for estimating system states through recursive model-data interoperation, it is targeted at linear dynamical systems which may not converge for nonlinear dynamics. More complicated KF variants may be necessary to satisfactorily estimate system states under nonlinearity. Furthermore, its Gaussian noise assumption on model noise and measurement noise may not be appropriate for some real-life systems embedded with non-Gaussian and non-independently and non-identically distributed complex noise, particularly in multi-sensor and multi-view subspace learning (Yue et al., 2020). It will be useful to develop more robust methods for data assimilation in highly nonlinear dynamical complex systems with complex noise.

9.3 Interoperability Between Models and Data in the Inverse Mapping Problem

As discussed above, dynamical models play an important role in designing an optimal sensor placement strategy to collect system states in the right place at the right time. Knowing the underlying dynamics will inform us about the optimal placement of sensors, the number of sensors, the sensor coverage map, and the response time for fast and slow dynamics (Fontanini et al., 2016). Based on the cityCFD discussed in Sect. 5.4 of Chapter 5, for example, we can devise a suitable sensor placement strategy to collect information about the dynamics of microclimates of a built environment, indoor pollution of a building, and outdoor air pollution of a city according to the dynamics of the airflow vector field in the entire domain. For instance, sensors should be placed near regions with low air speed, and regions in which buoyancy dominates the airflow field are harder to sense than regions with higher Reynolds numbers and inertial driven airflow. With appropriate sensor placement strategy in terms of sensor location, response time, and necessary number of sensors, we can get a better understanding and monitoring of the dynamics and formulate suitable strategies in case of emergency (Fontanini et al., 2016).

To create and update data-driven digital twins more efficiently, Kapteyn et al. (2020) developed a methodology that uses a library of component-based ROMs and interpretable optimal decision tree for digital-twin construction. The component-based models can scale to large and complex systems and the library such constructed can generate a dataset containing predicted observations under a large variety of system states in the state space. In their study, sensors were used to detect conditions of the physical asset/system, and in combination with the optimal decision tree (Bertsimas and Dunn, 2017), to efficiently estimate the best-fit model and update the digital twin. The model can identify the region of the input/data space where knowing the model results will be most beneficial to improve the accuracy and applicability of the digital twin. The methodology is a tell-tale realization of the function of model-data synchronization that makes dynamical models data-driven and data model-informed so that the digital twin can be dynamically evolved with respect to changing system conditions.

Within their framework (Kapteyn et al., 2020), the digital twin, d_t, at time t is defined by the following equation

$$d_t = T\left(\widetilde{\boldsymbol{x}}_t\right) \in \mathbf{M} \tag{9.16}$$

where $\widetilde{\boldsymbol{x}}_t$ *is* the set of observations of the physical asset at time t; $\mathbf{M}$ is the physics-based model library capturing a range of possible states of the physical system expressed via parametric ROM derived by a parametric component-based model reduction method (Huynh et al., 2013); and T is the data-driven model selector that is learned from the data set by some machine-learning methods—the optimal classification tree in this case (see Leung 2010) for a brief discussion on classification tree). In brief, the model selection attempts to solve the following inverse mapping problem

$$T : \mathbf{X} \rightarrow \mathbf{M} \tag{9.17}$$

The model selector T—the optimal classification tree that incorporates optimal feature/sensor selection—is trained by sampling on the following forward mapping

$$F : \mathbf{M} \rightarrow \mathbf{X} \tag{9.18}$$

to generate the dataset $\left\{\left(\boldsymbol{x}_{j,}\mathbf{M}_j\right), j = 1, \ldots, |\mathbf{M}|\right\}$, $\left|\mathbf{M}_j\right|$ being the cardinality of the model library $\mathbf{M}$ containing the ROM, $\mathbf{M}_j, j = 1, \ldots, |\mathbf{M}|$, where the parameterized model $\mathbf{M}_j \in \mathbf{M}$ is evaluated to predict the data $\boldsymbol{x}_j$. Under noisy observations, the inverse mapping problem can be defined as

$$\tilde{F} = \mathbf{M} \times V \rightarrow \mathbf{X} \tag{9.19}$$

where V is the space of possible noise due to, for example, sensor noise or observational measurement errors (see Sect. 10.3 of Chapter 10 for a discussion on measurement errors). The noise coming from a sensor is assumed to be an additive Gaussian noise with known bias and covariance. The resulting dataset is $\left\{(\boldsymbol{x}_j^k, \mathbf{M}_j), j = 1, \ldots, |\mathbf{M}|; k = 1, \ldots, s\right\}$, s being the number of noisy samples. All the datapoints are then vertically stacked together to form a matrix representation $(\mathbf{X}, \mathbf{M})$ which is used to learn the inverse mapping T via the following optimization problem

$$\min_{T} R(T) + \alpha|T| \tag{9.20}$$

where T is the classification tree; R (T) is the classification error of the tree; $|T|$ is the complexity of the tree measured by the number of splits; and α is the complexity parameter balancing the trade-off between accuracy and complexity. The predictions made by such an optimal classification tree are interpretable and is embedded with optimal selection of features or sensors contributing to a decision. Furthermore, it can shed light on the design of sensor network for optimal sensor placement and scheduling (see Sect. 10.2 of Chapter 10 for a discussion on sensor networks). As a result, the digital twin can be dynamically updated from new observations/an enriched library, with the possibility to extrapolate system states to unseen situations. Such an approach can be extended to manage digital twins of similar assets—like a fleet of vehicles, a cluster of rooms in a building, a cluster of similar buildings in a built environment, and a cluster of urban entities, etc.

9.4 Interoperability Between Dynamical Models and Time Series Data

As previously discussed, data-driven learning of dynamical models from time series data plays an important role in building digital twins of cities. On the other hand, the theory of nonlinear dynamical systems provides new concepts and methods for the characterization of time series data, particularly irregular time series. The analysis of time series from the perspective of nonlinear dynamics in which non-stationarity, chaos, and multifractality play a key role is a typical example. Therefore, the interoperability between theories and data are key to the study of city dynamics and complexity via digital twins of cities. Since the construction of ROMs for time-dependent dynamics hinges on the snapshots obtained from the data generated by discretized high-dimensional models if the underlying governing equations are known or assumed, as discussed in Chapter 3, the nature and accuracy of the snapshots of temporal dynamics are of great importance. The successful detection of long-range dependence or chaotic behavior in time series is of particular importance in employing LSTM and ROM to build digital twins of cities. For example, if we take snapshots of the time series of a chaotic system with intervals of various lengths, their behaviors should be similar across these intervals/scales. Sometimes, we do not even know the governing equations but just the historical observations over time generated by some unknown underlying dynamic processes. To come up with a simpler and more revealing model, we need to take the time series into consideration and try to unravel the hidden dynamics leading to such empirical expressions. In data assimilation, for instance, we need a time series archive for reanalysis and model updating. Therefore, we should collect and examine time series data from the perspective of dynamical systems.

9.4.1 Identifying characteristics of time series by empirical mode decomposition for learning underlying dynamics

Empirical mode decomposition (Huang et al., 1998) is an efficient and adaptive data-driven method for iteratively decomposing a non-stationary and nonlinear time series into a finite set of amplitude and/or frequency modulated components—coined the intrinsic mode functions (IMFs)/the EMD components—which represent oscillatory modes at different scales in the system-state space. It does not impose any requirement on the basis function, stationarity, or linearity assumptions about the time series. The IMFs are obtained through an iterative sifting process based on the local extrema of the time series. In brief, the sifting process first creates an envelope by interpolating between the identified local maxima and minima in the time series with a cubic spline. The average envelope is then obtained by calculating the mean of the upper and lower envelopes. By subtracting the mean envelope from the original time series, we obtain the high-frequency components of the time series—the oscillatory mode. We then decide whether it is an IMF. If not, the above steps are repeated iteratively until a stopping criterion is met. An IMF is a function with two properties: (1) the number of extrema differs from that of zero-crossings by no more than one, and (2) the envelop of either the local maxima or local minima has zero mean. If yes, we subtract the first IMF from the original time series. The residual time series represents a part of the signal which is oscillatory with a characteristic frequency and is treated as a new time series. The above sifting process is then applied to it to unravel the next IMF. The sifting process is repeated iteratively until all IMFs are unraveled. Thus, the EMD decomposes a time series into a finite number of IMFs capturing different oscillatory modes in the time series. Because of noise in the observational data, the state space representation might be corrupted. EMD gives a natural and empirical way to filter out the noise and generates components of a time series by sifting out rapidly oscillating components from the time series through iterative subtraction of slowly oscillating components. Though the sifting process is purely algorithmic, it is shown that it can be made partial-differential-equation-based by taking the function of a selective signal smoothing process (Niang et al., 2012).

The sifting procedure decomposes a complicated series into a finite and usually small number of IMFs, some with physical meanings (Zhou et al., 2012). The number of IMFs determines the dimensionality that is most appropriate to represent the data in reconstructing the state space. As a result, a time series **X** (t) can be decomposed as follows

$$\mathbf{X}(t) = \sum_{j=1}^{k} IMF_j + r_k \tag{9.21}$$

where r_k is the residue of the sifting process generating the k IMFs, indicating that no more IMFs can be extracted from the time series. Zhou and Leung (2010a), for example, employed EMD as a pre-detrending procedure to study sunspot cycles from sunspot series during the period 1749–2009 (Fig. 9.3) by extracting all IMFs (Fig. 9.4) and subject them to MFDFA to determine which IMFs carry real physical meanings about cycles of sunspot activities and scaling behaviors of the sunspot time series. We may be able to draw some insights into urban microclimates from the sunspot activity for climate resilient city planning.

Therefore, EMD can be in a way treated as an empirical method, a purely data-driven procedure, for building a ROM of the original data series that can be subjected to machine learning of the underlying dynamics. The IMFs can be considered as modes in a certain sense because they capture specific oscillatory behaviors with

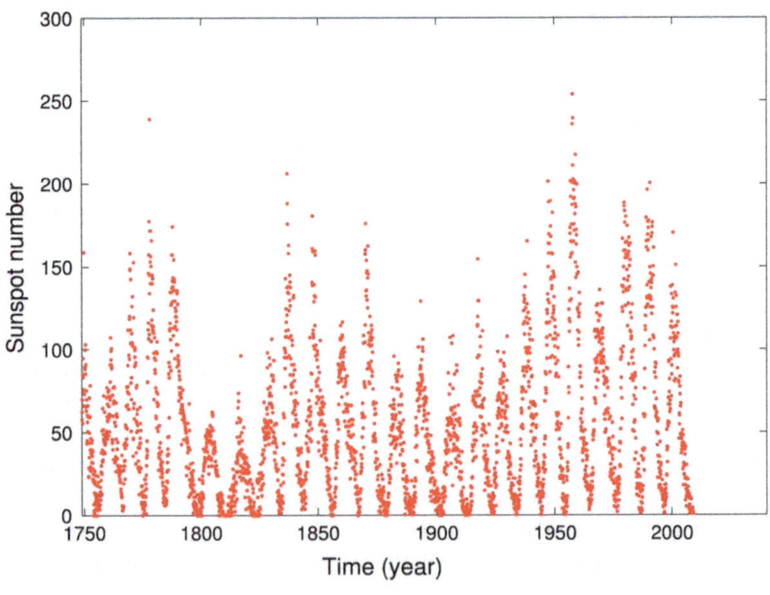

Fig. 9.3 The monthly sunspot time series, 1750–2009 (adopted from Zhou and Leung (2010a))

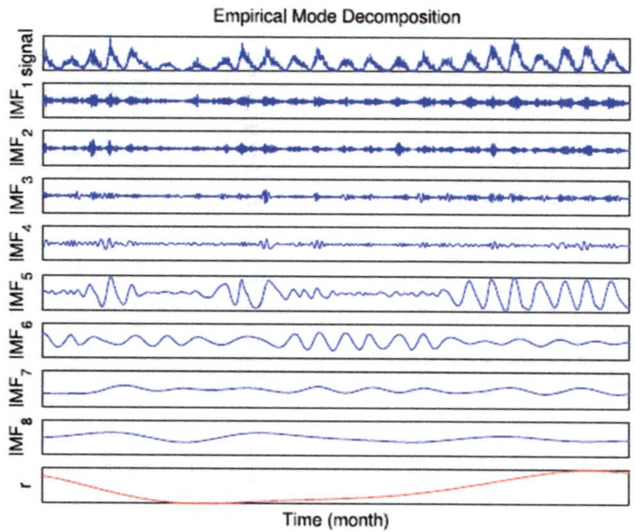

IMF	Corresponding period
IMF_2	the 153-day cycle of γ-ray flares and interplanetary magnetic fields
IMF_3 and IMF_4	the periods of 1.3–1.4 years, quasi-biennial oscillation
IMF_5 and IMF_6	the 11-year cycle
IMF_6	the Hale period
IMF_7	the double Hale period
IMF_8	the Gleissberg period

Fig. 9.4 Results of the empirical mode decomposition (EMD) of the original sunspot series (adopted and derived from Zhou and Leung (2010a))

physical meanings in the time series. By combining the IMFs, such as Eq. (9.21), we can reconstruct the original time series and analyze its characteristics at various scales and frequencies.

To mitigate the mode-mixing problem arising from the EMD procedure and to improve the physical significance of the modes, the ensemble EMD (EEMD) (Wu and Huang, 2009), involving multiple decompositions which add a white noise series to a time series such that a series—of a similar scale in a noisy data set is contained in one IMF—can be used to extract the EEMD IMFs with physical meanings in, for example, the concentration of PM2.5 in cities (Fig. 9.5) (Leung et al., 2019). The ensemble averaging procedure alleviates the impact of noise and enhances the stability and reliability of the IMFs across different realizations.

Remark. It should, however, be noted that the IMFs are not orthogonal or linearly independent, so they do not form a basis in the conventional and strict sense. The reconstructed time series may not be identical to the original time series because the IMFs are not orthogonal, and they may not capture all the minute details of the original noisy time series. Furthermore, the residual component may contain nuances of the original time series the IMFs fail to account for. We can assess the accuracy of EMD by examining the difference between the EMD-reconstructed time series with the original time series by metrics like MSE or correlation coefficients. To improve the accuracy of EMD, we can preprocess the time series data by reducing noise with some filtering methods before decomposition. To increase its stability and reliability, cross-validation methods can be applied to the time series data of various compositions. We can employ EMD to decompose a time series into IMFs and then apply MFDFA to study the impact of periodic and quasi-periodic trends on long-range correlation and multifractality embedded in time series data (Zhou and Leung, 2010b). These are useful information that can provide insights into the underlying dynamics of complex urban systems whose governing mechanisms—e.g. governing equations—are to be uncovered by learning methods discussed in this book. Knowing the system dynamics, on the other hand, will inform us on what to look for and measure in empirical time series to facilitate the identification of relevant governing mechanisms.

9.4.2 EMD and LSTM for Data-Driven Learning of Urban Dynamics

Besides the oscillatory modes, we may also want to detect whether the components are highly correlated—i.e. whether the series is long-range correlated—to give more information about the underlying dynamics embedded in time series. Leung et al. (2019) employed DFA (Peng et al., 1994) to detect autocorrelation in the underlying dynamics of a process. Given a time series, if the sum of autocorrelation $C(\tau)$ with time lag τ ranging from a finite value to infinity diverges, then the corresponding

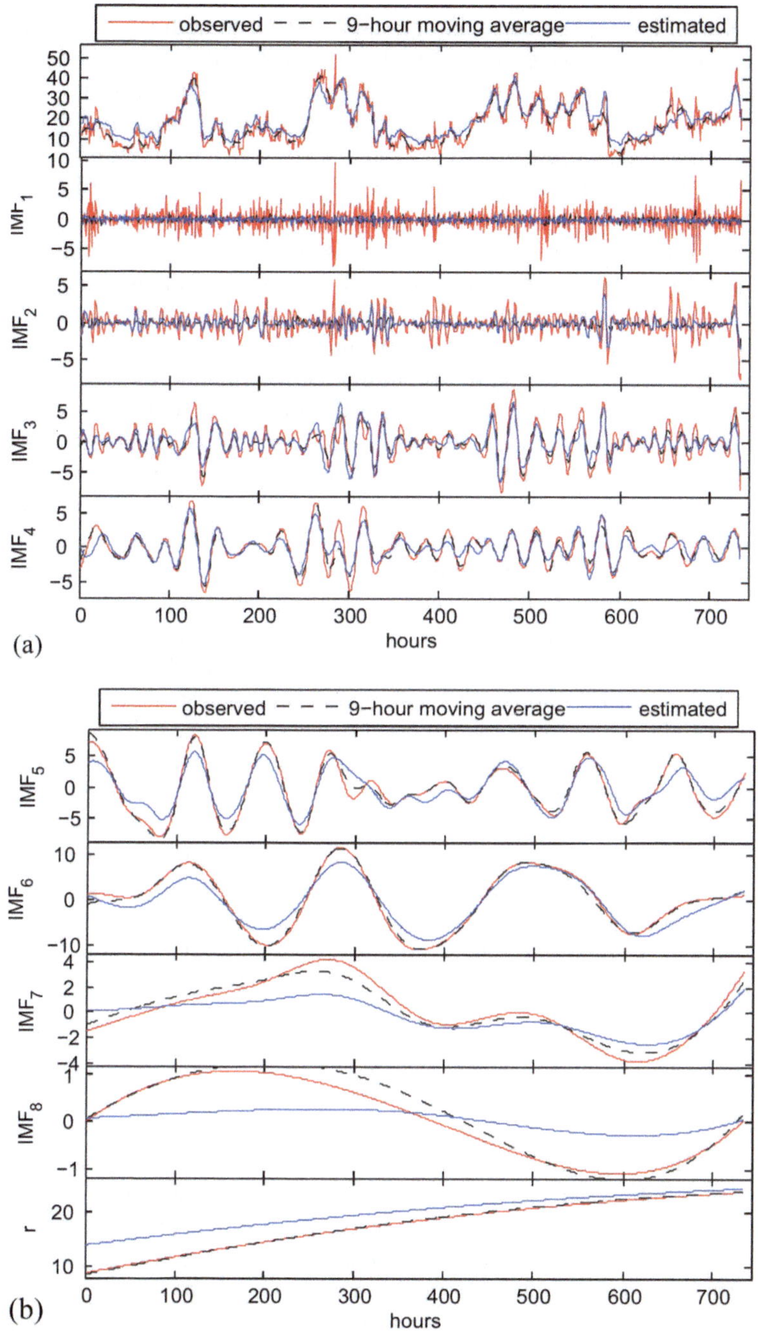

Fig. 9.5 The original series (a) and its EEMD components (b) of the observed, 9-h moving average, and estimated PM2.5 values at the Daemyeong district station in July 2017 (adopted from Leung et al. (2019))

process is with long-range correlation (Beran, 1994). In addition to the similarity detection of empirical modes, the DFA scaling behavior of the estimated series should also be close to that of the observed series if the two-step local regression estimation is appropriate (Leung et al., 2019). Such estimated series can characterize the observed data at different time scales—e.g. daily and weekly scales with respect to the EMD components and long-range correlation. The series can then be used to build the LSTM-ROM.

Since air pollutant concentration varies in space and time, modeling air quality with an adaptive utilization of spatiotemporal information from multiple air quality monitoring stations under a multiscale framework is thus crucial in building the corresponding digital twin. Without knowing the underlying dynamics, it is necessary to decompose the given series and to fuse multi-site information for its discovery. Shi et al. (2024) proposed a novel multiscale and multi-site modeling method, named the multivariate empirical mode decomposition and spatial cosine-attention-based long short-term memory (MEMD-SCA-LSTM), which first employs the MEMD to decompose the multi-site air quality series into the scale-aligned components and then models the components at different scales. The high-frequency components are modeled by a SCA-LSTM, which employs LSTM with residual blocks to extract the temporal information and utilizes a cosine-similarity attention mechanism to adaptively extract interactions among different sites; other relatively regular components are modeled by the LSTM. Figure 9.6 is the general framework of the MEMD-SCA-LSTM which adaptively utilizes spatiotemporal information about air pollution at multiple spatial sites and multiple temporal scales (Shi et al., 2024).

In brief, the multiscale framework contains two key constituent procedures: (1) decomposing the given series by MEMD and (2) modeling the individual components by SCA_LSTM. In decomposition, MEMD is used to catch the multiscale relationship at S stations to extract N groups of the matched common modes at the aligned temporal scales. Let $\mathbf{X} \epsilon \mathbb{R}^{T \times S} = [\boldsymbol{x}_1, \boldsymbol{x}_2, \ldots, \boldsymbol{x}_s]$ be the series of S stations, where $\mathbf{X}_i \in \mathbb{R}^T$ is a column vector representing the air pollution series at the i-th station. The series $\mathbf{X}$ is decomposed into N groups of the matched common components/modes $\boldsymbol{C}^{\mathrm{i}} \in \mathbb{R}^{T \times S}$ at the aligned temporal scales. We obtain

$$\mathbf{X} = \sum_{i=1}^{N} \boldsymbol{C}^i \tag{9.22}$$

Generally, MEMD adopts a concept of multivariate joint oscillation and directly processes the input series in a multidimensional domain by taking projections along different directions in the S-dimensional space. The resultant components/modes are jointly, synchronously, and coherently captured to guarantee the aligned temporal scales of the matched components/modes in the same group.

Typically, the low frequency components obtained by MEMD are smoother and more regular, and hence easier to model compared to the high-frequency components. Shi et al. (2024) used LSTM to model the low frequency components. For the more complex high-frequency components, they proposed the SCA-LSTM based

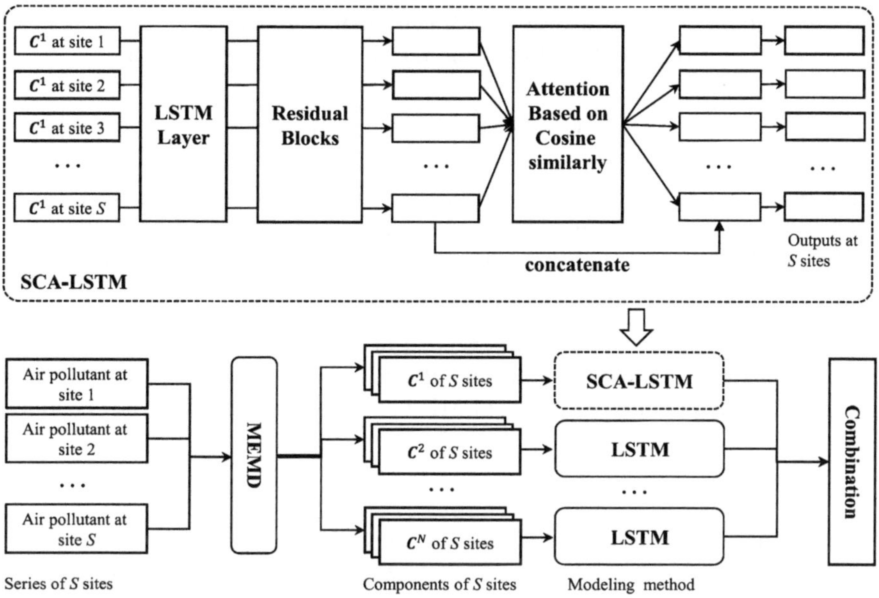

Fig. 9.6 The general framework of the multi-site and multi-time MEMD-SCA-LSTM for modeling city air pollution (adopted from Shi et al. (2024))

on the SA-LSTM, which uses the SA mechanism to fuse the multi-site information. Different from the canonical attention mechanism used in the SA-LSTM, they proposed a novel attention mechanism based on the cosine similarity between features at different sites, called spatial cosine-attention-based LSTM (SCA-LSTM). Because of its ability to handle long-term dependency of historical time series, the LSTM layer is used to extract the temporal feature of the individual MEMD components/modes. Accordingly, S LSTMs are used to model the temporal variations of each MEMD component/mode at the S stations. After the LSTM layer, three residual blocks are added to enrich the representational information. These residual blocks utilize short-cut connections with identified mappings to tackle the issue of degradation in training deep neural networks (He et al., 2016). In their study of $PM_{2.5}$ concentration in a city (Shi et al., 2024), each residual block consists of two linear projection layers and one short-cut connection, which is applied to each station separately and identically. The output of a residual block, R, is

$$\tilde{\mathbf{h}}_s = R(\mathbf{h}_s) = \mathbf{h}_s + f(\mathbf{h}_s) = \mathbf{W}_2\sigma(\mathbf{W}_1\mathbf{h}_s + \mathbf{b}_1) + \mathbf{b}_2 \tag{9.23}$$

where $\mathbf{h}_s$ is the output hidden state of the s-th LSTM; f is a feedforward neural network; σ is the ReLU activation function; $\mathbf{W}_2$ and $\mathbf{W}_1$ are the respective connection weight matrices; and $\mathbf{b}_1$ *and* $\mathbf{b}_2$ are the corresponding bias vectors. The three residual blocks are stacked consecutively on each $\mathbf{h}_s$. By concatenating the feature vector $\widetilde{\mathbf{h}}_s$ with the spatial attention mechanism $Att(\mathbf{h}_s)$, we can use a fully connected layer to obtain the output of the fusion module at station s, $1 \le s \le S$ as

$$y_s = \mathbf{W}\left[\widetilde{\mathbf{h}}_s, Att\left(\widetilde{\mathbf{h}}_s\right)\right] + \mathbf{b} \tag{9.24}$$

where **W** is the connection weight matrix of the fully connected layer which is kept the same for each state and site, and **b** is the bias term. Therefore, the MEMD-CSA-LSTM can shed light on the multi-site and multiscale spatiotemporal dynamics of air pollution of a city.

Remark. In EMD, more research is needed in the correct handling of the mode-mixing problems, mitigation of boundary effects, robustness to noise, and automatic selection of hyperparameters to make EMD-based learning effective and accurate.

9.4.3 Obtaining Model-Informed Time Series for the Learning of Dynamical Complex Urban Systems

Though Park et al. (2022) have shown the efficacy of EMD in recovering the chaotic dynamics of the Rossler attractor—a system of three parameterized nonlinear ordinary differential equations—and extreme hyper salinity events associated with ecological collapse from noisy data, EMD in general cannot be used to learn directly the governing equations of dynamical systems. However, it can provide valuable information to learn the underlying dynamics and the associated ROMs. With the IMFs, we can, for example, apply the phase reconstruction techniques discussed in Sect. 4.6 of Chapter 4 to obtain the RPS from which we can apply methods discussed in Chapters 3 to 5 to learn the underlying dynamics and the associated ROMs. When the governing equations of the dynamics of a complex system is known, for instance, the EMD and its variants constructed for various situations—such as those discussed above—can be subjected to low-dimensional manifold learning discussed in Chapter 3 to derive ROMs for complex urban dynamics. When we do not know the explicit description of the underlying dynamics, or we do not even know the governing equations of city evolutions, we can apply the data-driven approaches discussed in Chapter 4 to the EMD results to learn the underlying dynamics and the ROMs. To build urban theories into the EMD-based learning process, we can employ the urban theory-informed neural networks discussed in Chapter 5 to derive interpretable ROMs for highly nonlinear complex urban systems.

Some experimental studies have shown that EMD and its variants are effective in constructing ROMs for capturing dynamics of complex systems. Lee et al. (2010), for example, show that the slow-flow model of a strongly nonlinear aeroelastic response represented as time histories/series can be decomposed into a small number of IMFs via EMD to form a basis for expanding a multicomponent signal in terms of a series of mono-component signals related to the dominant frequency components. This forms a physically meaningful basis for constructing a ROM capable of capturing important interactions between substructures. The MEMD-SCA-LSTM discussed above can thus be employed to construct ROMs for multi-site and multiscale digital twins of dynamic urban systems without the knowledge of the governing equations. It will be interesting to investigate if the performance can be further improved if the recently developed xLSTM (Alharthi and Mahmood, 2024) is adopted to handle time series forecasting. Furthermore, as discussed in Chapter 5, we can make the process theory-informed if we can impose the physics of airflow or turbulence on the MEMD-SCA-LSTM learning so that the unraveled dynamics will respect the theory of chemical transport via atmospheric dispersion modeling—such as the Gaussian dispersion model. The results will then be interpretable, and the model can suggest optimal sensor placement strategy also.

To give another example of model-data interoperation, in the simulation of city microclimates discussed in Sect. 5.4 of Chapter 5, the cityFFD can only simulate the absolute velocity and temperature vector fields. Because of the chaotic behavior of the wind field, we need to obtain training data of dynamic speed and direction for a longer period. Furthermore, data with more morphological parameters such as building size, building density, and spatial layout of buildings need to be generated to enhance the generality of cityFFD. If near real-time or real-time observations can be made, we may be able to further enhance our capability in simulating dynamics and complexity of urban microclimates (Peng et al., 2024). With such feedback mechanism embedded in the interoperation between models and data, we can make our models data-informed/data-driven and our data model-informed in the modeling of city microclimate dynamics and complexity through digital twins of cities.

For further substantiation, urban traffic—particularly in high-density living—is a complex and chaotic system. To mitigate urban traffic congestion and the associated air pollution, successful prediction of the onset of congestion via the identification of emergence of chaotic occurrences between free flow and congestion is of great importance (Narh et al., 2016). However, to identify the emergence of chaos in traffic flow, which can happen within seconds in time and very short distance in space, we need to be able to capture high-resolution spatiotemporal data on the perturbations on links and intersections to employ chaos theory to accurately describe the transient states and asymptotic behavior of traffic flows over the transportation network. Therefore, chaos theory informs us that low-resolution spatiotemporal data are not capable of detecting short-term variability and anomaly of traffic flows caused by the variability of driving behaviors, driver interactions, vehicle speeds, irregular stop and go, roadside parking, loading and unloading, pedestrian crossing, etc., and the necessity of collecting high-resolution data in the right place at the right time via distributive sensors. The availability of high-resolution spatiotemporal data, on the other hand, enables us to employ chaos theory to understand and predict the dynamics of traffic congestion and the evolution of traffic conditions over a transportation network. Such understanding can facilitate us to design an appropriate traffic signal system and other mitigation measures to better prevent chaotic traffic congestion and hopefully guide the system to non-chaotic transition. It is such interoperability between models and data that we need to build into digital twins of urban transportation systems.

9.4.4 *Urban Dynamics Manifested by Long-Range Correlation and Multifractality in Time Series.*

As pointed out in Sect. 7.2 of Chapter 7, time series may be non-stationary exhibiting long-range correlation and multifractality. Knowledge about these features in the time series will help us learn appropriate dynamical models that generate the series. Reciprocally, knowing the dynamical models, we can design appropriate schemes to take observations of the complex non-stationary process. Detrended fluctuation analysis (DFA) is used to detect the presence of long-range correlations in time series. It provides a quantitative measure of the scaling properties of a time series and draws insights into the underlying dynamics and complexity of the system generating the data. In brief, DFA first establishes the profile by removing any trend present in the time series by, for example, fitting a polynomial to the data and subtracting it from the original time series. This establishes the profile for subsequent local detrending. The series is then divided into non-overlapping segments/windows of equal length which determines the range of time scales over which correlations are examined. A least-squares fit—the fitting polynomial can be linear, quadratic, cubic, or of higher order—is then applied to each segment to calculate the local trend. Since detrending is through the subtraction of the polynomial fits from the profile, DFA can use the scaling behavior of different orders with different capabilities in eliminating trends in the time series. The RMS fluctuation/variance is calculated for each segment and averaged over all segments at each time scale. To determine the scaling behavior of the fluctuation function, we plot it as the function of the segment size on a log–log scale and calculate the scaling exponent that indicates the extent of long-range correlation in the time series. When the scaling exponent equals 0.5, it implies that the series is uncorrelated. When it is greater than 0.5 and less than 1, it indicates that the time series has long-range correlation. When it is greater than 0 and less than 0.5, it implies that the series has short memory or long-range anti-correlation. Knowing this will shed light on the underlying system dynamics that generate the data and the way it might be learned.

Sometimes time series may possess multifractal properties with the presence of multiple scaling exponents across different time scales. To uncover multifractality and long-range correlation in non-stationary time series, multifractal detrended fluctuation analysis (MFDFA) (Kantelhardt et al. 2002)—the generalization DFA—has been proposed to identify long-range correlation and crossover time scales that separate different behavioral regimes embedded in time series. The procedure is essentially the same as DFA with the exception that the fluctuations are averaged over all segments (Fig. 9.7) to obtain the q-th order fluctuation function, and we are interested in how the generalized q-dependent fluctuation functions depend on the time scale for different values of q. All steps leading up to the averaging step must be repeated for several time scales. Subsequently the scaling behavior of the fluctuation functions is determined by analyzing the log–log plot of the q-th order fluctuation function against the segment length for each value of q. The generalized Hurst exponent is then calculated with interpretations parallel to that of the DFA. MFDFA has been applied to study the temporal scaling behavior of avian influenza A in cities (Leung et al., 2011), and a formal statistical procedure has been developed to detect crossover time scales in MFDFA (Ge and Leung, 2012). In time series, points near in time are generally more related than points some distance apart. Based on this rationale, multifractal temporally weighted detrended fluctuation analysis was proposed by Zhou and Leung (2010b) to analyze the scaling behavior of time series by incorporating temporal weighting to MFDFA, making it more sensitive to local fluctuations and crossover timescales. The ideas of moving windows and weighted moving windows are proposed for smoothing the log–log plot of the fluctuation function against the time scale so that local effects can be taken into consideration and crossover timescales, particularly large timescales, can be effectively detected. This also improve intelligibility and provides a basis for model editing discussed in Sect. 4. 8 of Chapter 4.

Remark. It is worth noting that DFA and MFDFA are basically used to characterize the scaling properties and/or multifractality of time series. They are not intended

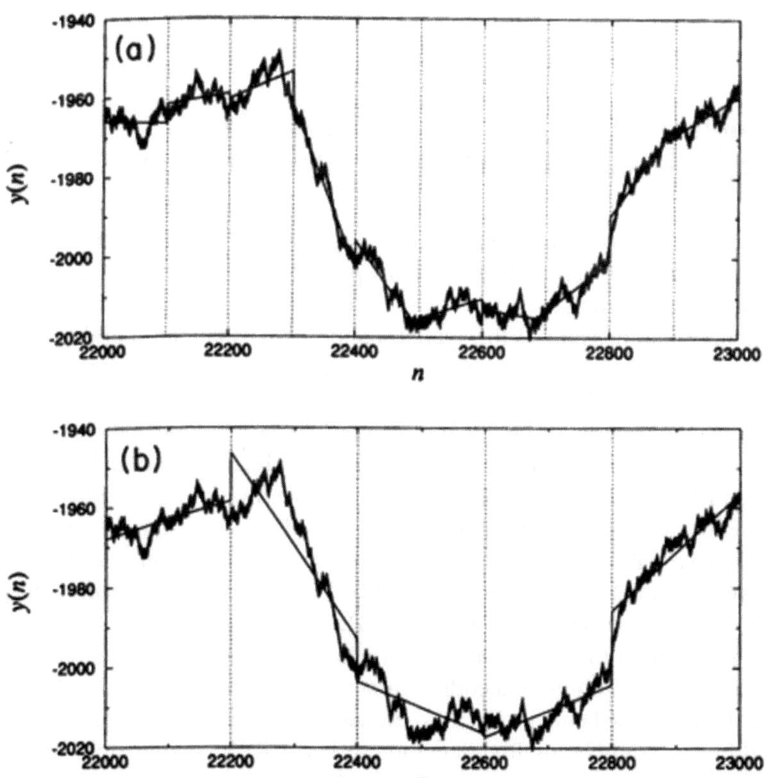

Fig. 9.7 Schematic illustration of multifractal detrended fluctuation analysis (MFDFA) with selected scales (**a**) box size 100 (**b**) box size 200, with within box least-squares fits (adopted from Peng et al. (1994))

for the learning of governing equations of system dynamics and the ROMS derived from them. However, these scaling behaviors/features can provide useful parameters for informing the selection of model structures to capture long-range correlations, multifractality, and phase space transition in time series and the derivation of ROMs of the underlying chaotic dynamics. To improve the estimation of the scaling exponent in DFA and MFDFA, adaptive segmenting/windowing of time series according to local properties will be useful to accurately capture the scaling behavior (Zhou and Leung, 2010b). More research is needed for further improvement. It is worth mentioning that both methods are sensitive to noise and outliers. Robust denoising methods will be useful for accurate detrending. Interoperability between dynamical models and DFA/MFDFA should be thoroughly investigated to facilitate mutual enhancement. In general, EMD, DFA, and MFDFA can provide insights into the underlying structure, correlations, and complexity of the data, facilitating our uncovering of the most appropriate dynamical model that generates the scaling behavior exhibited in the time series. Through data assimilation, the model can be updated and improved by current time series observations, and the power of predicting future trends and patterns can be enhanced by the constantly updated model.

9.5 Nonlinear Dynamics and Nonlinear Time Series—Issues in Model-Data Interoperability

To sum up, with respect to the interoperability between models and data, theories and models of dynamical complex systems provide a basis for the characterization of time series via characteristic features—for instance, in terms of dimension (to find the support of the measure of the spatial, temporal, or spatiotemporal process, e.g. correlation dimension to characterize self-similarity of a fractal process), Lyapunov exponents (to identify chaos), recurrence plot (to identify transience/non-transience), intermittency (to describe irregular alternations between chaotic and periodic behaviors, e.g. a spiky distribution generated by the multiplicative binomial cascade often exhibited in rainfall intensity and air pollutant concentration time series (Anh et al. (2005)), entropy (to measure the amount of disorder in a system/amount of information in a probability distribution of a time series), short-range and long-range correlations (to reflect scaling laws), DFA (to reveal mono-fractal scaling properties and long-range power-law correlation), MFDFA (to account for multifractality and long-range correlation), etc. And they inform how data should be observed/collected/measured in time and how embedding dimension and time delay should be determined so that specific behaviors of a dynamical system can be correctly captured and reflected in, for example, multivariate time series or RPS via time delay embedding discussed in Sect. 4.6 of Chapter 4, and snapshots for learning.

The correspondence between nonlinear dynamics and nonlinear time series plays an important role in this model-data interoperation (Tong, 1990; Kantz and Schreiber,

2004; Bradley and Kantz, 2015). In reciprocal, appropriately captured time series—e.g. correct sampling on real-world attractors and dynamical system behaviors—offer us the empirical time-ordered information to unravel or reconstruct governing mechanisms/equations and the microscopic and macroscopic drivers of the regular or irregular behaviors of the underlying system that might generate the data. It also renders an empirical basis for hypothesis testing and model verification of dynamic behaviors. To extend it to the spatiotemporal context, like the spatiotemporal dynamics of city air pollution discussed above, such interoperability between models and spatiotemporal data will play a pivotal role in the incorporation of dynamics and complexity into digital twins of cities. However, finding the correct correspondence between dynamical systems and time series is by no means straightforward, particularly under nonlinearity and complexity. The mapping between the two is very complicated in nonlinear dynamics. A fundamental question to ask is that given a time series, can we definitively find the corresponding dynamical model that generates it. Conversely, given a dynamical model, can we definitively find the time series corresponding to it? Specifically, is the mapping between the two one-to-one? one-to-many? many-to-one?

9.5.1 One-To-One Mapping Between Dynamical Models and Time Series

To find the one-to-one mapping between a time series and the corresponding dynamical model that generates it is often challenging and difficult because of nonlinearity and complexity of real-world urban systems. We need to have a complete time series of the system states and a lucid structure of the model to learn the unique one-to-one mapping between dynamical models and time series. The learning methods discussed in Chapters 3 and 4, for example, target such system identification problems by learning the corresponding ROMs through the time series of system states and inputs. Inappropriate model specification, incompleteness of time series, and improper design of learning methods will jeopardize the mapping task and result in learning failure. To obtain correct mappings, it is beneficial to consider the complex situations discussed as follows.

9.5.2 Many-To-One Mapping—From Dynamical Models to Time Series

Because of dynamical degeneracy and emergence, it is possible that the same time series with almost identical or similar behavior is generated by different dynamical models. Degeneracy is directly related to system complexity and is a source of system robustness. From the system perspective, we can achieve the same outcome by using different components in a large variety of ways. With nonlinear interactions and feedback loops, dynamical systems with distinct governing equations, structures, and parameters may converge to the same behavior giving rise to indistinguishable time series. Degeneracy implies that the one-to-one mapping between dynamical models and time series is impossible. This many-to-one mapping due to dynamical equivalence and degeneracy complicates the system identification problem. For example, the logistic map for population growth and the Tent map are different nonlinear dynamical models that exhibit chaotic behavior with similar bifurcation diagrams and chaotic attractors. The Lorenz system, Eq. (4.12), and the Rossler system have distinct governing equations but exhibit similar chaotic attractors sensitive to initial conditions. Though different in functional form and parameters, various versions of the Lotka–Volterra model in Eq. (7.1) exhibit similar oscillatory dynamics and populations cycles with periodic solutions. So, it is essentially a many-to-one situation that makes it challenging to derive a one-to-one mapping between the time series and the corresponding dynamical model. If we really want to differentiate the dynamical models that generate identical behavior in time series, we can check for the existence of characteristic features in time series by fitting each of the candidate dynamical models to the time series to choose the one with the best parameter estimates and most sensitive to parameter changes. For example, to confirm whether it is the Verhulst-Pearl equation, Eq. (3.12), that generates the population time series, we may check for changes in parameter estimates and evaluate whether the model estimations appear in the time series. Other characteristic features may be points of inflection, the logistic growth curve, and the asymptotic behavior in time series that match the model. We can also evaluate through bifurcation diagrams to see which dynamical system exhibits bifurcation patterns similar to that observed in the time series. Further insight may also be drawn by comparing the reconstructed attractors in the RPS of the candidate dynamical systems. For the identification of the Navier–Stokes equation, Eq. (5.33), we may look for whether the characteristic features—such as chaotic and irregular fluctuations, Reynolds number effects, vortices, and energy cascades—are exhibited in the time series. If these measures are insufficient, additional measures and more advanced data analysis methods may need to be utilized to identify the true dynamical model that generates the time series.

It should be mentioned that using the above methods to solve the many-to-one mapping problem assumes that we have the candidate dynamical models and their governing equations so that we can derive the corresponding characteristic features to check for their existence in the time series. However, in learning underlying urban dynamics from time series data, we may not know the dynamical models at all. Then the many-to-one mapping problem becomes even more challenging. If we suspect that it is a particular dynamical model that generates the time series, then we may employ the urban theory-informed neural network approach (Chapter 5) by building initial conditions and discerning characteristic features into the loss function to learn the underlying dynamical model and to assess whether the learned behavior matches that exhibited in the observed time series through hypothesis testing or goodness of fit test.

9.5.3 One-To-Many Mapping—From Dynamical Models to Time Series

Due to the nonlinear, chaotic, and sensitive nature of dynamical complex systems, it is possible that a single dynamical model can generate several time series of distinct behaviors through emergence. That is, a system can have multiple stable states. This is the well-known phenomenon of multistability in nonlinear dynamical complex systems—saying that we may have multiple stable states/attractors for the same set of parameters, depending on the initial conditions and historical development (Feudel, 1997; Kelso, 2012). Nonlinear interactions of system parts and processes result in non-equilibrium phase transition—the most primitive form of self-organization—that gives rise to multistability. The notion of bistability—a special case of multistability—indicates the coexistence of two stable states/equilibriums in a dynamical system. Bifurcation occurs when a small change in parameter values leads to sudden qualitative changes in the system behavior. It switches system behavior from bistability to monostability with respect to a parameter. Bistability and bifurcation set up the stage for multistability in the state space. A set of trajectories arising from a set of initial conditions that converge to the same attractor can be quite complicated in structure—fractals. Depending on the initial conditions and chosen parameters, the logistic population growth characterized by the Verhulst-Pearl equation—Eq. (3.12)—for example, can generate multiple time series exhibiting different behaviors such as periodicity, chaos, or convergence to stable equilibrium points representing different population levels. The Fisher-KPP equation, equation (3.16), exhibits multistability with multiple stable patterns of population distribution and wave-like diffusion. The Lotka–Volterra model, Eq. (7.1), models population dynamics exhibiting limit cycle oscillations representing predator–prey interactions and multistability when the predator and prey populations coexist in multiple stable equilibrium points manifesting dispersions of different populations in space. With small differences in initial conditions, the Lorenz model, Eq. (4.11), can generate significantly different time series and the emergence of multiple attractors of trajectories in the state space. Similarly, the Rossler model exhibits chaotic oscillations with numerous coexisting attractors possessing fractal properties—the Rossler attractors—similar in a certain way to the long-term system behavior of the Lorenz model. The Navier-Stoke equation, Eq. (5.33), exhibits multistability with multiple flow patterns or turbulent states.

Therefore, multistability, parameter dependence, and sensitivity to initial conditions will lead to the many-to-one mapping problem, making it difficult in system identification. To identify the unique dynamical model that generates all plausible time series with significantly different behaviors—i.e. to amass all possible time series generated by the same dynamical model for learning—we can methodically vary the parameters within a certain range and generate all plausible trajectories the system can exhibit. And we can make small variations of the initial conditions to identify main characteristic features that affect the system dynamics to avoid missing important behaviors and misidentifying time series. For the Verhulst-Pearl equation, for instance, we can systematically vary the rate of natural increase and the initial population size to explore behaviors changing from stable fixed points to chaotic attractors to capture all plausible trajectories generated by the same model. To identify the model that generates the multiple time series, we can empirically verify which model behavior is most similar to the behaviors of the time series in terms of indicators like periodicity and bifurcation diagram.

Multistability renders a basis for chaos control (Pisarchik and Feudel, 2014). In chaotic systems, we can have strange attractors with an infinite number of embedded unstable periodic orbits/invariance sets, resulting in time series with different behaviors. By local control of unstable orbits, we can either stabilize them or direct the system to desirable final state—from one attractor to another attractor—through non-equilibrium phase transition. Some long-term behaviors of dynamical urban systems may not be desirable, and we may want to steer the system to some preferred stable states that meet urban planning designs through coordinated phase transition. For instance, the process of land use transition exhibits multistability in different configurations of land use mix. By applying local financial or zoning controls, we may be able to steer the transition to desirable stable configurations. Similarly, the dynamics of urban transportation systems may exhibit multistability in having stable configurations of transportation networks. By shifting travel times, modal choice, or infrastructure investment, we may be able to channel the system to designated equilibrium points of networking. Without further elaborations, urban patterns or processes like urban microclimates, air pollution, and social networks could exhibit multistability, particularly spatial multistability creating adjacent spatial domains with different geometries and stationary frontiers. These systems are sensitive to perturbations. A thorough understanding of the above urban processes will play a crucial role in achieving urban resilience and sustainability.

With the possibility of having many-to-one and one-to-many mappings, the mapping between dynamical models and time series is not simple and straightforward. Identification of the correspondence between models and time series becomes very challenging under nonlinearity and multistability. Exploring and understanding these complex mappings will shed light on the construction of appropriate digital twins of cities to learn and model urban dynamics and complexity. That is why for correct system identification, no matter what approaches we are using, we must ensure that the time series from observations or experiments must be complete so that the state space it represents comprises all parameter configurations and initial conditions so that the characteristic features and all trajectories of the underlying dynamics can be effectively captured in the snapshots for learning. Multistability is crucial to the learning of behaviors of dynamical complex systems.

Understanding the intricacy of the above relationships between dynamical models and time series will be instrumental to the design of appropriate strategies for learning urban dynamics and complexity. It will guide us to collect/generate appropriate snapshots and find suitable projection methods for low-dimensional manifold learning discussed in Chapter 3. For system identification in the data-driven approach investigated in Chapter 4, it will help us build proper function libraries for sparse identification, construct the mixture distribution for Gaussian inference, and design the optimal neural network architecture for learning the underlying system dynamics. Similarly, multistability should be incorporated into digital twins of cities in the context of dynamical complex networks discussed in Chapter 6 and MAS examined in Chapter 7. It may also inspire us on the appropriate scale(s) on which urban dynamics and complexity shall be studied, as discussed in Chapter 8.

References

Alharthi M, Mahmood A (2024) xLSTMTime: long-term time series forecasting with xLSTM. *AI* 5(3):1482–1495. https://doi.org/10.3390/ai5030071.

Anh V, Leung Y, Lam KC, Yu ZG (2005) Multifractal characterization of Hong Kong air quality data. *Environmetrics* 16: 1-12.

Beran J (1994) *Statistics for long-memory processes.* Boca Raton: CRC Press.

Bertsimas D, Dunn J (2017) Optimal classification trees. *Machine Learning* 106(7): 1039–1082.

Bertsimas D, Dunn J (2019) *Machine Learning under a Modern Optimization Lens.* Charlestown: Dynamic Ideas LLC.

Bradley E, Kantz H (2015) Nonlinear time-series analysis revisited. *Chaos* 25(9), 097610. https://doi.org/10.1063/1.4917289.

Carrassi A, Bocquet M, Bertino L, Evensen G (2018) Data assimilation in the geosciences: an overview on methods, issues and perspectives. arXiv:1709.02798v3. https://doi.org/10.1002/wcc.535.

Feudel U, Grebogi C (1997) Multistability and the control of complexity. *Chaos* 7(4): 597-604.

Fontanini AD, Vaidya U, Ganapathysubramanian B (2016) A methodology for optimal placement of sensors in enclosed environments: a dynamical systems approach. *Building and Environment* 100: 145-161.

Ge EJ, Haining R, Li, Chi P, Yu ZG, Waye MY, Chu KH, Leung Y (2012) Using knowledge fusion to analyze avian influenza H5N1 in East and Southeast Asia. *PloS One* 7(5): e29617, 2012.

Huang NE, Shen Z, Long SR, Wu MC, Shih HH, Zheng Q, Yen NC, Tung CC, Liu HH (1998) The empirical mode decomposition and the Hilbert spectrum for nonlinear and non-stationary time series analysis. Proceedings of the Royal Society A: Mathematical, Physical and Engineering Sciences 454:903-995. DOI:10.1098/rspa.1998.0193.

He K, Zhang X, Ren S, Sun J (2016) Deep residual learning for image recognition. *Proceedings of the IEEE Conference on Computer Vision and Pattern Recognition*, 770–778.

Huynh DBP, Knezevic DJ, Patera1AT (2013) A static condensation reduced basis element method: approximation and a posteriori error estimation. *ESAIM: Mathematical Modelling and Numerical Analysis* M2AN 47: 213–251. https://doi.org/10.1051/m2an/2012022.

Kalman R. (1960) A new approach to linear filtering and prediction problems. *ASME Journal of Basic Engineering* 82: 35-45.

Kantelhardt JW, Zschiegner SA, Koscielny-Bunde E, Havlin S, Bunde A, Stanley HE (2002) Multifractal detrended fluctuation analysis of nonstationary time series. *Physica A: Statistical Mechanics and its Applications* 316(1–4): 87–114.

Kantz H, Schreiber T (2004) *Nonlinear Time Series Analysis.* Cambridge: Cambridge University Press.

Kapitaniak T (2000) Controlling Chaos. NY: Springer.

Kapteyn MG, Knezevic DJ, Willcox K (2020) Toward predictive digital twins via component-based reduced-order models and interpretable machine learning. *AIAA Scitech 2020 Forum.* https://doi.org/10.2514/6.2020-0418.

Kelso JAS (2012) Multistability and metastability: understanding dynamic coordination in the brain. *Philosophical Transactions of The Royal Society B* 367: 906–918.

Khodarahmi M, Maihami V (2023) A review on Kalman filter models. *Archives of Computational Methods in Engineering* 30:727–747.

Lee YS, Vakakis AF, McFarland DM, Bergman LA (2010) Non-linear system identification of the dynamics of aeroelastic instability suppression based on targeted energy transfers. *The Aeronautical Journal* 114(1152): 61 – 82.

Lendek Zs, Babuˇska R, and De Schutter B (2007) Distributed Kalman filtering for multiagent systems. *Proceedings of the European Control Conference*, 2193–2200.

Leung Y (2010) Knowledge Discovery in Spatial Data. Berlin: Springer-Verlag.

Leung Y, Ge EJ, Yu Z G (2011) Temporal scaling behavior of avian influenza A (H5N1): he multifractal detrended fluctuation analysis. *Annals of the Association of American Geographers* 101(2011): 1221 - 1240.

Leung, Y, Zhou Y, Lam KY, Fung T, Cheung KY, Kim TJ, Jung H (2019) Integration of air pollution data collected by mobile sensors and ground-based stations to derive a spatiotemporal air pollution profile of a city. *International Journal of Geographical Information Science* 33 (11): 2218–2240.

Narh AT, Thorpe N, Bell MC, Hill GA (2016) Do new sources of traffic data make the application of chaos theory to traffic management a realistic possibility? *Transport Reviews* 36(5): 635-658. https://doi.org/10.1080/01441647.2016.1140687.

Niang O, Thioune A, El Gueirea MC, Deléchelle E, Lemoine J (2012) Partial differential equation-based approach for empirical mode decomposition: application on image analysis. *IEEE Transactions on Image Processing* 21 (9): 1057-7149.

Park J, Pao GM, Sugihara G, Stabenau E, Lorimer T (2022) Empirical mode modelling: A data-driven approach to recover and forecast nonlinear dynamics from noisy data. Nonlinear Dynamics 108: 2147–2160. https://doi.org/10.1007/s11071-022-07311-y.

Peng CK, Buldyrev SV, Havtin S, Simons M, Stanley HE, Goldbergerz AL (1994) Mosaic organization of DNA nucleotides. *Physical Review E* 49(2): 1685-1689.

Peng W, Qin S, Yang S, Wang J, Liu X, Wang L (2024) Fourier neural operator for real-time simulation of 3D dynamic urban microclimate. *Building and Environment* 248: 111063. https://doi.org/10.1016/j.buildenv.2023.111063.

Pisarchik AN, Feudel U (2014) Control of multistability. *Physics Reports* 540 (4): 167-218.

Shi G, Leung Y, Zhang JS, Zhou Y (2024) Modeling the air pollution process using a novel multi-site and multi-scale method with adaptive utilization of spatio-temporal information. *Chemosphere* 349:140799.

Tong H (1990) *Non-linear Time Series*. New York: Oxford University Press.

Wang S, Zhan X, Zhai Y, Shen J, Wang H (2021) Performance estimation for Kalman filter based multi-agent cooperative navigation by employing graph theory. *Aerospace Science and Technology* 112, 106628.

Wu Z, Huang NE (2009) Ensemble empirical mode decomposition: a noise-assisted data analysis method. *Advances in Adaptive Data Analysis* 01(01): 1–41.

Yue ZS, Yong HW, Meng DY, Zhao Q, Leung Y, Zhang L (2020) Robust multiview subspace learning with nonindependently and nonidentically distributed complex noise. *IEEE Transactions on Neural Network and Learning Systems* 31(4):1070-1083. https://doi.org/10.1109/TNNLS.2019.2917328.

Zhou Y, Leung Y (2010a) Empirical mode decomposition and long-range correlation analysis of sunspot time series. *Journal of Statistical Mechanics: Theory and Experiment* 12: P06021. https://doi.org/10.1088/1742-5468/2010/12/P12006.

Zhou Y, Leung Y (2010b) Multifractal temporally weighted detrended fluctuation analysis and its application in the analysis of scaling behavior in temperature series. *Journal of Statistical Mechanics: Theory and Experiment* 06: P06021. https://doi.org/10.1088/1742-5468/2010/06/P06021.

Zhou Y, Leung Y, Ma JM (2012) Empirical study of the scaling behavior of the amplitude-frequency distribution of the Hilbert-Huang transform and its application in sunspot time series analysis. *Physica A* 392:1336-1346.

Chapter 10
Sensor Network and Data Quality Assurance for Digital Twins of Cities

10.1 On Urban Sensing with Sensors and IoT

As discussed above, the construction of digital twins of cities relies largely on spatiotemporal data coming from empirical simulations or real-life monitoring. Real-time or near real-time data obtained via IoT devices and stationary or mobile sensors are particularly important for machine learning of system dynamics, responsive monitoring, and control of urban entities or phenomena such as traffic flows under emergency, urban microclimates, and air pollutant concentrations. In urban sensing, besides conventional sources of georeferenced information, sensors and IoT devices have become ubiquitous means to collect information about the dynamics of various spatiotemporal phenomena (Cuff et al. 2008; Ghahramani et al. 2020). They are especially important to real-time human movement and traffic sensing, and timely response to emergencies and sporadic disasters. IoT devices such as mobile phones collect the hourly, daily, weekly, monthly, seasonal, etc., dynamics of travel behaviors across time scales (Wang et al. 2018). Crowdsensing that collects information from and metes out instructions to the crowd can play a key role in intelligent route guidance, parking, and crowd movement management. To provide backdraft sensing for buildings, for instance, we need to appropriately locate multiple temperature and gas sensors in various rooms of a building to detect the presence of fires and hazardous gases (Hasan and Ali 2012). Deploying good enough number of sensors to measure and deliver the right information to the right place at the right time has become a key issue in the interoperation between models and data over sensor networks. However, it should be noted that some learning models like PINN can work with limited data collected by sparse sensors. How and where to place limited number of sensors to collect relevant training data again calls for the interoperation between models and data discussed in Chap. 9. By integrating LLMs with sensing technologies, we can perhaps develop multimodal human-centric urban sensing with human cognition, commonsense, and world view for human-based urban planning (Hou et al. 2025).

Y. Leung, *Digital Twins of Cities*, Advances in Spatial Science,
https://doi.org/10.1007/978-3-032-07966-4_10

Since data in general and sensor data in particular are often noisy embedded with errors due to human mistakes or erroneous measurements in instruments—particularly measurements made by ubiquitous sensors, how to handle noisy data and how to propagate errors in data processing and machine learning have become a fundamental issue in data science and AI. It in turn constitutes a crucial issue in building digital twins of cities. I give a brief discussion of the above two issues in the following sections, respectively.

10.2 Dynamic Urban Sensing via Sensor Networks

Development of information technology has enabled the construction of large-scale sensor networks to monitor our physical systems/twins and the environment to accomplish challenging sensing tasks (Culler et al. 2004). In the estimation of system state, for example, the Kalman filter, discussed in Sect. 9.2 of Chap. 9, is a method that fuses estimates coming from different sensors to obtain the final estimate of some unknown system states. IoT and/or various types of sensors generally form a sensor network to collect data about urban dynamics. For instance, data coming from sensors via a Lagrangian framework for traffic estimation and river flow estimation has been developed (Rudy et al. 2017). In addition to stationary sensors, we often need to deploy mobile sensors to collect data about distributions of certain urban phenomena such as harmful gases emitted from industrial complexes, or poisonous gases from accidental spills in the transportation of hazardous wastes (Li and Leung 2011). To derive air pollution profiles of a city in time and space, for instance, Leung et al. (2019) proposed a rigorous framework for the integration of air pollutant concentration data with varying spatial and temporal scales coming from ground-based stations, which are spatially sparse but temporally dense, and mobile sensors, which are spatially dense but temporally sparse. With the ubiquitous deployment of mobile sensors or IoT for city monitoring, it is of great importance to integrate such data with those collected via conventional means to form a comprehensive database, which is now relatively dense in space and time, for constructing digital twins of cities for urban analysis and prediction. A two-step regression (Yan and Mei 2014) was applied to the integrated database to estimate air pollutant concentrations for specified locations and moments in time. The regression model is used to explore the spatiotemporal variation of air pollutants in a city. It combines geographically weighted regression (Fotheringham et al. 2002) and local smoothing to handle both spatial and temporal information. The time series such estimated are then subjected to performance evaluations by examining (1) whether the estimated and observed series have the same empirical mode decomposition (EMD) components/modes, and (2) whether the corresponding components are highly autocorrelated (Leung et al. 2019).

Over the years, great progress has been made on a variety of sensor designs (Gazis et al. 2025). Mobile phones, for example, have served as sensors for the study of travel behavior in space and time (Wang et al. 2018). A modular plug-and-play sensor system that can be carried by people or mounted on board of vehicles or unmanned aerial vehicles has been built for 2D and 3-D multi-sensor measurements of city air pollution (Yi et al. 2016, 2018). Wireless sensor networks have also been developed for air pollution monitoring (Yi et al. 2015, 2016), and a system for personalized health care targeting the analysis of ECG and EEG signals through the integration of on-body wearable mobile sensors and even in-body sensors, if available. Through mobile application and web interface, urban residents and their doctors/health advisors can use the system to keep track of their health information. They can communicate through the system anywhere and anytime (Tong et al. 2017). If they can also carry the modular plug-and-play sensor system, we can also correlate air pollution exposure and health condition in cities.

To enable sensor networks to dynamically discharge and enlist sensors according to needs and model instructions over time and space, Leung et al. (2013) formulated a multitarget tracking sensor network to track time-varying number of targets in a cluttered environment by the probability hypothesis density (PHD) filter based on finite set statistics within the Bayesian framework. To further achieve energy efficiency, a prediction-based sensor selection scheme was formulated under a quantized energy-efficiency criterion. Sensors are selected by minimizing energy consumption and communication or deployment costs. Since the activation and hibernation mechanisms are instrumental to saving energy and prolonging the lifetime of a sensor network, a prediction-based approach was constructed for the sensor selection scheme (Wu et al. 2020). The PHD filter is thus more appropriate and robust than the time periodic Kalman filter (Liu et al. 2014) or other filters (Bar-Shalom and Li 1995) for the design of sensor networks dealing with interacting multiple targets and uncertainty. The PHD filter treats the set of targets and measurements as random finite sets and circumvents the problem of data association. It tracks the time-varying number of targets by fusing together data coming from the distributed source sensors. Therefore, it is suitable for addressing uncertainty encountered in multi-target tracking systems.

The algorithm consists of a sequential PHD-filter-based hierarchical fusion architecture within a two-level fusion scheme running respectively at the cluster heads (CHs) and the central base station (CBS) of the locally decentralized network. The sensor network comprises a position-aware central base station and multiple sensors, where the source sensors directly communicate with the corresponding cluster heads which act as local information fusion centers (Fig. 10.2) in the sensing environment subdivided according to the underlying dynamics (Fig. 10.1). This is to cater for the fact that digital twins centralize data to some extent by collecting comprehensive sensor data from the local cluster heads, and aggregate and store the data in an easily accessible data hub for learning and data assimilation.

Since the activation and hibernation mechanisms are instrumental to saving energy and prolonging the lifetime of a sensor network, a prediction-based quantized energy-efficiency criterion is further designed to dynamically select a suitable number of sensors to reduce energy consumption under a tracking accuracy requirement (Wu et al., 2020). Sensors stay in the hibernation state until they are activated by messages sent from the corresponding cluster heads to perform their sensing tasks. The cluster

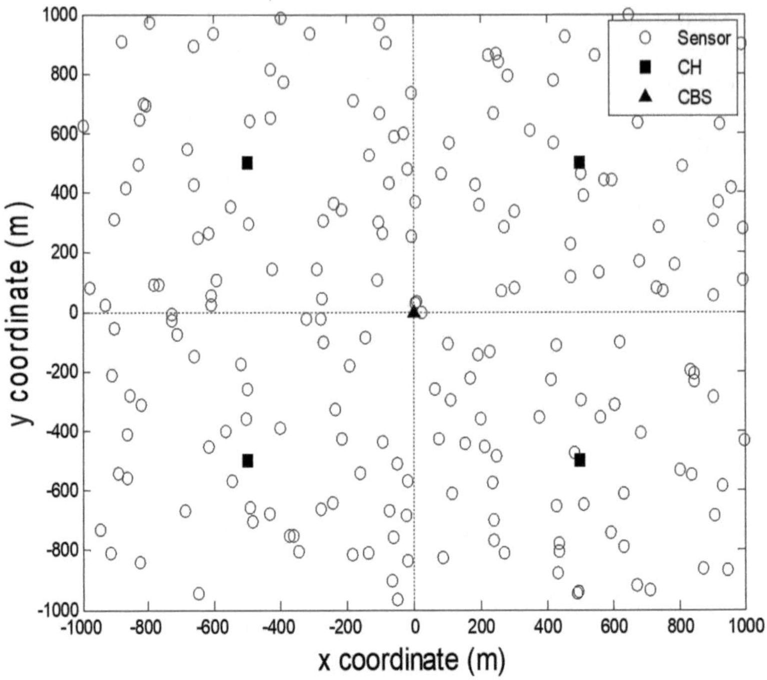

Fig. 10.1 The cluster-based hierarchical sensor network (adopted from Leung et al. [2013])

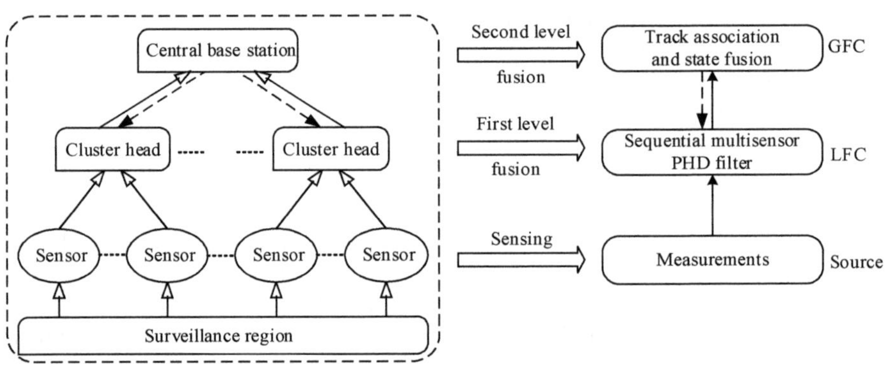

Fig. 10.2 The hierarchical fusion architecture with a two-level fusion scheme for multitarget tracking sensor networks (adopted from Wu et al. [2020])

heads receive data from their cluster members and use the measurements to perform signal processing. They then forward the locally aggregated data to the central base station for global fusion. The design strikes a good balance between estimation accuracy and sensor activation/hibernation in periodic sensor scheduling throughout the observation period of a dynamical urban system.

Target tracking problems can be treated as a target-state estimation problem involving many sensors with energy constraints. Energy efficient sensing and optimal dynamic sensor selection are two main concerns in the design of sensor network for dynamical systems. State-space model has been commonly employed for target tracking system (Bar-Shalom and Li 1995). It models the process of tracking by estimating on-line the target states with noisy measurement. In the discrete-time system, the unknown target state x_k at time k is expressed as $x_k = [L_{x,k}, v_{x,k}, L_{y,k}, v_{y,k}]^T$, where $L_{t,k} = [L_{x,k}, L_{y,k}]^T$ is the target positions, and $v_{t,k} = [v_{x,k}, v_{y,k}]^T$ is the velocities in the x and y directions. Then, the state-space model can be specified by the following target-motion model and range-based measurement model:

$$x_k = F_k(x_{k-1}, w_k) \tag{10.1}$$

$$z_k^{[s]} = H_k^{[s]}\left(x_k, v_k^{[s]}(x_k)\right), s = 1, \ldots, N_s \tag{10.2}$$

where $F_k(x_{k-1}, w_k)$ and $H_k^{[s]}\left(x_k, v_k^{[s]}(x_k)\right)$ are the target-state transition and sensor measurement functions, respectively, and w_k and $v_k^{[s]}(x_k)$ are the white Gaussian-process noise and measurement noise, respectively. The system estimates the target states with noisy measurements made by the tracking technologies. The multitarget state at time k can be described as the union of the survived targets $S_{k|k-1}(x)$ with probability $p_{S,k}(x)$, spawned targets $B_{k|k-1}(x)$, and spontaneous birth targets Γ_k as follows (Mahler 2003; Vo et al. 2005; Vo and Wan 2006)

$$X_k = \left(\bigcup_{x \in X_{k-1}} S_{k|k-1}(x)\right) \cup \left(\bigcup_{x \in X_{k-1}} B_{k|k-1}(x)\right) \cup \Gamma_k \tag{10.3}$$

This computationally efficient PHD filter can be implemented through the approximation of the multitarget density using recursively their first-order moments $D(x)$ in time instead of the posterior itself. Specifically, with a single sensor, it is implemented according to the following steps.

Prediction step

$$D_{k|k-1}(x) = \int p_{S,k}(\zeta) f_{k|k-1}(x|\zeta) D_{k-1}(\zeta) d\zeta + \int b_{k|k-1}(x|\zeta) f_{k|k-1}(x|\zeta) \\ D_{k-1}(\zeta) \mathrm{d}\zeta + \gamma_k(x) \tag{10.4}$$

Update step

$$D_k(x) = \left[\sum\nolimits_{z \in Z_k} \frac{p_{D,k}(x) f_k(z|x)}{\kappa_k(z) + \int p_{D,k}(\zeta) f_k(z|\zeta) D_{k|k-1}(\zeta) \mathrm{d}} \zeta + 1 - p_{D,k}(x)\right] D_{k|k-1}(x) \tag{10.5}$$

where the first-order moment $D_k(x)$ is the PHD of the multitarget state radio frequency sensor (RFS); $\gamma_k(x)$ is the PHD of spontaneous target birth RFS; $b_{k|k-1}(x|\zeta)$ is the PHD of the target RFS spawned by a target of previous state ζ at time $k-1$; $p_{S,k}(\zeta)$ and $p_{D,k}(x)$ are the survival and detection probabilities, respectively; and $\kappa_k(z)$ is the PHD of the clutter RFS.

For N_s number of sensors, suppose there are N_s independent measurements $Z_k^{[1]}, \ldots, Z_k^{[N_s]}$ at time k, where

$$Z_k^{[s]} = \left(\bigcup_{x \in X_k} \Theta_k^{[s]}(x) \right) \cup K_k^{[s]} = \{z_1^{[s]}, \ldots, z_{N_{m,k}^{[s]}}^{[s]}\}, s = 1, \ldots, N_s \tag{10.6}$$

and $N_{m,k}^{[s]}$ denotes the number of measurements in a single sensor s. Then, measurements from different sensors are sequentially used to update the PHD (Pham et al. 2007; Zhang et al. 2010):

$$D_k(x) = f_k^{[N_s]}(Z_k^{[N_s]}|x) \cdots f_k^{[1]}(Z_k^{[1]}|x) D_{k|k-1}(x) \tag{10.7}$$

where

$$f_k^{[s]}\left(Z_k^{[s]}|x\right) = 1 - p_{D,k}^{[s]}(x) + \sum_{z \in Z_k^{[s]}} \frac{p_{D,k}^{[s]}(x) f_k^{[s]}(z|x)}{\kappa_k(z) + \int p_{D,k}^{[s]}(\zeta) f_k^{[s]}(z|\zeta) D_{k|k-1}^{s-1}(\zeta) d\zeta} \tag{10.8}$$

$$D_{k|k-1}^0(x) = D_{k|k-1}(x) \tag{10.9}$$

In this manner, the sequential multi-sensor PHD filter approach can fuse data coming from multiple sensors. Therefore, according to the dynamical model requirements, we can deploy time-varying number of sensors in an urban environment at designated times and locations to collect relevant information to update or improve the digital twins of cities.

To obtain more information to improve model accuracy, we ideally should use as many sensors as possible in the network. Nevertheless, given the constraint on energy consumption, only a small number of sensors could be used at any point in time. Sensor selection then becomes a key issue in multitarget tracking in an uncertain environment. It hinges on the selection of a subset of necessary sensors while simultaneously keeping most of the other sensors in hibernation mode until their services are called for by the cluster heads. In what follows, we concentrate on the sensor selection scheme in sensor networks for our multitarget tracking algorithm.

First, the total energy consumption of the whole sensing system at time k is given by:

$$E_{\text{total}}(k) = \sum_{j=1}^{N_c} \left[E_{\text{CH-consum}}(j, k) + \sum_{s \in \mathbf{N}_s^j} E_{\text{sensor-consum}}(s, k) \right] \tag{10.10}$$

where

$$\begin{aligned} E_{CH-consum}(j,k) &= E_{T-control}(j,k) + E_R(j,k) + E_{process}(j,k) + E_T(j,k) \\ &= \sum_{s \in \mathbf{N}_s^j} \left[E_{elec}\; l_{control} + E_{amp}\; d_{to-CH}^{\rho}(s) \right] + E_{elec}\; l\; |Z_{k|k-1}^{[s]}| \\ &\quad + E_{process} + \left[E_{elec} + E_{amp} d_{to-CBS}^{\rho}(j) \right] l \end{aligned} \tag{10.11}$$

is the energy consumption of the j-th cluster head at time k—in which the energy consumption of the j-th, $j = 1, \ldots, N_C$, cluster head is partitioned into four parts: (1) energy consumption in transmitting controlled messages to the source sensors, denoted by $E_{T-control}(j,k)$, (2) energy consumption in receiving the measurement set, denoted by $E_R(j,k)$, (3) energy consumption in processing, denoted by $E_{process}(j,k)$, and (4) energy consumption in transmitting the local estimated data to the central base station, denoted by $E_T(j,k)$.

And the energy consumption of an activated source sensor s at time k is.

$$\begin{aligned} E_{sensor-consum}(s,k) &= E_{R-control}(s,k) + E_{sensing}(s,k) + E_{commu}(s,k) \\ &= E_{elec}\; l_{control} + E_{sensing} + \left[2E_{elec} + E_{amp} d_{to-CH}^{\rho}(s) \right] l\; |Z_{k|k-1}^{[s]}| \end{aligned} \tag{10.12}$$

The energy consumption of the source sensor is partitioned into three parts (1) energy consumption in receiving the controlled message from the cluster head, denoted by $E_{R-control}(s,k)$, where $l_{control}$ is the size of the control message, and l is the size of the data message; (2) energy consumption in sensing, denoted by $E_{sensing}(s,k)$; and (3) energy consumption in receiving and transmitting data, denoted by $E_{sensing}(s,k)$, which is computed according to the overall energy consumption in transmitting l bit data over a distance d based on the Euclidian distance $d_{to-CH}(s)$ from sensor s to its cluster head

$$E_{\text{comm}}(l,d) = (2E_{\text{elec}} + E_{\text{amp}} d^{\rho})\; l \tag{10.13}$$

where E_{amp} is the energy needed to transmit one bit over a distance d in achieving an acceptable signal-to-noise ratio at the destination, and ρ is the exponent of the path loss;

$$E_{T_{x-elec}} = E_{R_{x-elec}} = E_{\text{elec}} \tag{10.14}$$

where $E_{T_{x-elec}}$ is a distance independent term for the transmitter electronics, and $E_{R_{x-elec}}$ is a distance independent term for the receiver electronics. The volume of data is assumed to be proportional to the cardinality of PIMS $|z_{kk-1}^{[s]}|$. For simplicity, we assume that all sensors have the same energy consumption for receiving the controlled message and sensing.

In short, at a given time step, after receiving the feedback from the central base station at the last time step, each cluster head carries out the sensor selection scheme according to the above prediction-based quantized energy-efficiency criterion to locally determine the activated sensors and transmit control activation messages to invoke them. The source sensors are activated to perform sensing after the control activation messages have been received. Then they transmit the measurement data—along with some sensor specific parameters, such as the energy level condition—to their cluster heads. The cluster heads receive measurements from the activated sensors and fuse these data to estimate the local states using the sequential multi-sensor PHD filter. After that, the cluster heads communicate the local tracks to the central base station for global fusion. The central base station carries out track association and state fusion on these local data. Finally, the central base station transmits the estimated global states to each cluster head as feedback. This process is repeated until the sensors in the system are exhausted.

It should be noted that in the above multi-target tracking scheme, a fixed number of clusters is adopted, and the source sensors are organized into clusters by the static nearest-neighbor clustering algorithm. To be more flexible and energy efficient, we can dynamically determine the number of clusters and explore various ways to deploy the clustering architecture in an ad hoc and network-self-organization manner. We can also explore other filtering methods to further enhance the capability of the sensor network. By leveraging ROMs for the high-dimensional dynamics previously discussed, we can explore data-driven sparse sensor placement strategy for signal reconstruction to minimize data collection cost by reducing the number of sensors for compressed sensing (Manohar et al. 2018; Clark et al. 2019). This again promotes the interoperability between models and data discussed in Chap. 9.

Remark. Though the advancement of information technology enables us to acquire big data for our analysis, data are still sparse in space and time for process learning under many circumstances. Digital twins, however, can assist to generate data to train AI models like neural networks under different conditions. This is another reason why we need to promote the interoperability between models and data.

10.3 Error Analysis and Error Propagation in Digital Twins of Cities

To make simulations and predictions of digital twins reliable, besides having a model which correctly captures the underlying dynamics of physical systems, accuracy of data which is used to learn the dynamics by the digital twins is pivotal to their trustworthiness, particularly for chaotic systems which are sensitive to small errors in initial conditions. Of course, this is not unique to digital twins but a general issue in all scientific modeling. Such data quality concerns have been raised in the geoinformation community, particularly the GIS community, dealing with digital twins (Goodchild et al. 2024; SPARC 2023). Taking that all measurements, including conventional measurements and measurements made by sensors and IoT, generally contain errors, the issue is then on how to do error analysis and error propagation in digital twins so that errors in the final result can be determined by the propagation of errors from the inputs, the GIS operations, the dynamical models, or visualization. With respect to measurement-based GIS, Leung et al. (2004a, 2004b, 2004c, 2004d) formulated a rigorous statistical framework for error analysis and error propagation briefly recapitulated as follows.

10.3.1 Propagation of Errors in Data Measurements

The basic measurement error (ME) model for indirect measurement can simply be expressed as

$$y = f(x) \tag{10.15}$$

$$x = \mu_x + \varepsilon_x, \varepsilon_x \sim (0, \Sigma_x) \tag{10.16}$$

where μ_x is the true-value vector; x is the random measurement-value vector; y is the indirect measurement-value vector obtained by the transformation function f; and ε_x is the random measurement error vector with zero mean $\mathbf{0}$ and variance–covariance matrix Σ_x. Once x is measured and f is known, y and the associated error distribution are uniquely and automatically determined. The inverse of f is denoted by f^{-1}, that is, the function that allows measurements x to be determined from the quantities y. This reciprocal relationship between x and y proved to be instrumental in error analysis and database maintenance. Apparently, y is random and its error covariance matrix Σ_y—propagated from Σ_x—also depends on the true-value vector μ_x. Based on this, we establish the following laws for error propagation:

$$\Sigma_y = \mathbf{B}\Sigma_x\mathbf{B}^T, \textit{ if } f(x) \textit{ is linear in } x, f(x) = a + \mathbf{B}x \tag{10.17}$$

$$\Sigma_y \approx \tilde{\Sigma}_y \equiv \mathbf{B}_\mu \Sigma_x \mathbf{B}_\mu^T, \textit{ if } f(x) \textit{ is nonlinear in } x \tag{10.18}$$

where $x \in \mathbb{R}^P$ is a set of p measurements which can be measured directly; $y \in \mathbb{R}^q$ is a set of q quantities to be measured; $\mathbf{a} \in \mathbb{R}^p$ is a point; $\mathbf{B}$ is a Jacobian matrix of partial derivatives with respect to each of the components; and f is the transformation function representing a specific GIS operation such as calculating the length of a line segment, estimating the intersection point of two line segments, determining point in polygon, performing polygon overlays, estimating area, etc. Under nonlinearity, Taylor series expansion is employed for linearization (Leung et al. 2004a).

Based on the law of error propagation, rigorous statistical level of confidence for the end results of the operations can be established by the errors propagated from the inputs. Figure 10.3 depicts the propagation of errors throughout a sequential operation process involving various tasks in measurement-based GIS. Figure 10.4 summarizes the analytical results of error propagations in various GIS operations obtained by the rigorous statistical analysis in Leung et al. (2004a, 2004b, 2004c, 2004d). The framework can also be extended to handle uncertainty in space-time prisms for spatiotemporal movements (Leung et al. 2016) and crowd-sourced georeferenced measurements (Zhang et al. 2019). If error is a mixture of fuzziness and randomness—due to fuzzy/random points, lines, and polygons—error propagation can still be performed in the operations on such error-embedded georeferenced data (Leung and Yan 1997) in which sentiments and opinions are generally fuzzy in connotation and voluntary geographical information are error bound under randomness.

In data assimilation, we need to combine data from various sources. The propagation of errors in data taken from various sources in time and space is essential to data quality control in the assimilation process. In such data fusion process, we need to propagate errors from various sources to obtain the error in the fused measurement (Leung et al. 2010). Assume that there are r independent sources, denoted by $s_1, s_2, \ldots, s_r$, of measurement data. Let x be the true value, and the measurement X_i from s_i is unbiased with an additive random error, i.e. $E[X_i] = x$ and $VAR[X_i] = \sigma_i^2, i = 1, 2, \ldots, r$. Then the fused measurement estimator is

$$X = \lambda_1 X_1 + \lambda_2 X_2 + \cdots \lambda_r X_r = \sum_{i=1}^{r} \lambda_i X_i \tag{10.19}$$

where λ_i is the weight assigned to measurement X_i, and X is a weighted average satisfying $\sum_{i=1}^{r} \lambda_i = 1, \lambda_i \geq 0, i = 1, 2, \ldots, r$.

Under such transformation, X is still unbiased with

$$E[X] = \lambda_1 E[X_1] + \lambda_2 E[X_2] + \cdots + \lambda_r E[X_r] = x \tag{10.20}$$

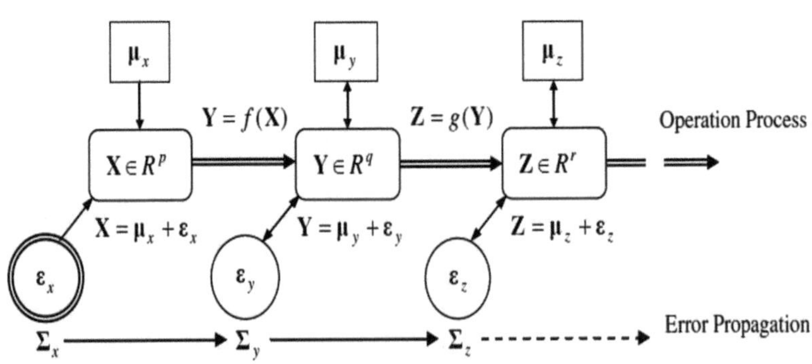

Fig. 10.3 Schematic representation of error propagation in measurement-based GIS (adopted from Leung et al. [2004a])

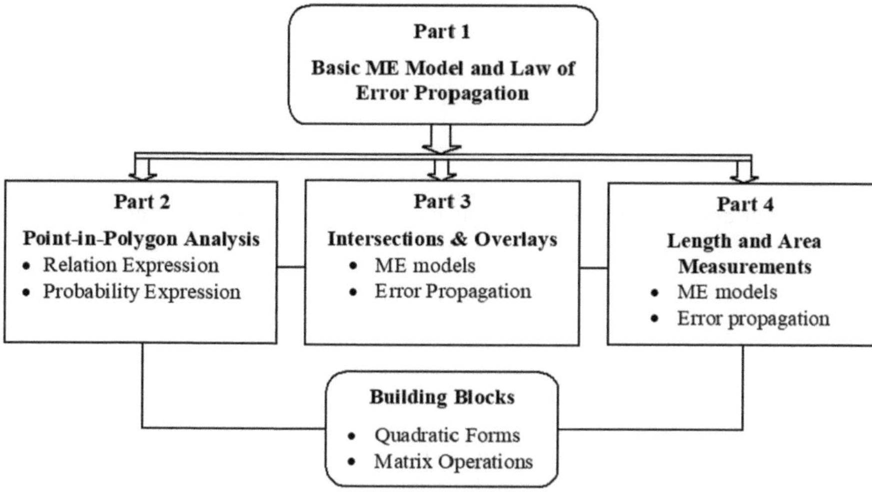

Fig. 10.4 Fundamental results of error propagation in selected GIS operations (adopted from Leung et al. [2004a])

$$VAR[X] = \lambda_1^2 VAR[X_1] + \lambda_2^2 VAR[X_2] + \cdots + \lambda_r^2 VAR[X_r] = \sum_{i=1}^{r} \lambda_i^2 \sigma_i^2 \tag{10.21}$$

To obtain λ_i, $i = 1, 2, \ldots, r$, so that Eq. (10.21) is minimized, we solve the following optimization problem

$$\begin{aligned} &\min f(\lambda_1, \lambda_2, \ldots, \lambda_m) = \textstyle\sum_{i=1}^{r} \lambda_i^2 \sigma_i^2 \\ &\text{s.t.} \quad \textstyle\sum_{i=1}^{r} \lambda_i = 1, \lambda_i \geq 0, i = 1, 2, \ldots r \end{aligned} \tag{10.22}$$

The solution is

$$\tilde{\lambda}_i = \left(\sum_{k=1}^{r} \frac{I}{\sigma_k^2} \right)^{-1} \frac{1}{\sigma_i^2}, \; i = 1, 2, \ldots, r \tag{10.23}$$

where $\left(\sigma_i^2\right)^{-1}$ is a precision measure of the measurement from the i-th data source—the larger the variance, the smaller the weight. The weight $\tilde{\lambda}_i$ assigned to measurement i is proportional to its precision.

If all the variances are known, then the variance of the fused measurement estimator

$$\tilde{X} = \sum_{i=1}^{r} \tilde{\lambda}_i X_i \tag{10.24}$$

is

$$VAR[\tilde{X}] = \left(\sum_{k=1}^{r} \frac{I}{\sigma_k^2}\right)^{-1} \tag{10.25}$$

In case the variances are unknown, we can use a plug-in fused measurement estimator

$$\widehat{X} = \sum_{i=1}^{r} \widehat{\lambda}_i X_i \tag{10.26}$$

where

$$\widehat{\lambda}_i = \left(\sum_{k=1}^{r} \frac{I}{\widehat{\sigma}_k^2}\right)^{-1} \frac{1}{\widehat{\sigma}_i^2}, i = 1, 2, \ldots, r \tag{10.27}$$

The exact variance is complicated in this situation but can be approximated as

$$VAR\left[\widehat{X}\right] = \left(\sum_{k=1}^{r} \frac{I}{\widehat{\sigma}_k^2}\right)^{-1} \tag{10.28}$$

10.3.2 Propagation of Errors in Dynamical Processes

In the context of using digital twins of cities to model the dynamics of urban systems, the transformation function can be any of the learning algorithms that we previously discussed. For example, the closure problem in representing dynamics in terms of a partial observation $\boldsymbol{y}$ of a full state $\boldsymbol{x}$ involves errors in data and their propagation in the learning of a nonlinear dynamical systems (Pan and Duraisamy 2018). Here, $\dot{\boldsymbol{x}}(t) = f(\boldsymbol{x}(t); \boldsymbol{\mu})$ are the nonlinear PDEs depicting the dynamical system; $\boldsymbol{y}(t) = g(\boldsymbol{x}(t)) + \boldsymbol{\varepsilon}; f$ is the nonlinear function; and ε is the error. The error will then be propagated to the approximate dynamical system $\dot{z}(t) = \widehat{f}\left(z(t); \widehat{\boldsymbol{\mu}}\right)$, where $z(t) = \psi(\boldsymbol{y}(t))$. For instance, in the projection-based approaches discussed in Chap. 3, we can derive system-theoretic error bounds and error estimates for the ROMs in the time or frequency domains. In the discovery of hidden chaotic dynamics in highly contaminated data using RCMD discussed in Sect. 4.6 of Chap. 4, errors are transmitted from the prior to the posterior in the mixture distribution through which we can establish statistical bounds for the end result. In the low-rank approximation of a random graph discussed in Sect. 6.3 of Chap. 6, noise in the adjacency matrix is propagated to the random graph through the low-rank matrix. In the derivation of ROMs, errors are propagated through dimension reduction also. In data assimilation, errors of measurements and errors of processes are propagated to the variance of future system-state estimation along a chain of prediction-estimation steps within a destinated time domain.

With respect to the neural network approach to the construction of digital twins of cities, the optimal encodings for biased association in linear associative memory proposed by Leung et al. (1998) would be useful to trace error propagation from inputs to outputs. Let $\mathbf{X} = [\boldsymbol{x}_{1,}, \boldsymbol{x}_{2,} \ldots, \boldsymbol{x}_r]$ and $\mathbf{Y} = [\boldsymbol{y}_1, \boldsymbol{y}_2, \ldots, \boldsymbol{y}_r]$ be the set of input and output vectors, respectively. We say that the network encoding $\mathbf{W}$ is unbiased if it satisfies $\mathbf{Y} = \mathbf{XW}$. Given $\tilde{\boldsymbol{x}}_i = \boldsymbol{x}_i + \boldsymbol{\varepsilon}_i$, $\boldsymbol{\varepsilon} = [\boldsymbol{\varepsilon}_1, \boldsymbol{\varepsilon}_2, \ldots, \boldsymbol{\varepsilon}_r]$, where $\boldsymbol{x}_i$ is the input vector and $\boldsymbol{\varepsilon}_i$ is the measurement error vector, the output of the linear associative memory—a feedforward neural network: $\tilde{\boldsymbol{y}}_i = \boldsymbol{W}\tilde{\boldsymbol{x}}_i$—should be kept as close to $\boldsymbol{y}_i$ as possible. Therefore, the encoding $\mathbf{W}$ is obtained by minimizing the following mean squared error:

$$MSE(\boldsymbol{W}) = E\left[\sum_{i=1}^{r} \|\boldsymbol{y}^i - \tilde{\boldsymbol{y}}_i\|^2\right] = E\left[\sum_{i=1}^{r} \|\boldsymbol{y}_i - \mathbf{W}(\boldsymbol{x}_i + \boldsymbol{\varepsilon}_i)\|^2\right] \tag{10.29}$$

Based on such formulation, Leung et al. (1998) derived the optimal encoding scheme to perform biased association for the white noise and non-white noise situations. This is how error in the input can be propagated to the error in the output in the data-driven approach to build digital twins of cities. By minimizing Eq. (10.29), we learn the neural network by simultaneously handling error propagation and error minimization in one go. Such method can be extended to deep learning by multilayer feedforward neural networks with measurement errors in the inputs.

Since intelligent systems often involve reasoning with concepts rather than vector or raster in conventional GIS, it may be an opportune time to reopen the issue and give further thoughts to the object-oriented GIS, advocated by Leung et al. (1999), where GIS is concept-based and on scale, and yet a connection can be built to link vector- and raster-based data to concepts to take advantage of their data processing capabilities. We can extend this framework to build into the spatial concept lattice subjective human and social dimensions from social sensing for a more embracing urban information infrastructure. With such object-oriented GIS, it will facilitate the integration of concepts of urbanism and social space into geographical space to study social issues in digital twins of cities, particularly the LLM-based urban MAS. Since there is a hierarchical structure of concepts in object-oriented GIS, error can be propagated and analyzed along the conceptual hierarchy.

Besides the error issue about data, there are other conceptual issues such as privacy, liability, security, ethical issues, etc. about data—particularly IoT and social sensing data—that have been discussed in the urban sensing, digital twins of cities, and GIS communities (Cuff et al. 2008; SPARC 2023; Goodchild 2024). It will not be discussed here.

References

Bar-Shalom Y, Li XR (1995) *Multitarget-Multisensor Tracking: Principles and Techniques*. Denver: YBS Publishing.

Clark E, Askham T, Brunton SL, Kutz JN (2019) Greedy sensor placement with cost constraints. *IEEE Sensors Journal* 19(7): 2642 – 2656. https://doi.org/10.1109/JSEN.2018.2887044.

Cuff D, Hansen M, Kang J (2008) Urban Sensing: Out of the Woods. *Communications of the ACM* 51(3): 24–33.

Culler D, Estrin D, Srivastava M (2004) Overview of sensor networks. *IEEE Computer* 37(8): 41–49.

Fotheringham AS, Brunsdon C, Charlton M (2002) *Geographically Weighted Regression – The Analysis of Spatially Varying Relationships*. Chichester: Wiley.

Gazis A, Papadongonas I, Andriopoulos A, Zioudas C, Vavouras T (2025) A comprehensive review of sensor technologies, instrumentation, and signal processing solutions for low-power Internet of Things systems with mini-computing devices. arXiv:2503.13466.

Ghahramani M, Zhou M, Wang G (2020) Urban sensing based on mobile phone data: approaches, applications and challenges. https://doi.org/10.48550/arXiv.2008.12992.

Goodchild MF, Connor D, Fotheringham AS, Frazier A, Kedron P, Li W, Tong D *(2024)* Digital twins in urban informatics. *Urban Informatics 3:16*. https://doi.org/10.1007/s44212-024-000 48-6.

Hasan MM, Ali MN (2012). A new approach of preventing backdraft explosion in commercial buildings by implementing sensor technology. *International Journal of Information and Electronics Engineering,* 2(4): 625–629. https://doi.org/10.7763/IJIEE. 2012.V2.174.

Hou C, Zhang F, Li Y, Li H, Mai G, Kang Y, Yao L, Yu W, Yao Y, Gao S, Chen M, Liu Y (2025) Urban sensing in the era of large language models. *The Innovation* 6(1): 100749.

Leung Y, Dong TX, Xu ZB (1998) The optimal encodings for biased association in linear associative memory. *Neural Networks* 11: 877–884.

Leung Y, Leung KS, He JZ (1999) A generic concept-based object-oriented geographical information system. *International Journal of Geographical Information Science* 13:475–498.

Leung Y, Ma JH, Fung T (2010) Error propagation for the fusion of multi-source and multi-scale spatial data. (unpublished paper)

Leung Y, Ma JH, Goodchild MF (2004a) A general framework for error analysis in measurement-based GIS, part 1: The basic measurement-error model and related concepts. *Journal of Geographical Systems* 6: 325–354.

Leung Y, Ma JH, Goodchild MF (2004b) A general framework for error analysis in measurement-based GIS, part 2: The algebra-based probability model for point-in-polygon analysis. *Journal of Geographical Systems* 6: 355–380.

Leung Y, Ma JH, Goodchild MF (2004c) A general framework for error analysis in measurement-based GIS, part 3: Error analysis in intersections and overlays. *Journal of Geographical Systems* 6: 381–402.

Leung Y, Ma JH, Goodchild MF (2004d) A general framework for error analysis in measurement-based GIS, part 4: Error analysis in length and area measurements. *Journal of Geographical Systems* 6: 403–428.

Leung Y, Wu TJ, Ma JH (2013) A PHD-filter-based multitarget tracking algorithm for sensor networks. *Proceedings of 13th International Conference on Computational Science and Applications (ICCSA 2013)* 4: 93–107.

Leung Y, Yan JP (1997) Point-in-polygon analysis under certainty and uncertainty. *GeoInformatica* 1: 93-114.

Leung Y, Zhao Z, Ma JH (2016) Uncertainty analysis of space–time prisms based on the moment-design method. *International Journal of Geographical Information Science* 30: 1336–1358.

Leung, Y, Zhou Y, Lam KY, Fung T, Cheung KY, Kim TJ, Jung H (2019) Integration of air pollution data collected by mobile sensors and ground-based stations to derive a spatiotemporal air pollution profile of a city. *International Journal of Geographical Information Science* 33 (11): 2218–2240.

Li RR, Leung, Y (2011) Multi-objective route planning for dangerous goods using compromise programming. *Journal of Geographical Systems*, 13: 249–271.

Liu S, Fardad M; Masazade E, Varshney PK (2014) Optimal Periodic Sensor Scheduling in Networks of Dynamical Systems. *IEEE Transactions on Signal Processing*. 62 (12). https://doi.org/10.1109/TSP.2014.2320455.

Mahler R (2003) Multitarget Bayes filtering via first-order multitarget moments. IEEE *Transaction on Aerospace and Electronic system* 39(4): 1152–1178.

Manohar K, Brunton BW, Kutz JN, Brunton SL (2018) Data-driven sparse sensor placement for reconstruction. *IEEE Control Systems Magazine* 38(3) 63. https://doi.org/10.1109/MCS.2018.2810460.

Pan S, Duraisamy K (2018) Data-driven discovery of closure models. *SIAM Journal on Applied Dynamical Systems* 17(4): 2381–2413.

Pham NT, Huang W, Ong SH (2007) Multiple sensor multiple object tracking with GMPHD filter. *Proceedings of the 10th International Conference on Information Fusion.*

Rudy SH, Brunton SL, Proctor JL, Kutz JN (2017) Data-driven discovery of partial differential equations. *Science Advances* 3(4). https://doi.org/10.1126/sciadv.1602614.

SPARC (2023) Digital Twins in Geospatial Research. *Report of the SPARC Workshop held at ASU's Tempe campus in 2023.* SPARC Digital Twins Workshop Final Report.pdf.

Tong KK, Leung KS, Leung Y (2017) A system for personalized health care with ECG and EEG signals for analysis. *Proceedings of 2017 International Smart Cities Conference (ISC2).* https://doi.org/10.1109/ISC2.2017.8090793.

Vo B.-N, Ma WK (2006) The Gaussian mixture probability hypothesis density filter. *IEEE Transactions on Signal Process.* 54(7): 2652–1661.

Vo B.-N, Singh S, Doucet A (2005) Sequential Monte Carlo methods for multitarget filtering with random finite sets. *IEEE Trans. Aerospace and Electronic Systems* 41(4): 1224–1245.

Wang Z, He SY, Leung Y (2018) Applying mobile phone data to travel behaviour research: a literature review. *Travel Behaviour and Society* 11: 141–155.

Wu TJ, Leung Y, Ma JH, Fang JW (2020) Multitarget tracking in sensor networks based on the PHD filter and a quantized energy-efficiency criterion. (unpublished paper)

Yan N, Mei CL (2014) A two-step local smoothing approach for exploring spatio-temporal patterns with application to the analysis of precipitation in the mainland of China during 1986–2005. *Environmental and Ecological Statistics* 21: 373–390.

Yi WY, Leung KS, Leung Y (2018) A modular Plug-And-Play sensor system for urban air pollution monitoring: design, implementation and evaluation. *Sensors 18(1): 7.*

Yi WY, Leung KS, Leung Y, Meng ML, Mak T (2016) Modular sensor system (MSS) for urban air pollution monitoring. *2016 IEEE Sensors* https://doi.org/10.1109/ICSENS.2016.7808924.

Yi WY, Lo KM, Mak T, Leung KS, Leung Y, Meng ML (2015) A survey of wireless sensor network based air pollution monitoring systems. *Sensors* 15(12): 31392–31427.

Zhang HJ, Liang ZL, Hu SQ (2010) Localization of multiple emitters based on the sequential PHD filter. *Signal Processing* 90(1): 34–43.

Zhang WB, Leung Y, Ma JH (2019) Analysis of Positional Uncertainty of Road Networks in Volunteered Geographic Information with a Statistically defined Buffer-Zone Method. *International Journal of Geographical Information Science* 33 (2019): 1807–1828. https://doi.org/10.1080/13658816.2019.1606430.

Chapter 11
Summary and Conclusion

11.1 Summary

The fundamental idea of building digital twins of cities is to learn the simplest models that capture effectively the dynamics and complexity of city evolution so that we can reliably and efficiently model, analyze, simulate, predict, and manage dynamics and complexity of urban entities/processes and our cities throughout their life cycles. To recapitulate what we have discussed in this book, I summarize in Fig. 11.1 the general framework proposed in this study. When the governing equations of city dynamics are known, we build digital twins of cities by learning ROMs of much lower dimensions with low-dimensional manifold learning from snapshots generated by solving or simulating the corresponding high-dimensional models, and we can also learn ROMs of parametric dynamical models via different projections onto the low-dimensional space (Chapter 3). When we have very limited knowledge or no idea about the governing equations, we build digital twins of cities by learning with sparse identification, neural networks, or statistical distributions the ROMs from spatiotemporal time series obtained in observational or experimental settings using data-driven methods (Chapter 4). To make the data-driven approach interpretable and observe certain urban theories, we inject urban theories into data-driven learning to make it urban theory informed (Chapter 5). These are essentially the macroscopic approaches to the incorporation of dynamics and complexity into digital twins of cities. In case we model cities as dynamical complex networks, ROMs can also be derived through low-dimensional manifold learning (Chapter 6). To address emergence arising from interactions of individual city agents on the microscopic level, we incorporate dynamics and complexity into digital twins of cities by learning ROMs of adaptive dynamical networks with agents interacting within complex network communication topologies (Chapter 7). It is worth reemphasizing the feedback loops between models and data as well as between the high-dimensional models and the corresponding ROMs depicted in Fig. 11.1. The former indicates the importance of making models and data mutually informed and the latter highlights the continual

Y. Leung, *Digital Twins of Cities*, Advances in Spatial Science,
https://doi.org/10.1007/978-3-032-07966-4_11

improvement in modeling complex dynamical urban systems through dimension reduction of high-dimensional models and discovery of elusive processes through data-driven approaches that in turn advance our understanding of the dynamics and complexity of city evolution via digital twins of cities.

In this book, I have also given conceptual arguments for building digital twins of cities on a multiscale basis so that cross-scale dynamics and complexity can be incorporated and perhaps synchronized (Chapter 8). To stress the importance of model-data synchrony, I have proposed the trilateral interoperation between the real world (the physical twin), the model (the virtual twin), and the data in building digital twins of cities, together with a new general definition for digital twins (Chapter 9). Concerning data and quality assurance, I have given a brief discussion on sensor networks and data quality assurance and suggested a way to do error analysis and error propagation to make digital twins of cities accountable and reliable (Chapter 10). In this concluding chapter, I also propose some main directions for further research on digital twins of cities. I hope the proposed framework is general enough for the incorporation and modeling of deterministic and stochastic urban dynamics and complexity via digital twins of cities. Because of space limitation, depth is traded off for breadth, and technical details of the proposed methods are either briefly discussed or omitted in our deliberation.

11.2 Directions for Further Research

Besides the research issues and outstanding problems that I have highlighted under various approaches in our above discussion, for future research—as a general direction—we must further elaborate and strengthen the theoretical underpinnings of the approaches embedded in this proposed framework and experimentally verify and validate them in synthetic simulations and real-life applications. Digital twin itself is a dynamical system that should evolve over time to achieve general intelligence. To make our digital-twin learning adaptive, robust, and forward looking, we should consider using various learning strategies such as reinforcement learning (Mnih et al. 2015)—to select actions that maximize long-term cumulated reward in learning; meta-learning (Peng 2020)—to adapt learning models to unseen tasks for out-of-sample predictions; transfer learning (Pan and Yang 2010)—to capitalize on knowledge gained through one task/dataset to enhance performance on another related task/dataset; self-supervised learning (Liu et al. 2021)—to reduce the dependence on manual labeling the training data; ensemble deep learning (Ganaie et al. 2022)—to combine individual models to form an ensemble digital-twin model for better generalization; incremental learning (van de Ven et al. 2022)—to acquire new knowledge with continual learning from non-stationary data stream; and federated learning (Zhang et al. 2021)—to allow multiple digital twins to collaborate to solve city dynamics and complexity problems in our ever-changing city environment.

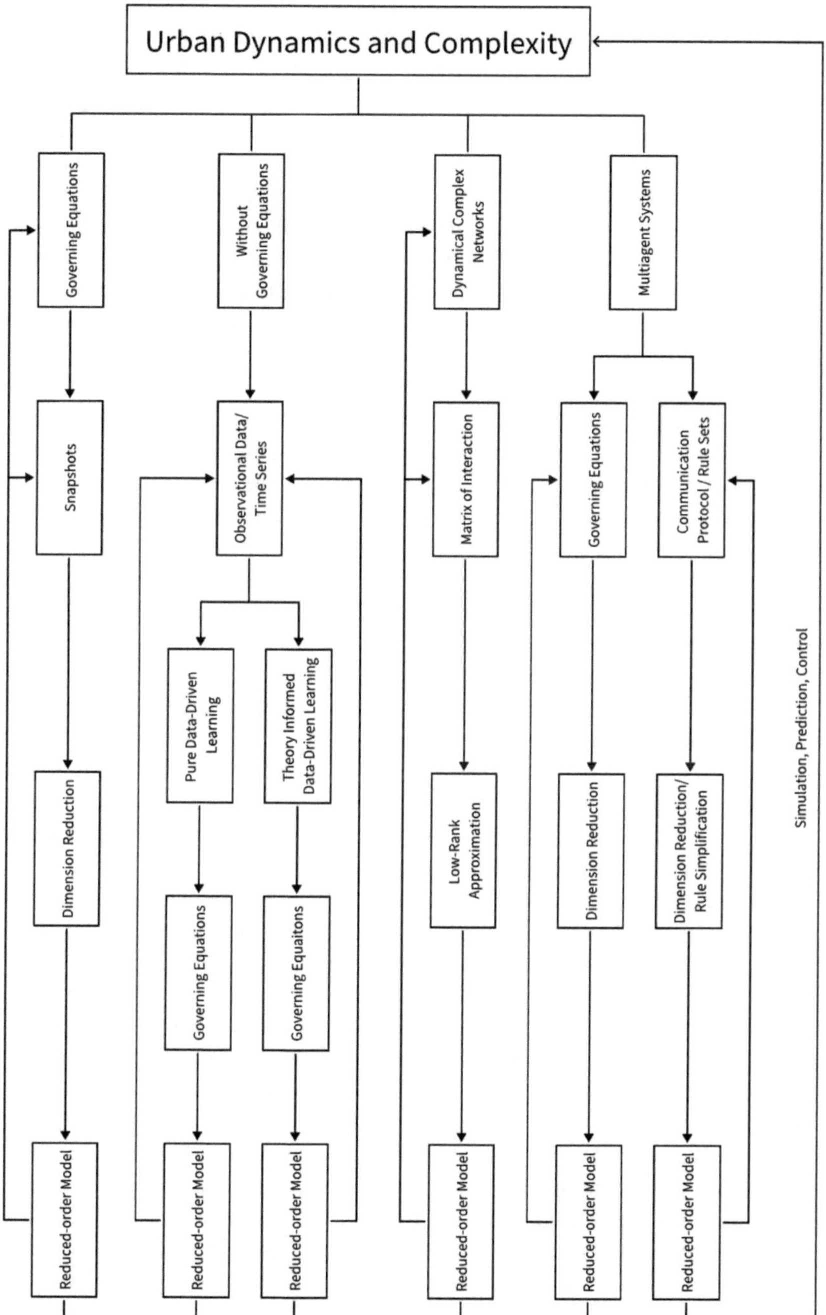

Fig. 11.1 General framework for the incorporation and modeling of urban dynamics and complexity via digital twins of cities

With respect to the instantaneous and voluminous data streams, it will be useful to develop methods to learn the low-dimensional manifold of the extremely high-dimensional data to achieve data parsimony beneficial to digital-twin construction and learning. For instance, we may want to apply the scale-space filtering method to obtain natural clusters in a high-dimensional data set along the scale (Leung et al. 2000) and employ the method of nonlinear dimensionality reduction of data lying on multi-cluster manifold (Meng et al. 2008) to achieve low-dimensional representations of data. It should be noted that many learning methods target data clustering/segmentations in which cluster characterization and identification in data—e.g. clustering data into different dynamic behaviors/regimes for the construction of corresponding ROMs—play a key role. As an example, the neural network approach to convex hull computation can facilitate real-time identification of natural clusters (Leung et al. 1997; Leung 2010).

To facilitate our decision-making—particularly real-time or near real-time decision—effort should also be made to build an intelligent infrastructure for the simulation, prediction, and management of large-scale urban systems with continuous knowledge and data flows among the physical city entities, the corresponding digital twins, and the data hubs in a synchronized and timely manner. It is the construction of such digital threads (Pang et al. 2021) that channel data, information, and knowledge from all parts of the urban system to support human and machine intelligence in making diagnoses of and providing solutions to the management of life-cycle city development problems in space and time.

Decision-making involving digital twins of cities, particularly a group of interrelated digital twins, can get to be very immersive and complicated. It may involve reasoning with multiple evidence—often conflicting—in an urban-politic group decision-making context. An integrated information fusion approach based on evidence theory and group decision-making may be profitable for making reliable decision under uncertainty when evidence coming from various sources are of varying degrees of believability and sometimes highly conflicting. Leung et al. (2013) incorporated the ideas of information fusion and group decision-making into Dempster-Shafer theory of evidence (Shafer 1976; Leung 1997) and proposed decision rules such as the veto-by-one rule, majority rule, and compromise rule for decision-making under multiple evidence. This may be an effective way to model decision-making involving a group of digital twins who interact with their physical twins and the environment consisting of other digital twins in a distributive city system. Decision-making in multiple AI agent collaboration discussed in Sects. 7.3 and 7.4 of Chapter 7, and integration of a group of LLMs/SLMs or distillated LLMs to sequentially solve interrelated tasks and learning problems discussed in Sect. 5.6 of Chapter 5 are typical examples. Through multiple AI agents, we can integrate social dimensions into digital twins of cities to model and simulate social dynamics and decision-making involving multiple stakeholders and their virtual twins. We can efficiently simulate social scenarios and evaluate plausible impacts of urban policies and interventions before their actual implementations. Together with the information fusion and group decision-making approach in Leung et al. (2013) discussed above, we can effectively and efficiently model and address the dynamic and complex processes of urbanism involving interaction between, feedback from, and decision-making of individuals, communities, and the physical city environments. Successful integration of the social and physical fabrics into the theoretical and technical framework of digital twins of cities will be instumental to the solution of problems arising in the life-cycle development of our ever-evolving cities. It will also encourage citizen participation in the transparent and bottom-up process of inclusive city goverance with a macro perspective in a theory and/or data driven setting.

Since the quantitative revolution in geography and spatial analysis, we are at another crossroad of theoretically and pragmatically modeling geographical systems in general and the dynamics and complexity of urban systems in particular. Our success will hinge on our being able to harness the power of AI in general and machine learning in particular, and to maneuver and capitalize on rich information provided by IoT and big spatiotemporal data. We however must avoid jumping on the bandwagon without a thorough understanding of what it means and what it takes to address the genuine needs in our investigations. We should not be mesmerized by the recent euphoria on big data—including IoT—and AI. Equipping us with big data, state-of-the-art information technology, and AI algorithms alone will not make us much more intelligent in advancing urban science in general and building useful digital twins of cities in particular. The ultimate power rests on urban theories. Digital twins of cities should be built so that we can model effectively our city development processes and render methods for their efficient simulation, prediction, control, and management. Urban theories, particularly those on dynamics and complexity, should be our guiding light in search for appropriate urban forms and processes, urban resilience, and sustainable development. In our tool kit, we should have optimization, classical and contemporary dynamical analysis, complexity analysis including emergence, machine learning including deep learning, stochastic and statistical learning theory, and other biologically inspired approaches such as genetic algorithms, neural networks, cellular automata, multiagent methods, and whatever methods that we genuinely need and to be developed. Depending on the circumstances, we should take advantage of the complementarity and synchrony of various approaches to build our digital twins that are intelligent and scale well.

I have raised in this book a considerable number of issues/questions whose solutions/answers need rigorous theoretical underpinning and empirical investigation. There is a host of theoretical and applied research lying in front of us. A lot of formidable but worthy scientific and technical challenges we need to take up in future research (as echoed in Wilson 2024). It is an exciting undertaking in novel modeling in the era of explosive growth of AI and big multisource, multitype, and multiscale spatiotemporal data that goes beyond geography, urban planning, and regional science. If we can successfully ride the tide of conceptual and theoretical development in urban science, advancement in information technology, and fast evolution of AI, which I am optimistic, it will take us to a new frontier of modeling geographical systems in general and urban systems, together with their digital twins, in particular. It will also break new grounds in interdisciplinary research involving academia, industry, government, and practicing professionals in the study of human and physical systems that are ever evolving in space and time.

References

Ganaie MA, Hu M, Malik AK, Tanveer M (2022) Ensemble deep learning: a review. *Engineering Applications of Artificial Intelligence* 115: 105151.

Leung Y (1997) *Intelligent Spatial Decision Support Systems*. Berlin: Springer-Verlag.

Leung Y (2010) *Knowledge Discovery in Spatial Data*. Berlin: Springer-Verlag.

Leung Y, Ji NN, Ma JH (2013) An integrated information fusion approach based on the theory of evidence and group decision-making. *Information Fusion* 14: 410–422.

Leung Y, Zhang JS, Xu ZB (1997) Neural networks for convex hull computation. *IEEE Transactions on Neural Networks* 8: 601–611.

Leung Y, Zhang JS, Xu ZB (2000) Clustering by scale-space filtering. *IEEE Transactions on Pattern Analysis and Machine Intelligence* 22: 1396–1410.

Liu X, Zhang F, Hou Z; Mian L, Wang Z, Zhang J (2021) Self-supervised learning: generative or contrastive. *IEEE Transactions on Knowledge and Data Engineering* 35(1): 857 – 876.

Meng DY, Leung Y, Fung T, Xu ZB (2008) Nonlinear dimensionality reduction of data lying on the multicluster manifold. *IEEE Transactions on Systems, Man, and Cybernetics, Part B: Cybernetics* 38: 1111–1122.

Mnih V, Kavukcuoglu K, Silver D, Rusu AA, Veness J, Bellemare, MG, Graves A , Riedmiller M , Fidjeland AK, Ostrovski G, Petersen S, Beattie C, Sadik A, Antonoglou I, King H, Kumaran D , Wierstra D , Legg S , Hassabis D (2015) Human-level control through deep reinforcement learning. *Nature* 518(7540): 529–533.

Pan S, Yang Q (2010) A survey on transfer learning. *IEEE Transactions on Knowledge and Data Engineering* 22(10): 1345–1359. https://doi.org/10.1109/TKDE.2009.191.

Pang TY, Pelaez Restrepo JD, Cheng CT, Yasin A, Lim H, Miletic M (2021) Developing a digital twin and digital thread framework for an 'Industry 4.0' shipyard. *Applied Sciences* 11:1097. https://doi.org/10.3390/app11031097.

Peng H (2020) A comprehensive overview and survey of recent advances in meta-learning. arXiv: 2004.11149.

Shafer GA (1976) *A Mathematical Theory of Evidence*. Princeton: Princeton University Press.

van de Ven GM, Tuytelaars T, Tolias AS (2022) Three types of incremental learning. *Nature Machine Intelligence* 4:1185–1197. https://doi.org/10.1038/s42256-022-00568-3.

Wilson AG (2024) The future of urban modelling: from BLV to AI. *Networks and Spatial Economics*. https://doi.org/10.1007/s11067-024-09658-8.

Zhang C, Xie Y, Bai H, Yu B, Li W, Gao Y (2021) A survey on federated learning. *Knowledge-Based Systems* 216(1): 106775. https://doi.org/10.1016/j.knosys.2021.106775.

Index

Y. Leung, *Digital Twins of Cities*, Advances in Spatial Science,
https://doi.org/10.1007/978-3-032-07966-4

E

T

MIX
Papier aus verantwortungsvollen Quellen
Paper from responsible sources
FSC® C105338

If you have any concerns about our products,
you can contact us on
ProductSafety@springernature.com

In case Publisher is established outside the EU,
the EU authorized representative is:
Springer Nature Customer Service Center GmbH
Europaplatz 3, 69115 Heidelberg, Germany

Printed by Libri Plureos GmbH
in Hamburg, Germany